SEGREGATED SABBATHS

Mother Bethel A.M.E. Church, Philadelphia

SEGREGATED SABBATHS

RICHARD ALLEN AND THE EMERGENCE OF INDEPENDENT BLACK CHURCHES 1760–1840

CAROL V. R. GEORGE

NEW YORK
OXFORD UNIVERSITY PRESS
London   1973   Toronto

For Bill

PREFACE

When he wrote *The Souls of Black Folk* in 1903, W. E..B. Dubois included an essay that analyzed the black religious experience, called "Of the Faith of the Fathers." Many of his comments were harshly critical of those churches that he believed had failed to serve the real needs of the people, and had ministered instead to "cold, fashionable devotees," and members whose interests were only in "information and amusement." But whenever he referred to the African Methodist Episcopal Church, he described it as "great," or "the greatest Negro organization in the world," and its bishops as being included "among the most powerful Negro rulers in the world." A teacher, author, scholar and race leader, DuBois was in a better position than most of his contemporaries, whether black or white, to view the black church objectively, and it seemed clear that he was willing to place the A.M.E. Church in a class by itself.

This study is an account of the development of that church, focused on the life of its founder, Richard Allen. It is not a denominational history, however, but rather a description of the people and circumstances that encouraged not only black Methodists, but other denominational groups as well, to develop racially separate churches. The period during which these churches was born, that is, from 1787 when Allen led the withdrawal of a group of black Methodists from the predominately white congregation with whom they had worshiped, until his death in 1831, was a tumultuous one for most Northern freedmen. As the egalitarian claims of the Revolutionary War generation gradually died out, they were replaced by other voices calling for measures to deal with the growing free black population that had increased as a result of the adoption of gradual emancipation laws. White politicians and community leaders, particularly after 1800, considered restrictive legislative and social policies, and a recently revived scheme, colonization, attracted a sizable body of supporters. Within racially mixed congregations, freedmen recognized the manifestations of these ideas in their religious life and began to look for other alternatives. If some white churchmen encouraged black members to organize separate congregations, in many cases, notably Allen's, freedmen planned for their own autonomous religious societies in spite of white demands to desist. The struggle that ensued between Allen's black Methodist supporters and their white Methodist opponents forms a chapter in the history of American race relations. The result of that confrontation, the formation of the African Methodist Episcopal Church, should guarantee Allen a position alongside those who, like Roger Williams, Jonathan Edwards, John Carroll, Francis Asbury, and the rest, have already had a place claimed for them in American church history.

There are two areas in which a few words of explanation may be helpful. The first has to do with the persistent problem of "present-mindedness"; of superimposing recent views and interpretations on historical events, a constant temptation in a work of this nature. James Cone's analysis of black theology is a case in point. It was clear, after reading the sermons of black churchmen, that what they were saying was quite different from what their white colleagues were emphasizing: Cone's description of black theology seemed to apply to that difference which I had recognized. In general, I was aware of the problem, and realized the threat it posed to objectivity. The second area involves the meaning given to certain terms, specifically, moral reform. By moral reform is meant that which appeals to the moral sense or moral sensibilities of individuals, whose response is in keeping with the nature of the appeal, that is, an individual willingness to act on the basis of what one perceives to be right conduct, or sanctioned by one's conscience. It is not necessarily opposed to political action, though it can be: in the case of the debate over temperance, for example, there were, in addition to the ones who saw it as a moral issue requiring a moral solution, those who identified it as a moral problem but favored a political response. If even this explanation seems vague, it might be useful to recall that it was the controversy over the implications of these terms— where moral suasion left off and where political action took over— that divided the abolitionists in the 1840's.

I am happy to acknowledge the assistance I have received, in the form of grants and a fellowship, to help me with my work. Grants in aid from the American Philosophical Society, the Research Foundation of the State University of New York, and the American Council of Learned Societies made it possible for me to undertake additional research, and a fellowship from the National Endowment for the Humanities freed me from teaching responsibilities to draft the manuscript.

I have accumulated a large debt to the librarians, ministers, church secretaries, and sextons who have helped me find material. In particular, I would like to mention the staff at Bethel Church, Philadelphia, who allowed me to reproduce the Journal of Proceedings, and the Rev. David Licorish, of Abyssinian Baptist Church, New York City, who suggested some useful leads. The librarians I encountered were generally pleasant and generous with their time, although some were unusually helpful and that included: the staffs of the Schomberg Collection of New York Public Library, Syracuse University Library, the Manuscripts Division of Boston Public Library, Cornell University Library, and the Methodist Historical Society, Philadelphia.

The entire project, originally a doctoral dissertation, was carried out under the direction of Nelson M. Blake, Maxwell Distinguished Professor of History at Syracuse University. His critical comments and seemingly limitless patience sharpened my thinking and improved the manuscript as it went through each revision. Professor Otey Scruggs, also of Syracuse University, not only read and commented on several drafts of the manuscript, but asked the kinds of basic questions that led me to reconsider, and ultimately revise, some of my original assumptions.

Other people have offered assistance at various stages in my work: Dorothy Farrell carefully typed several drafts of the manuscript; my mother, though she may not realize it, developed my interest in church history; **D. B. Robertson** of Syracuse University offered advice on the manuscript; and Mr. and Mrs. W. B. George, Sr., helped me by assuming some of the responsibilities that would otherwise have been mine. Hollis Lynch, general editor of this series, gave the manuscript a critical reading, and I have profited from his extensive knowledge of the field. Herbert Mann and Sally Dufek of Oxford University Press both read the manuscript and offered assistance in innumerable ways.

My greatest debt, however, is to my family, whose patience and good humor I sorely taxed. They have not only understood my problems and frustrations, but have willingly accepted all the inconveniences that my erratic schedule created. To all of them, —my husband, and Glynis, Billy, and David—I am, and shall continue to be, deeply grateful.

C. V. R. G.

Baldwinsville, New York
April 1, 1973

CONTENTS

SEGREGATED SABBATHS

INTRODUCTION: WHY A SEPARATE BLACK CHURCH

A CASE FOR BLACK THEOLOGY

ONE DAY, after he had lived in the city for about twenty years, Richard Allen was stopped on the street in Philadelphia by a slave catcher who had come to town looking for some black bounty. The slaver claimed that the African preacher was his runaway bondsman, and he meant to take him back to his work. It was not an uncommon occurrence: Northern freemen often found their status challenged by those who thought they saw a chance to gain a slave—either their own fugitive or simply a random choice—easily and inexpensively. Since the burden of proof rested on the freeman, who had to produce freedom papers or other adequate testimony to support his contentions, the odds in such cases clearly favored the accuser. But the slaver who singled out Allen had chosen unwisely: he had selected, indiscriminately, a preacher who was known in the white community and respected in the black, and whose friends were willing to testify that they had known him as a free man for nearly two decades. So this time the shoe was on the other foot, as the white man was charged with making false accusations and sentenced to a jail term. After he had served part of his sentence, Allen decided he had been sufficiently punished, and asked to have him released and sent home. The entire episode was dismissed as an unfortunate incident by all save the principals involved, and a few Quakers and members of the preacher's congregation who knew what had happened. There is no indication that Allen himself ever referred to the event again, and there was no change in his behavior to suggest that he was intimidated by the experience:

he continued to serve his parishioners at Bethel Church and the black residents of the city just as he had before, as active and outspoken as he had always been.

But it was still not an experience one could take lightly; his silence may have covered his anger and aspects of psychological bruising, but it could not wipe out the implications of the encounter. No freeman, regardless of his local reputation or occupation, could consider his freedom secure as long as some people were slaves and others were slave hunters. The freeman's future was inexorably linked to the peculiar institution, and even if a man became a bishop, as Allen did, he was constantly reminded of just how tenuous his situation really was. He could anticipate a daily portion of sometimes subtle, sometimes direct, insults, slights, and discriminatory treatment, but more than that, he could have all his efforts to make a better life for himself wiped out by one capricious challenge from a dealer in the slave business.

That particular encounter alone would set Allen's episcopacy apart from those of other American bishops. To be sure, some white bishops suffered from forms of personal and professional insecurity as a result of supporting unpopular doctrinal positions, but the price they might be forced to pay for their witness—rebuke, and possible removal from office—involved a qualitatively different fear from the kind that Allen knew. But this first black American bishop was also different from his white colleagues in other respects: born a slave, he spent the first twenty years of his life in bondage before he was elected as the founding bishop of the African Methodist Episcopal Church. An account of his life, therefore, is not necessarily prima facie evidence of the kind of scholarly elitism criticized by those who prefer to have history written from "the bottom up," that is, from the perspective of the so-called "man-in-the-street." It is, of course, true that Allen occupied a unique place in his own time and in ours, but it is equally true that his seemingly impressive title failed to relieve him of the anxieties and tensions that were the common lot of all freemen. No mere black variation on the Horatio Alger, rags-to-riches success story, he was never able to enjoy the emoluments of ecclesiastical office or ignore the political attacks that threatened to undo his religious organization. His theological perspective was obviously molded by such experience, and it was here that he made his special contributions to black religious life. These fell into basically two complementary areas: in the first instance, he recognized the distinctive religious and theological needs of black people; and in the second, he applied his theological views to the practical solution of immediate physical and social problems. Black clerical leadership in matters of social reform may now be taken for granted, and it may even represent to some activists a political technique they have rejected, but this was not the case in Allen's day when the precedent for involvement had been neither established nor accepted. His recognition of black religious expectations, an almost intuitive ideological expression of what has recently been termed "black theology," developed out of his personal experiences into a commitment to black religious separatism.[1] Reared as a traditional Methodist, Allen came to the conclusion that if Methodist theology refused to be identified with solutions to social and political injustice, then it was meaningless and irrelevant to the pressing needs of black people. Theology, in its practical manifestation, should mean the liberation from oppression and injustice of people whose hopes had previously been directed to the City of God rather than the City of Man. He seemed to conclude that a separate and independent black church, served by black clergymen, could provide the most effective mission to Afro-Americans by utilizing not only its physical resources of buildings, committees, and such, but by also invoking the powerful philosophical resource implicit in a theology of liberation. He had his pietistic side too, which was revealed in the kind of other-wordly "God-talk" common to most nineteenth-century preachers: he did, for example, offer frequent admonitions on the disastrous results of scandalous living, and he preached, on at least one occasion, on the joys awaiting the faithful in "everlasting mansions of glory."

---

[1] James Cone, *Liberation: A Black Theology of Liberation* (Philadelphia: Lippincott, 1970). See, for example, 59: "The organizing of the African Methodist Episcopal Church, the African Methodist Episcopal Zion Church, the Christian Methodist Church, the Baptist Churches and many other black churches is a visible manifestation of Black Theology."

But he spoke from a particular frame of reference: to those who readily observed his kinship, he was a brother who knew first-hand the oppression of slavery, the continuing insecurity of a quasi-free life, and the suppressed expectation of ultimate liberation here as well as hereafter. Such an orientation gave even his semingly pious platitudes a ring of urgency and immediacy.

Doctrinally, Allen remained a lifelong Methodist, but after 1815 he was known officially as Bishop of the African Methodist Episcopal Church, rather than, say, as African Bishop of the Methodist Episcopal Church. And that distinction was significant: if the universality of the Christian gospel was as comprehensive as the Methodists proclaimed it to be, if in fact they believed that in "Christ there is neither Jew nor Greek, neither bond nor free, but all are one," then there would be no need for segregated worship facilities. The churches, however, *were* segregated and black members *were* denied full participation in ways that reflected the racial attitudes of their social environment. It was to overcome such immediate, humiliating oppression that Allen walked out in protest from white St. George's Methodist Church to organize a separate African denomination, and not because of any doctrinal reservations he had about Methodism.

The second distinguishing feature of his ministry, that of active secular involvement, was an inevitable extension of the first; that is, his personal theology was inseparable from the impulse to apply such thinking to practical matters of liberation. Instead of employing the more forceful rhetoric of a David Walker or Nat Turner, Allen chose to combat institutionalized prejudice through a variety of specific channels; he attacked the American Colonization Society and its program of sponsored African emigration, he supported the Free Produce Society (an organization that sold goods produced by free rather than slave labor), he arranged for the meeting of the First National Negro Convention in 1830, and also managed to involve himself and his church in numerous other projects. He died in 1831, before the abolitionist movement had developed into a national crusade, but it soon became apparent that his interpretation of black theology was shared by his clerical colleagues who survived him in the campaign.

This is not to say that Allen initiated a kind of nineteenth-century black Social Gospel movement. The application of theology, or spiritual beliefs, to immediate social ills was not a new concept in the black worshipping community; scholars such as Melville Herskovits and W. E. B. Dubois have suggested that the practice may have an historic tradition, arising in Africa, where the priestly role was assumed to include control over natural events as well as supernatural phenomena.[2] And even on a practical, experiential level Allen's actions were anticipated by other black preachers who had earlier tried to organize racially separate churches in the American South—George Liele in Silver Bluff, South Carolina around 1773 and Andrew Bryan in Savannah, Georgia, shortly thereafter—but their efforts were limited or suppressed by the conditions of slavery. The significance of Allen's ministry, therefore, was not so much that he introduced a radically new concept to black worship, but rather that he was able to manipulate the winds of social change that whirled about him to achieve a relatively safe and theologically satisfying spiritual home for black people. The desire to segregate church facilities was current near the turn of the nineteenth century, and that impulse was being implemented within Methodist circles even as Allen walked out of St. George's. He recognized these intentions, using the fact of segregation as the basis for his confrontation with white Methodists, severed all ties with the denomination, and institutionalized black religious separatism with the creation of the A.M.E. Church. Allen never renounced his religious debt to Methodism, and it is possible that he might have considered remaining within the denomination if its leaders and members had indicated a willingness to deal with the problems of black injustice; he had, after all, joined the church at a time when it was the most vocal religious group attacking slavery. But as time went on, he saw a growing discrepancy between what the official

[2] See W. E. B. DuBois, *The Negro Church* (Atlanta: Atlanta University Press, 1903); also, Melville Herskovits, *The Myth of the Negro Past* (6th ed.; Boston: Beacon Press, 1968), especially Chap. VII. DuBois is concerned primarily with the scope of the priestly role, while Herskovits focuses on the degree to which local control limited that role.

An investigation of the religious history and practices of West Africa before and during the period of the slave trade could provide some valuable insights into the development of Afro-American church history.

church Discipline (which was the codification of denominational polity and theology) maintained was policy and what individual churches practiced, until it became reasonably clear that Methodist theology was not going to be applied to the solution of black problems. If that was to be the case, then such theology was meaningless ideology to Allen and his friends, who could simultaneously appreciate the essence of Methodism while they rejected its social behavior toward blacks. A theology that failed to deal with earthly oppression was not a viable one, from their point of view. And so they organized a separate denomination that qualified Methodist Discipline to the extent that the A.M.E. group limited membership to Africans and vigorously attacked slavery and the slave trade.

That Allen was eager to establish black religious separatism seemed evident; he worked to organize new branches of African Methodism whenever he had a chance, and tried, unsuccessfully, for years to effect a merger with the A.M.E. Zionists in New York. His psychological motivation for doing so is less clear, however, and in any case is beyond the scope of this study. Like most people, his motivations appeared complex, and occasionally contradictory, with the result that later observers who have attempted to assess his career have been able to come to very different, frequently conflicting, conclusions.[3] Psychological analysis of historical figures can produce some fascinating results, as studies of Martin Luther and Mahatma Gandhi have indicated, but in Allen's case the lack of substantial evidence dealing with his personal life makes such efforts an exercise in futility. His brief personal recollections provide some insights into what he regarded as significant events in his life, and coupled with the activities and achievements of his ministry, can support certain observations. The two characteristics that seem to define his professional career are ambition and leadership, and they may actually be two different aspects of what was a singular charismatic quality. His ambition manifested itself in quantitative as well as qualitative

---

[3] Howard Holman Bell, *A Survey of the Negro Convention Movement, 1830-1861* (reprint, New York: Arno Press, 1970), 14-18; Benjamin T. Tanner, *An Apology for African Methodism* (Baltimore: n.p., 1867), 63. Bell thought that Allen was frequently motivated by personal ambition; Tanner regarded him as a courageous leader. See also Chapter VIII.

ways. He had a seemingly inexhaustible store of energy which was usually diverted into filling the demands of the various jobs he held, many simultaneously, while his professional desires were hinged to A.M.E. growth. Inevitably, his personal ambition offended some who chose to interpret it as hunger for power—and that unfortunately included a black separatist group he was trying to attract—but it was an undeniable asset to his denomination at a time when politicians seemed anxious to curtail its activities. His leadership qualities can only be assumed, but the evidence suggests that it is a safe assumption. He attracted thousands into the membership of Bethel Church, and his position at the head of the church and the denomination was never questioned by those who relied on his direction. He was apparently endowed with the kind of presence, or charisma, that set him apart from his peers. In most other respects he was not particularly unusual; he was moderate in dress, usually cautious in speech and behavior, often stern and paternal in dealing with black parishioners, and if the situation required it, he could be diplomatic and evasive in negotiating with white spokesmen. He was a churchman, not an intellectual, although he read, wrote, and enjoyed attending local lectures whenever he could find the time.

His cultural inheritance, a seemingly incompatible mixture of diverse elements, had the capacity for inducing intellectual schizophrenia in anyone who lacked the ability to create some kind of sensible order out of the disparate parts. He was born during the religious revivals of the Great Awakening, and his birthright included eighteenth-century slavery along with the Afro-American religious tradition. He adopted Methodist doctrine and imbibed the philosophical preferences of Revolutionary America. He heard of slaveholding politicians who declaimed on the theme of liberty while they also discredited itinerant preachers who conducted emotional revivals for inter-racial audiences. It was a tumultuous, unpredictable era, and the man and his ministry cannot be understood apart from the cultural milieu of the period.

THE FAILURE OF INTEGRATED WORSHIP

> Christian theology is a theology of liberation. . . . In
> fact, theology ceases to be a theology of the gospel when it
> fails to arise out of the community of the oppressed. For it
> is impossible to speak of the God of Israelite history, who is
> the God who revealed himself in Jesus Christ, without
> recognizing that he is the God of and for those who labor
> and are heavy laden.
>
> The black church in America was founded on the belief
> that God condemned slavery and that Christian freedom
> meant political emancipation.
>
> James Cone
> *A Black Theology of Liberation*

A religious man by inclination and profession, Allen was a slave
before he was a Methodist, a descendant of the Afro-American
tradition before he was a Christian. That there are African prece-
dents for certain forms of black spiritual expression has already
been suggested, although it is difficult to establish the extent to
which these practices survived the ordeals of the Middle Passage
and the depersonalizing experience of institutionalized slavery.[4]
There is some evidence to indicate, however, that those who
resided in the slave quarters practiced a variety of forms of
spiritual expression that included magic, superstition, ancestor
worship, and voodoo, incorporated with a strain of acquired
Christianity.

African slaves gradually accepted Christianity during the seventeenth century as a result of two developments: first, their apparent reluctance to accept the master's faith was slowly overcome
through the process of indoctrination and acculturation; and secondly, owners began to abandon the time-honored belief that
Christian baptism automatically conferred emancipation. It thus

---

[4] Included among those who cite evidence to support a relatively high degree of retention of African religious customs are Herskovits, in *Myth of the
Negro Past,* and DuBois, in *The Negro Church.*

Their positions are contradicted by E. Franklin Frazier in *The Negro
Church in America* (New York: Schocken, 1963) and Stanley Elkins in *Slavery:
A Problem in American Institutional and Social Life* (Chicago: University of
Chicago Press, 1959).

became possible for masters to send missionaries among the slaves, baptize them, and still retain them as permanent bondsmen. Nevertheless, the number of baptized slaves in the seventeenth century was small, and of those few it is difficult to determine how many merely decided it was expedient to accept the form, but not the substance, of the new faith.[5]

The colonial religious situation begs the question of just how it was possible for a supposedly Christian group of people who presumably set great store in the concept of personal religious freedom to agree to the enslavement of other Christians. The answer to the question is probably mixed in the tangled web of white racial attitudes, although economic considerations seem to describe the dominant pattern that emerges. Recent studies suggest some other interesting alternative possibilities, and while it is doubtful that any explanation will be generally regarded as definitive, clearly it is a subject that calls for more detailed investigation.[6]

Among some Protestant groups, the clergy and members alike seemed to regard missionary activity as an effective substitute for any kind of moral indictment of slavery and the slave trade. There were occasional dissenters, who, troubled by the obvious incompatibility between their religious ideas and their slaveholding status, made their views known, but they represented special cases. Quakers generally tended to be more outspoken critics of slavery than members of other groups, particularly during the eighteenth century when their corporate policy was moving in that direction. But by and large most church groups seemed more concerned with the slave's market value than with his spiritual

[5] Lorenzo Johnston Greene, in *The Negro in Colonial New England* (New York: 2d ed.; Atheneum, 1968), indicates that there were few real converts to be found among slaves. See also Gerald F. DeJong, "The Dutch Reformed Church and Negro Slavery in Colonial America," *Church History*, XL (December 1971), 430.

[6] The subject of white motivation in racial matters is discussed in psychosexual terms in Winthrop Jordan's book, *White Over Black* (Chapel Hill: University of North Carolina Press, 1968), 574 ff., and in Frantz Fanon's *Black Skin White Masks*, trans. Charles Lam Markmann (New York: Grove Press, 1952), 165, 167. Economic factors figure more prominently in the following books: Lorenzo Johnston Greene, *The Negro in Colonial New England* (New York: Atheneum, 1968), Chap. X, and Edgar J. McManus, *A History of Negro Slavery in New York* (Syracuse: Syracuse University Press, 1966), 193.

value. And if some of them retained legal reservations about the
function of baptism, six colonial legislatures responded to assuage
their fears; between 1664 and 1706 Maryland, Virginia, North
Carolina, South Carolina, New York, and New Jersey all passed
measures that ended the traditional linking of baptism with
emancipation.[7] Despite the comforting effects on owners of this
piece of class legislation, many still remained puzzled about the
practical problems that could result from a general effort to secure slave conversion: that is, were converts automatically church
members? In those colonies that restricted the vote to church
members, were black converts to be enfranchised? Would knowledge of Christianity encourage slaves to be discontented and re-
bellious? To what extent should black members participate in
worship services? Would slaves comprehend the gospel message of
brotherly love and attempt to apply it to situations of social in-
equity? Never able to answer these questions to their own satisfaction, church officials nevertheless embarked on a program to
secure slave conversions during the eighteenth century.

The Anglican Church, traditionally regarded as the church of
the planters, initiated the effort in 1701 with the creation of the
Society for the Propagation of the Gospel in Foreign Parts
(S.P.G.) as a missionary outreach aimed at converting "the Negro
and Indian slaves." The Bishop of London, the church official
who supervised the religious life of the colonies, finally resolved
the baptism issue for Anglicans in a statement announcing that
". . . the embracing of the Gospel [did] not make the least Alteration in Civil Property. . . ."[8] The church also advised S.P.G.
missionaries to persuade owners to give slaves time off to attend
schools and classes sponsored by the Society. But the slaveholders
who disregarded the Bishop's advice usually went unnoticed and

---

[7] Greene, *The Negro in Colonial New England*, 260.

[8] Bishop of London, *Letters of the Bishop of London: The First, To the
Masters & Mistresses of Families in the English Plantations abroad; Exhorting
them to Encourage & Promote the Instruction of their Negroes in the Christian Faith. The Second, To the Missionaries There. To Which is Prefix'd An
Address to Serious Christians Among Ourselves* (London: Joseph Downing,
1729), 21-22.

The Bishop's announcement included an appeal to owners to permit their
slaves to attend S.P.G. schools, but it also said that baptism conferred "Freedom . . . from the Bondage of Sin," but not freedom from the control of the
master. *Letters of the Bishop of London*, 1729.

infractions often passed undetected; most owners preferred to have local S.P.G. missionaries who would preach on topics that would make slaves contented with their lot and "reconcile them to their poor estate."[9] In spite of its proselyting efforts, however, the Anglican Church attracted comparatively few black converts, for reasons that probably included its identification with the planter, its austere service, and its failure to explain the intricacies of its involved ritual. In later years, the church's unwillingness to take a stand on the antislavery issue, which it regarded as a political problem, also discouraged black members. An eighteenth-century Anglican priest complained that the religious instruction of slaves was considered complete if they were able to "gabber over the apostles creed" and have a minister "throw some water in their faces."[10] And for those slaves who were converted to Anglicanism, the churches, whether in the North or the South, provided segregated seating arrangements in galleries or special pews in the rear, thus ensuring that they would be the last to receive the elements at Communion.

The Congregationalists, concentrated in New England where there were few slaves, attempted to match the centrally organized Anglican effort to convert the Afro-American with localized church drives. A few individuals publicly denounced slavery—notably Judge Samuel Sewall—but the churches as a whole generally ignored the issue. Local congregations occasionally conducted classes for black workers in the area, and from time to time a black convert was admitted to membership: although it was a general policy to allow all white members to vote on church matters, it was a privilege not usually extended to black members, though individual churches may have made exceptions.

If the Congregational and Anglican churches languished in their efforts to attract black converts, at mid-eighteenth century, they, and other churches as well, also failed to post significant white membership gains. The picture changed somewhat after 1740, as the revivals of the Great Awakening drew large crowds, only some of which yielded potential church members.

9 The Rev. Thomas Bacon, *Sermons Addressed to Masters & Servants* (Winchester, Va.: John Heiskell, 1743), 1.

10 Society for the Propagation of the Gospel in Foreign Parts, *Classified Digest of the Records, 1701-1872* (London: Spottiswoode and Co., 1893), 64. See also Knox, *Three Tracts*, 33.

The Great Awakening moved across the colonies like an out-
going tide, picking up momentum and energy as it moved further
away from the eastern coast. It offered a new style of preaching—
enthusiastic and often extemporaneous—and introduced a new
emotionalism, which has admittedly sometimes been exaggerated,
into religious services as a replacement for the austere formalism of
the past. It produced itinerant preachers who took their appeals for
conversion to small towns and rural hamlets, much to the chagrin
of the more traditional clergymen. Stories spread about the emotional outbursts that took place at revivals, causing the shocked
clerical elite to label the revivalists illiterates, firebrands, lunatics,
and worse. The most unsettling aspect of the movement from the
point of view of the regular clergy was not so much its emotional
mysticism as it was its challenge to the social order. The meetings
usually attracted a curious looking assortment of people. Slaves, indentured servants, recent immigrants, and back-country farmers
were among the most noticeable, and they all seemed to react favor-
ably to the unconventional nature of the gatherings. The preacher's primary task was to inspire conversion, not social criticism,
often through an emotional appeal for mystical communion with
God. But the very nature of the meetings implied a rejection of
traditional religious and social conventions.

The intangible results of the movement are difficult to ascer-
tain. It is undoubtedly true that the Great Awakening stimulated
the growth of two struggling denominations in the colonies, the
Baptists and the Methodists, and it was these two groups that had
the greatest appeal for the unprivileged and working classes. It is
also apparent that the nature and structure of the revivals represented a criticism of prevailing religious practices, and thus, perhaps, encouraged the conclusion that the strength of this opposition served as a temporary bond uniting the participants in spite
of racial and national differences. Some basic questions, however
—again dealing with motivation or intent—will have to remain
unanswered for the present. Did the revivals encourage a new
spirit of egalitarianism, evident in the natural rights doctrine of
the Deists, and later manifested in the Declaration of Independence? Did the movement serve to undermine the obviously hierarchical structure of a society that consigned blacks to the bottom-

most rung? Did the revivalists regard black people first as
bondsmen or as brothers in Christ? And why did blacks willingly
join Baptist and Methodists groups? Was it because they met an
emotional need not filled elsewhere, or was there a cultural attraction based on a recognized or remembered resemblance to
African tribal customs, as, for example, the Baptist emphasis on
the cleansing effect of river immersion?[11] If specific answers to
these questions are elusive, a single generalization may serve to
summarize the sense of the movement as it related to black people:
through its unconventional revivals, its challenge to social norms,
and its appeal to the lower and middle classes, it encouraged
alienated blacks to believe that society was on the verge of a major transformation that would hasten their liberation.

The period that the Great Awakening ushered in has been referred to as one that offered "Christianity for All," implying that
the movement comprehended members of different racial, ethnic
and social groups.[12] The Presbyterian Church, particularly in sec-
tions of Virginia, reported an increase in black membership, largely
the result of the efforts of the Rev. Samuel Davies,[13] but among
the other denominations that noted some gains it was the Baptist
and Methodist churches that reaped the greatest harvest of black
converts. The black people who joined those two groups during
the latter half of the eighteenth century might have sensed an
openness on matters relating to racial improvements; they were certainly less restricted and relatively freer to develop their personal
religious options then than they were after the turn of the century. While it was practically unheard of to have a black preacher
address an interracial audience during the four decades preceding
the Civil War, it was not so unusual in the period following the
Great Awakening. There were men like Harry Hosier, known to
history as Black Harry, who spoke to integrated groups of Methodists, and in Harry's case, substituted for the Bishop, Francis
Asbury, when the Bishop himself was not available. Harry's ora-

---

[11] See Herskovits, *The Myth of the Negro Past,* for a fuller discussion of
African influence on specific forms of religious behavior and belief.

[12] Luther P. Jackson uses the term in "Religious Development of the Negro
in Virginia from 1760 to 1860," *Journal of Negro History* (hereafter cited as
JNH), XVI (1931), 174.

[13] *Ibid.,* 171.

torical ability was reportedly quite impressive, but there were others whose talents may have equalled his but failed to gain the same kind of recognition because they didn't travel with Asbury as Harry did.[14] John Chavis, for example, was a Presbyterian preacher from North Carolina who served racially mixed congregations until state laws prohibited him from continuing and he turned his talents to teaching.[15] Henry Evans was a Methodist exhorter in Fayetteville, North Carolina, around 1800, whose preaching ability was attested to by the large crowds of black and white listeners he attracted; eventually, however, public opinion silenced him as well.[16] And while Moses and Gowan Pamphlet served as itinerants to predominately black congregations in the vicinity of Williamsburg, Virginia, a black clergyman worked as a staff member of the Baptist Church in Richmond.[17] Other black preachers followed their calling in various kinds of religious activities, engaged in work that was frequently subjected to the same kind of supervision that extended over everything else in their lives. But the possibility that these token forms of acceptance could assume substantive dimensions in the Revolutionary atmosphere of the period seemed to end with the close of the century; in the succeeding decades evidences of fraternal cooperation between black and white churchmen diminished markedly.

American Methodism was one of those movements that flourished in the wake of the Great Awakening, and during the eighteenth century it attracted more black people than the Baptists or any other denomination.

The reasons for Methodism's popularity are related to its early history in America and have as much to do with its social implications as with its theology, particularly since doctrinal issues were not a major concern for the first followers of Wesley. Meth-

[14] *Ibid.*, 176; Carter Woodson, *The History of the Negro Church* (Washington: Associated Publishers, 1921), 56-57. Dr. Benjamin Rush thought that Harry Hosier was "the greatest orator in America"; Woodson, 57.

[15] Woodson, *The History of the Negro Church*, 67-70; John Hope Franklin, *The Free Negro in North Carolina; 1790-1860* (Chapel Hill: University of North Carolina Press, 1943), 170.

[16] Woodson, *The History of the Negro Church*, 56; DuBois, *The Negro Church*, 36.

[17] Jackson, "Religious Development of the Negro in Virginia from 1760 to 1860," *JNH*, XVI (1931), 176.

odist Arminian theology, freed from the more obvious restraints of Calvinistic predeterminism, emphasized individual conversion: for the black people who attended Methodist gatherings, the sermons that held out a brighter future for the converted—both spiritually and materially—were a refreshing change from the somber advice they used to hear about accepting one's status as a slave because it was God's will. They also received from the preachers some very practical guides for "respectable" living: they were advised to work steadily, and avoid luxuries, intemperateness, and sensual pleasures. That such a regimen met with universal appeal is doubtful, but most potential black members responded enthusiastically to the informal, evangelistic services, and particularly to the denomination's avowedly antislavery policy. The Quakers also opposed slavery, but the Friends' unique type of worship and their hesitancy in soliciting black supporters affected their popularity. The Methodists, on the other hand, seemed to take their cue from John Wesley, who had announced his opposition to slavery and privately recorded in his *Journal* his opinion that the slave trade was the "execrable sum of all villanies . . . [that] infinitely exceeds in every instance of barbarity, whatever Christian slaves suffer in Mahometan [*sic*] countries."[18] Wesley's lieutenants in the New World, the men subsequently designated Bishops, Coke and Asbury, communicated his antislavery witness to the new constituency. Their stand on the issue—and Coke was reportedly given to "fiery" outbursts on the subject—was regarded as intemperate and ill advised by Southern planters, who believed it might taint their slaves with a gospel of potential insurrection.[19] Black folks responded by swelling the attendance at Methodist meetings, but to little avail. By 1800, the planters began to have their way, and the church gradually

[18] John Wesley, *The Journal of John Wesley*, ed. Nehemiah Curnock (London: Epworth Press, 1938), V (1772), 445-46.

[19] Jackson, "Religious Development of the Negro in Virginia from 1760 to 1860," *JNH*, XVI (1931), 235; Francis Asbury, *Journal and Letters of Francis Asbury*, ed. Elmer T. Clarke (Nashville: Abingdon Press, 1958), I, 488; II, 215; Donald Mathews, *Slavery and Methodism: A Chapter in American Morality, 1780-1845* (Princeton: Princeton University Press, 1965), 11, 15, 20-21. Mathews says that Coke's "undiplomatic" antislavery statements provoked "violent opposition" in Virginia, North Carolina, and South Carolina.

modified its antislavery stand to accommodate its Southern supporters, who by then were beginning to attract some Northern sympathizers.

When Richard Allen was born in 1760, the seed of American Methodism had been planted, but its full flower was not yet apparent. Just when and where the Methodist movement first began in the colonies is open to speculation because of the absence of conclusive documentary evidence to support the claims for a specific time and place. It is quite possible that George Whitefield, the English evangelical, cultivated the field for the later harvest of Methodism when he toured the colonies between 1739 and 1741. Whitefield had been a member of Wesley's "Holy Club" while a student at Oxford and, although subsequently ordained an Anglican priest, he retained his sympathy for the doctrines that he had learned earlier. During his colonial travels, he stayed for a time in Philadelphia and later preached in the Southern colonies as well as in New England, which was then in the throes of the Great Awakening. In the course of his excited sermons, he transmitted some of the ideas of Wesley and a great deal of the personality of Whitefield, leaving in his wake small units of devotees which subsequently nourished the spiritual seeds he had planted. These early groups then, in Philadelphia, New York, and Maryland, may be said to represent the first faint signs of Methodism in America. But it was not until 1769, when Wesley dispatched two preachers, Joseph Pilmoor and Richard Boardman, whose responsibility it was to minister to the spiritual needs of these essentially formless groups, that organized Methodism actually took root. At the time that Allen was born in Philadelphia, the religious scene there was dominated basically by two groups, the Anglicans and the Quakers, with just enough small sects around to give the city theological variety. Methodism contributed its distinctive share to the intellectual diversity of the City of Brotherly Love.

But in 1760, Philadelphia blacks knew slavery as a far more immediate fact of life than they did Methodism. Slavery in the Middle Colonies differed from the Southern variety, owing to the absence of the plantation system, but if it was milder in the North, it was simply a matter of degree to those affected; families

were still separated for sale, slaves were uprooted without warning, and special laws dealt with such things as the punishment of
pauperism, the use of firearms and liquor, intermarriage, and
public meetings.[20] Instead of living in separate quarters, slaves
were often housed within the owner's home, an arrangement of
doubtful value to the servants: their health and personal needs
might receive careful attention, but so did other aspects of their
life, and they were pressured to conform to white standards. It
has been estimated that in 1770, ten years after Allen's birth, the
number of blacks in the colonies accounted for 20 per cent of the
total population, and 90 per cent of these passed their lives in
slavery.[21] In the absence of specific colonial population figures, a
rough estimate would place the number of blacks in Pennsylvania in 1760 at somewhere between 3,000 and 4,000, and a majority resided in Philadelphia.[22] In 1780 the state passed its first
gradual emancipation law, but prior to that time, and in spite of
Quaker protestations, slaves were sold with impunity—either separately or as families—usually when household budgets revealed
a need for economy. Since slaves were usually employed at domestic tasks, or were hired out as artisans, their services were regarded as luxuries rather than necessities, making their continued
maintenance uneconomic during periods of financial strain. It
was, in fact, the unprofitability of slavery in the Middle States
that led to its eventual abolition.[23]

When the Attorney-General of Pennsylvania, Benjamin Chew,
took as his second wife Elizabeth Oswald, he was little concerned
about the economics of slavery. His recent bride was obliged to

[20] W. E. B. DuBois, *The Philadelphia Negro: A Social Study* (Philadelphia:
University of Pennsylvania Press, 1899), 13.

[21] Norman A. Graebner, Gilbert C. Fite, Philip L. White, *A History of the
American People* (New York: McGraw-Hill, 1970), 86-87.

[22] Department of Commerce, Bureau of the Census, *Negro Population, 1790-
1915* (Washington: Government Printing Office, 1918), 57. In the first national
census taken in 1790 there were approximately 10,000 Black people living in
Pennsylvania. After 1780, with the adoption of the state's first gradual emancipation law, the area became more attractive to fugitives and freedmen.

[23] DuBois, *The Philadelphia Negro;* also McManus, *A History of Negro
Slavery in New York,* 193. McManus says that the argument explaining Northern abolition on the basis of morality is a rationalization; the system had simply become uneconomic.

support his social standing, and she faced an imposing task for a new wife: she had to raise his four daughters from his previous marriage and also care for their own son, who was born the following year. As a good eighteenth-century husband, Chew saw to it that she was well provided with household help. Even if convenience did not require it, social convention seemed to demand it: the Attorney-General's position singled him out as a leader in Pennsylvania politics, and his wife's family connections identified her with the prestigious commercial firm of Joseph Turner and Chief Justice William Allen. And before Chew's private practice began to fall off in 1768, he saw fit to establish his growing family in a beautiful summer estate elegantly named "Cliveden." Situated on sixty acres of rolling land, Cliveden gradually acquired a coach house, stables, and artistically arranged landscaping, all of which had to be cared for in a manner in keeping with the owner's social status. Indentured servants were a possibility—and Chew may have employed some—but they were limited by their contracts to a given number of years' service, and their leaving could come at an inconvenient time, such as the birth of another child. It made for a more efficiently run household, from Chew's point of view, to keep slaves who were bound for perpetuity and well acquainted with the needs and idiosyncracies of the family. Chew, former Quaker turned Anglican, kept at least one family of slaves—the Allen family—and he may have kept more.[24]

[24] For information on Chew, see the *Dictionary of American Biography*, and Burton Alva Konckle, *Benjamin Chew, 1722-1810* (Philadelphia: University of Pennsylvania Press, 1932), 81-117.

I

SETTLING IN PHILADELPHIA

By the close of the third quarter of the eighteenth century the most significant humanitarian achievements of the Enlightenment were to be found in the American colonies, and especially at Philadelphia, their capital city. While the movement embraced both sides of the Atlantic, and speculation and sermonizing were rife in Europe as in America, it was at Philadelphia, more than anywhere else, that practice kept pace with theory. Here men generally accepted the proposition that poverty, disease and cruelty were intrinsically bad and socially inefficient, and that all were anachronisms in a community where progress was a demonstrable fact.

Perhaps Philadelphia's principal contribution to the "Age of Benevolence" was its crusade for humane treatment of the Negro.

CARL BRIDENBAUGH
Rebels and Gentlemen

I was born in the year of our Lord 1760, on February 14th, a slave to Benjamin Chew, of Philadelphia. My mother and father and four children of us were sold into Delaware state, near Dover. . . .

RICHARD ALLEN
Life Experience and Gospel Labors

FEBRUARY 14, 1760 WAS AN IMPORTANT DAY for the Allen family, but one little different from any other for the Benjamin Chews. On that day the Allens became the parents of a newborn son, Richard, whose appearance provided a temporary bright spot in their otherwise bleak lives. For the Chews, however, the birth of another black baby in their household was scarcely an event to celebrate: the temporary disability of the infant's mother, the matriarch of the resident black family, seemed more of an inconvenience to Mrs. Chew, who now had to care for the needs of her own five children without her customary help. And Master Chew himself could hardly be expected to regard it otherwise: he had, after all, refused to let his own wedding a few years earlier interfere with professional commitments he had previously made with the Governor and Council for that same day.[1] He was a busy lawyer, politically ambitious and socially active, an efficiently organized man who kept slaves to assist his wife and not because he was interested in turning a profit in the slavetrading business. The new black baby might rate an admiring glance, but little more; he was, at the moment, just another mouth to feed and his future value to Chew seemed indeterminate.

Unlike Chew, the Allens had no way of controlling their own child's future, although they may have entertained the hope that he would escape the drudgery of their existence. The family lived in Chew's household and did his domestic work, but they enjoyed none of the social advantages attached to being identified with an influential and aspiring lawyer; indeed, the uncertainty of Chew's practice and political fortune made their own future seem insecure. For as Chew grew more aware of increasing tensions between the colonies and the Mother Country, he became more of a Loyalist, and in a city where anti-British sentiments ran high, such a position was not likely to produce new clients or political preferment. The Allens could justifiably be concerned with the economic health of Chew's practice.

As the decade of the 60's wore on, Philadelphia suffered from a general economic crisis, and while Chew's family increased in size, his law practice lost its position of leadership to the youthful

---

[1] Konckle, *Benjamin Chew, 1722-1810*, 81.

Quaker, Nicholas Waln, and others.[2] Something had to be done to maintain the solvency of his family, and so, rather than forfeit houses or land, he sold his family of slaves.

Chew's solution to his fiscal problem was not an unusual one among slaveholders in the Middle Colonies. Slavery there was largely a domestic affair, limited generally to one or two mature household slaves who were valued for the social or economic advantages they conferred on their owners. They were usually required to perform a variety of tasks, the majority being employed as house servants, shopkeepers, or farm hands, while a few were hired out as skilled craftsmen.[3] These versatile bondsmen provided their Northern owners with a degree of ease and prestige, as in Chew's case, but rarely with sufficient profits to warrant their continued maintenance in hard times. For many owners, the answer to their problem was sale, rather than manumission, although a few, notably Quakers, took the opportunity to free their former slaves. Chew had been associated with the Friends until 1758 when he became an Anglican and a communicant of Christ Church, but the Quaker position on slavery apparently had little effect on him because he acquired another slave family to replace the Allens as soon as his fortunes improved.

The Allen family was to be sold—in this case as a unit, which offered them some small comfort—but where they were going and to whom would only be known when they reached their destination. They were part of that group of nameless, indistinguishable black workers who were shuttled about the colonies in response to economic fluctuations. The Allens were, typically, anonymous; no one, including their son, recorded their names, ages, or birth places, nor, for that matter, the total number of members who remained in the family after additional children were born and some were sold off. Neither is it known if any of the children were baptized, a matter of some speculation, since Chew had seen to it that all five of his own offspring were baptized at Christ Church when they renounced Quakerism in 1758.[4]

The family of six; mother, father, and four children; left Phila-

[2] *Ibid.,* 117.
[3] DuBois, *The Philadelphia Negro: A Social Study,* 16.
[4] Konckle, *Benjamin Chew,* 81.

delphia sometime around 1768. Richard later remembered only that when he "was a child" he was sold "into Delaware state, near Dover. . . ."[5] Chew had practiced law for a time in Dover before moving to Philadelphia about 1754, and his business dealings kept alive his contacts there. Richard Allen would eventually return to Philadelphia in 1786 to make it his permanent home; a move that, after an absence of nearly twenty years, appeared to be the result of a deliberate choice rather than a convenient coincidence. Whatever youthful memories he retained of his birthplace must have been relatively pleasant; one did not often hear, for example, of manumitted slaves returning to hometowns like Charleston or Savannah.

When the Allens arrived in Dover they found a situation quite unlike the one they had left behind. Their new owner, Master Stokeley, was not a lawyer but a farmer, and they were expected to work as farm hands rather than as domestics. It was a far cry from the urban atmosphere of Chew's townhouse. But like most black workers, the Allens had accepted the need to be flexible and versatile, and Richard eventually became acclimated to his new location and master, and may even have come to like the old man.[6]

Richard lived at Stokeley's place longer than most other members of his family—he probably spent a total of about thirteen years there—during which time he experienced some rather profound changes that affected the rest of his life.

The first had to do with the disruption of his family. The Allens adjusted to their rural environment and learned to perform the farm chores that Stokeley expected of them. Richard's mother, a mulatto woman whom he described as being "very pious," gave birth to several more children after her removal to

[5] As an old man, Allen dictated his memoirs, along with several addresses, to his young son, Richard, Jr. His account is obviously subject to the vagaries of age and memory, but it is the only source of information for his early life. His recollections are as important for what they include as for what they omit—in this case, any mention of his family. See Richard Allen, *The Life Experience and Gospel Labors of the Rt. Rev. Richard Allen* (2d ed.; Nashville: Abingdon Press, 1960), 15.

[6] *Ibid.*, 16. Allen said of Stokeley that he was a "good master . . . more like a father to his slaves than anything else."

Delaware, incidentally providing Stokeley with additional slaves for the future or the potential for a cash exchange. But things were not going well financially for Stokeley, and the arrival of more Allen children who would be dependent and non-productive for several more years could only add to his worries. He was caught in the downturn of the business cycle, and unless his fortunes improved, some of the slaves would have to be sold again. He reached the same decision that Chew had, but unlike the Philadelphian, he was willing to sell individual members of the family separately if the circumstances required it. And apparently Stokeley thought they did, because Richard and a brother and sister near his own age were retained, while the rest of the family were sold. Richard, an adolescent at the time, apparently lost all contact with them after the sale, since there is no record of his ever having referred to them again.[7]

If the separation was traumatic, he never revealed it; he may have found it too painful to recall, or he may have become so inured to unexplained and unanticipated disruptions that he regarded it as one of the hardships that made slavery such a "bitter pill." But the loss of his parents at a highly impressionable time in his life may have encouraged him to look for emotional compensation in some other form, such as the enthusiastic religion of eighteenth-century Methodism.

He seemed, indeed, to find it there. Methodism first arrived in the vicinity of Stokeley's farm in the same way that it came to other rural areas, that is, with the appearance of the circuit rider. Richard and his brother followed the other local farm hands to the gatherings in the woods to observe the novel scene, but like so many others, they were soon converted from observers to believers. This second change in his adolescent life, unlike the first, was one that he recalled many times in the future.

The event was an emotional one for the two youths, combining a powerful appeal for conversion with an emphasis on individual responsibility. And punctuating the entire message were deliberate strikes at slavery and slaveholding. They had never

---

[7] Allen never mentioned his own father, a revealing omission. It seems likely that if the elder Allen had remained behind on the farm that his son would have referred to him when he finally took leave of Stokeley.

been exposed to anything quite like it before, and they were understandably captivated by the preacher's approach, his style, appearance, and especially his message. Richard recorded his personal conversion experience in his memoirs many years later in language that seems to suggest that the event signaled a release from slavery as much as it implied an escape from sin.

> . . . I was [he said] awakened and brought to see myself, poor, wretched and undone, and without the mercy of God must be lost. Shortly after, I obtained mercy through the blood of Christ, and was constrained to exhort my old companions to seek the Lord. I went rejoicing for several days and was happy in the Lord, in conversing with many old, experienced Christians. I was brought under doubts, and was tempted to believe I was deceived, and was constrained to seek the Lord afresh. I went with my head bowed down for many days. My sins were a heavy burden. I was tempted to believe there was no mercy for me. I cried to the Lord both night and day. One night I thought hell would be my portion. I cried unto Him who delighteth to hear the prayers of a poor sinner, and all of a sudden my dungeon shook, my chains flew off, and, glory to God, I cried. My soul was filled. I cried, enough for me—the Saviour died. Now my confidence was strengthened that the Lord, for Christ's sake, had heard my prayers and pardoned all my sins.[8]

From the time of their conversion on, the young boys became frequent participants in revivals held in the woods, but they never let their spiritual life interfere with their farm chores. If they got behind in their work, they would forego the meeting for that week. They could count on the fact that, despite the disruption produced by the war, some Methodist preacher would usually manage to make it to the vicinity of Stokeley's place the following week.

That kind of confidence revealed more than the simple faith of a recent convert; it was a witness to the general and growing popularity of Methodism itself. For although the war with England inevitably created new hazards for all travelers, Methodist circuit riders seemed quite willing to assume whatever risks were involved in reaching new prospects. The itinerant preacher was paradoxically becoming a pillar of the church, a development en-

---

[8] Allen, *Life Experience*, 15-16. Allen's account of his conversion followed a pattern not uncommon among those who reported similar experiences.

couraged by denominational leaders like Francis Asbury, who later singled him out for recognition, usually at the expense of the minister who had turned in his saddle bags for a settled parish. And since their business was more clearly identified with the conversion of souls rather than political affairs, they could be relatively more detached from internal colonial feuding than the Anglicans, who were frequently caught in the crossfire between their patriot congregations on one side, and their Loyalist ties to England on the other. Methodists themselves were not entirely free from political entanglements, however, since John Wesley, who was politically a conservative Tory, published his views attacking the American cause.[9] But Methodist preachers seemed to be less dependent on their English sponsor than the Anglicans were on the Bishop of London. Officially still described as a movement within the Anglican Church, Methodism tended to be regarded as a separate entity among its colonial supporters. Most of the circuit riders tried to continue on their weekly rounds, making only those deferences to the exigencies of war that were absolutely essential. That kind of regimen, regular and predictable, could not fail to impress recent or potential converts, like the Allen brothers, whose lives were similarly scheduled in a way they assumed no clergyman would ever accept.

The young men decided to demonstrate to Stokeley the remarkable manifestations of their new belief by adopting an unwritten set of resolves. They determined first to work harder for Stokeley, then to convert the old master, and eventually, to purchase their own freedom. It seemed like an ambitious program, but within a rather surprisingly short space of time they were able to accomplish all three objectives. Their desire to be more diligent about their chores was inspired in part by the Methodist emphasis on the value of hard work, and in part by a concern to impress Stokeley with one of the practical results of conversion. Their program produced results more impressive than even they could have anticipated, for not only was Stokeley convinced that "reli-

---

[9] Some writers suggest that Wesley's pamphlet, *A Calm Address to the American Colonies,* cost him his influence in America, an influence that passed to Asbury, Elmer T. Clark, Introduction, *Journal and Letters of Francis Asbury* (Nashville: Abingdon Press, 1958), xi.

gion made slaves better and not worse . . ." but he was sufficiently moved to invite the well-known Methodist exhorter, Free-
born Garrettson, to speak at the farm. Garrettson was an ideal
choice because his preaching, emotional and direct, was liberally
laced with vigorous attacks on slavery and the slave trade. His
sermon overwhelmed the old farmer, who was still adjusting to
the change he had witnessed in the lives of the young men, and
helped to make a convert of him. Consistent with current Methodist attitudes on slavery, Stokeley then offered them the opportunity to purchase their own freedom. They had finally achieved
what they had initially set out to do, and after brief negotiations,
they arranged the terms of their freedom with their former
master:

> . . . he [Stokeley] proposed to me and my brother buying our times,
> to pay him 60£ gold and silver, or $2000, continental money, which
> we complied with in the year 17— [*sic*].[10]

Probably just past the age of twenty, Richard, along with his
brother, was set free, to manage for himself in a marketplace to
which he had previously been denied access. But he recalled his
feelings at the time when he set down his memoirs as an old man:
"I had it often impressed upon my mind that I should one day
enjoy my freedom, for slavery is a bitter pill, notwithstanding we
had a good master."[11]

Paternalistic masters had done little to mitigate the sting of
slavery for Allen, whose experience with the Middle Colonies'
variety had included the loss of his family, and his own removal
to strange, new surroundings. When he left Stokeley's farm,
empty handed and on foot, he took with him the psychic baggage
that he had accumulated during his years in slavery.

But those years he spent working for Stokeley had failed to provide him with the skills he needed to compete for a job in the
free world. He confessed that he faced an awesome task because
he did not know "what business I should follow to pay my master

---

[10] Allen, *Life Experience*, 17. It was probably in 1781 that Allen received his
freedom from Stokeley, since it took him almost five years to accumulate the
money to pay off his debt to his former master.

[11] *Ibid.*, 18.

and get my living."[12] With no formal education and very little practical knowledge of marketable skills, he was obliged to make his way as best he could, accepting odd jobs as opportunities came along. His work kept him on the move for the next five years, during which time he stopped at various spots in New Jersey, Delaware, and Pennsylvania.

Allen was now more than a physically free man, however; he was also a converted Methodist, a spiritually liberated believer, whose zeal for his new-found faith inspired a decision to preach. Like Garrettson and the others, Allen learned to travel the circuit, combining his preaching with more remunerative work that would sustain him. The decision to become a preacher, even a part time one, was apparently reached spontaneously, and with little noticeable regard for the problems he might face as a black itinerant.

It was a brash decision for an unskilled, uneducated, recently freed slave to make. The inspiration for his choice can only be conjectured, but probably had something to do with the fact that his conversion and his freedom were achieved almost simultaneously: psychologically, he might readily identify Methodism with a form of spiritual renewal or liberation. To be sure, the variety of Methodism that he heard preached supported a strong antislavery appeal, and he had seen his own master transformed by its demands. If this new message had the power to convert Stokeley, and to bring his brother and himself a recognition and acceptance of their individuality, a sense of self-esteem, then couldn't it have the same effect on others who were bound by sin and sinful society? Few Methodist preachers had accepted their "call" to the ministry on the basis of a reasoned response—a practice not inconsistent with the denomination's emphasis on personal commitment rather than doctrine—and in Allen's case the decision seems prompted by a natural youthful enthusiasm for a seemingly irresistible and dynamic appeal that offered physical as well as spiritual freedom. If other black people could be exposed to the message by someone who had personally shared their experiences, then they, too, might enjoy a new way of life.

[12] *Ibid.*

But Allen's itinerant preaching alone during these years was hardly enough to support him. He spoke frequently, usually to racially mixed audiences, and he reported the comment of an enthusiastic listener who said, "[T]his man must be a man of God. I never heard such preaching before."[13] Such magnanimous congregational approval was not matched by equally generous donations, however, and Allen was forced to accept whatever work was available locally: he worked in a brickyard for $50 a month, drove wagons loaded with salt during the Revolution, and labored for a time as a woodcutter. None of his jobs could be considered lucrative, and it was not until someone gave him a scrawny horse, which he later traded for a blind, healthy one, that he was able to alternate riding with walking. The donor of the horse he subsequently repaid, but the hospitality of friends and strangers he accepted freely as a contribution to his ministry, with the result that he was able to accumulate enough money to pay off his purchase price to Stokeley out of his meager and insecure income. Careful planning and extreme frugality had made the difference. "My hands," he said, "administered to my necessities."[14]

If he encountered racial animosity during his preaching tour, he didn't regard it as worth reporting in his memoirs, although he apparently lived in constant anticipation of such problems developing. His congregations were largely white; his overnight hosts, whom he identified by name rather than color, were probably sometimes black and sometimes white. His message may have sounded like typical Methodist exhortation to his white audiences, but to his black listeners certain favorite texts had special relevance; one that he recalled as being particularly effective was, "Come unto me, all ye that are weary and heavy laden, and I will give you rest." When he finished with his sermon based on the text he concluded, "Glory be to God! and now I know he was a God at hand and not afar off."[15] God, for Allen, was concerned about man's immediate and personal problems—about the weary

13 *Ibid.*, 21. He also recorded, however, that during this time he "had many trials to pass through," 23.
14 *Ibid.*, 23.
15 *Ibid.*, 21.

and heavy laden—and it was this existential quality that he thought black people needed to appreciate. Conversion implied liberation from sin and acceptance of individual responsibility, and these prospects were "at hand and not afar off."

Allen traveled the circuit with some of the most popular figures in eighteenth-century Methodism, and their reaction to his color was seemingly characteristic of the class-conscious paternalism of the period. He himself frequently referred to his well-known traveling companions as "fathers," a term in keeping with the Methodist practice of addressing each other by familial terms. It was a designation he used to refer not only to old Master Stokeley, but also to the evangelist Benjamin Abbott and the subsequent bishop, the Rev. Richard Whatcoat.

Allen apparently had the opportunity to get to know Abbott and Whatcoat reasonably well. The two were very different types of churchmen: Abbott was a fiery evangelist; Whatcoat a diplomatic church leader and organizer; together they offered an interesting study of the contemporary clergy. Allen admired Abbott for the similarity he bore to Garrettson: both were powerful preachers and outspoken antislavery advocates. But Abbott was a particularly unusual man, even among Methodist itinerants who generally tended to contradict the conventional image of clergymen. A preacher of overwhelming emotionalism, he had

> . . . large shaggy eyebrows, and eyes of flame, of powerful frame, and great extent of voice, which he exerted to the utmost, while preaching and praying, which, with an occasional stamp with his foot, made the church ring. . . . His words ran like fire sparks through the assembly, and "those who came to laugh" stood *aghast* upon the benches—looking down upon the slain and the wounded, while to use a favorite expression of his, "The shout of the king was in the camp."[16]

Whatcoat was a more traditional type of preacher than either Garrettson or Abbott, but Allen regarded him similarly; he was "a father in Israel." Together they traveled the Baltimore circuit

---

[16] G. W. Watson, *Annals of Philadelphia* (Philadelphia: Carey & Hart, 1830), I (1790), 456. See also, *Dictionary of American Biography*, which says that Abbott was "an ignorant zealot, on the verge of madness, but converted many to Methodism."

in 1785; the young unordained black itinerant who held no church title, and the white denominational leader.

The most obvious confrontation with racial awareness that he encountered among the clergy came from an unexpected source, Francis Asbury, one of the two original bishops of American Methodism. Asbury's attitude seemed to suggest the kind of hard-headed practicality of the administrator who thought he had grasped all the implications involved in a potentially sensitive situation. He reportedly sent for the young man and asked him to be his traveling companion, a precedent perhaps established when Harry Hosier, known as "Black Harry," accompanied the Bishop.[17] Asbury's offer presented Allen with the facts of Southern life as the older man saw them: Allen would be supplied with his food and clothing, but when they were traveling in the South, he was not to mix with slaves and would sometimes be required to sleep in the carriage. In rejecting the Bishop's arrangement, Allen explained that he could not accept the conditions, even though it meant a steady maintenance from the denomination at a time when it paid him nothing. But he was also planning for his future: deprived of associations with slaves, he would have no one to care for him if he got sick, and he was convinced that "people ought to lay up something while they were able, to support themselves in time of sickness or old age."[18] Traveling, even in the North, inevitably renewed the ugly manifestations of the race issue, and he decided to forego it entirely in favor of a settled place. When the Methodist elder in charge of Philadelphia sent for him to preach in the city, he accepted the invitation. He noted that the date was February 1786 when he returned to the place in which he had been born.

Philadelphia became Allen's permanent home, and during his long residence there its social milieu changed quite markedly. In 1786 when he returned it symbolized to many observers the social conscience of eighteenth-century Enlightenment liberalism. It was

----

[17] See Introduction, pp. 15-16, for discussion of Harry Hosier. It is not clear whether Hosier served as Asbury's personal servant or his ministerial assistant. If the former, then Allen's rejection of the Bishop's offer may have been prompted in part by this consideration.

[18] Allen, *Life Experience*, 23.

also the symbolic birthplace of American Methodism, and was even then recognized as a center for denominational operations. A cosmopolitan city, religiously active and apparently aware of social problems, it seemed to offer the best possible base of operation for the young black evangelist. But the claims that were made for the city in 1786 would have sounded disingenuous if made in 1831, the year of Allen's death.

The city that he returned to was quite unlike the place that Allen had left nearly twenty years earlier, not only in its physical manifestations, but also in its social and cultural aspects. Very possibly as he looked around he observed a kaliedoscopic range of activities that hinted of a faint but pervasive black influence. The anonymous black mass of his boyhood days was giving way to a readily discernible group of people determined to make their own choices and control their own future.

A city that had seen war and its devastation, the now peaceful place was in the process of being rebuilt, this time of brick rather than wood, and its port was opening its wharves to the increasing traffic from abroad. Benjamin Franklin, the town's best-known citizen and reminder of the past, shuffled along the street beside the chimney sweeps who hawked their skills with the traditional cries of "Sweep, oh!"[19] The city was in a transitional stage, and its pace of activity inspired visitors with a sense of awe and admiration. The reputation of the area acquired such legendary proportions that certain local residents, like Chief Justice Allen, were encouraged to describe the entire state as "the best poor man's country in the world," and French observers were prone to regard it as " 'l'Age d'Or de Pennsylvanie.' "[20]

A number of factors combined to produce the heady atmosphere of the city. The site of significant decision-making conferences for the colonies, Philadelphia acquired a cosmopolitanism that was fostered by the diversity of its economic and social life, and mellowed by the appearance of numerous social reform groups. The city had, of course, borne the impress of Quaker in-

[19] James Hosmer Penniman, *Philadelphia in the Early Eighteen Hundreds* (Philadelphia: St. Stephen's Church, 1923), 34-35.

[20] Carl Bridenbaugh, *Rebels and Gentlemen* (New York: Oxford University Press, 1942), 260-61.

fluence for generations, and the presence of the Friends contributed to the notion that the place had a social conscience, albeit
one tempered by practicality. The Quakers in 1712, were the first
organized group to go on record in opposition to the slave trade,
and it was they who continued to press for high import duties on
slaves to discourage the traffic. Their presence may have occasionally served to tip the balance on crucial issues: when the legislature in 1761 announced a rise in the duty on slaves to £10, local
employers and slaveowners who were feeling the pinch of a tight
labor market voiced their objections, but ultimately to no avail.[21]
Most numerous among the middle class and aspiring aristocracy,
Quakers were often resented by laborers who felt that their economic future would be jeopardized by the availability of freedmen's labor, if the aristocratic merchants and idealistic Friends
had their way.[22] But still the image persisted of a city concerned
about eradicating one of the most blatant forms of social injustice.

That image was advanced by the regular appearance of numerous social crusaders in the area. Along with the politically motivated, there were others whose altruism seemed quite sincere, including men like Anthony Benezet and Benjamin Rush. Benezet,
for example, was a conscientious Quaker whose humanitarian activities indicated his wide range of social concerns; an articulate
abolitionist, he personally funded an evening school for black
children beginning in 1770, while he also circulated petitions and
tracts opposing war, liquor, and cruelty to animals and prisoners.
One of his antislavery accounts reached John Wesley, who incorporated some of its material in his *Thoughts Upon Slavery*.[23] And
the Presbyterian physician, Dr. Rush, while usually less conspicuous than his Quaker friend, was no less zealous. Both ardent reformers, they attempted to deal with a full spectrum of social
injustice, from penal reform to abolition, on the basis of a philosophical approach to human need. That frame of reference was
rooted in a natural rights philosophy that merged the sentiments

[21] DuBois, *The Philadelphia Negro*, 16.

[22] *Hazard's Register*, V, 114. In 1722, "day labourers" sent a petition to the
Pennslyvania General Assembly stating that it "was a great disadvantage to
them who had emigrated from Europe for the purpose of obtaining a liveli-
hood" to employ blacks in their stead.

[23] Bridenbaugh, *Rebels and Gentlemen*, 258.

raised by the Great Awakening with the issues raised by the whole Revolutionary movement.[24] And it served alike for politician and reformer.

The work of these crusaders—humanitarians with more than a faint hint of paternalism—produced some highly visible results by the time Allen returned to the city. Their most significant claim had come in 1780, when they were able to announce that their state was the first to adopt a gradual emancipation law. Although this piece of legislation produced the most profound change that greeted the returning native son, the reformers who organized the Abolition Society in 1775 continued to work for a more effective law. The pace of their activities and the publicity given the Society created the impression that the generality of the population was, if not actually abolitionist, at least sympathetic to emancipation.

But there was another apparent change that had taken place, one that was in part a result of the recent war. The increase in the free black population—a partial product of a war policy that offered freedom to black recruits—led to a comparable rise in substandard housing, ghetto-like conditions, disease, and pauperism. Returning black soldiers might have lost their visible chains in the war, but they were in danger of replacing them with the immobility imposed by inadequate economic and social conditions.

One explanation for the apparent contradiction between civic intentions and social realities had to do with the general upheaval of the times. The war had not only brought into being a new nation, but a whole new social perspective that questioned old habits and conventions. In spite of some rather noble attempts to surmount traditional class-conscious distinctions, however, these differences remained and made communication among the social groups extremely difficult. While Quaker merchants, some of whom were inspired by the testimony at their meetings and others by those in the marketplace, were agitating for antislavery legislation, recent immigrants who feared the job competition of free black laborers were supporting new forms of economic discrimination. Local newspapers continued to publish notices advertis-

24 *Ibid.*, 257-61.

ing rewards for the return of runaway slaves, and masters with the necessary resources devised ingenious methods of circumventing the 1780 law—such as sending pregnant slave women out of state so that their offspring would not be born free.[25] A black skin was generally regarded as a badge of inferiority, and the extraordinary Henry Moss, who claimed he experienced a color change from black to white, was not only considered a work of the "Almighty Hand of Omnipotence," but also a kind of circus curiosity who could be seen on exhibit for two shillings by adults and for one shilling by children.[26] Benjamin Rush was not the sort who would visit such a side show, but there were obviously many who delighted in spending their shillings on such a curious spectacle, and it was they who regarded the freedman as a problem rather than a promise.

But if the motives of the patrician humanitarians were somewhat suspect, the fears of white laborers and artisans could be understood in terms of the cultural liabilities they lived with. Schooling for them was a haphazard affair, and their religious affiliation—which was usually with the Baptists, Methodists, or one of the smaller sects—described their social standing as surely as the clothes they wore. The plain clothes of the Baptists and Methodists, similar in style but different in color from the drab grayness of the Friends, provided an interesting but telling contrast with the elegant attire of the Episcopalians and the almost as elegant Presbyterians, who also affected the powdered wig and lace cuffs.[27] For these people, obviously labeled as members of the lower social strata of society, the postwar situation led to a frustration of their hopes by promising more than it delivered. Their frustrations reached the political establishment in widely distorted forms, and the objectives of civic leaders were, in turn, rarely communicated to working men in meaningful, substantive ways. Class consciousness had been dulled by the war and the passions it called up, but now it was returning, slowly and in slightly

[25] Stanley I. Kutler, "Pennsylvania Courts, the Abolition Act and Negro Rights," *Pennsylvania History*, XXX (1963), 14-15.

[26] *The Minerva and Mercantile Evening Advertiser*, New York, July 12, 1796, October 10, 1796. Moss was first exhibited in New York and then in Philadelphia.

[27] Watson's *Annals of Philadelphia*, I (1790), 458-59.

different guise, but potentially divisive nevertheless. Said General Washington near the close of the Revolution, "It is not the public but the private interest which influences the generality of mankind, nor can Americans any longer boast an exception."[28]

If the results of the Revolution were something less than white supporters had anticipated, they became even more disappointing to black people as time went on. Black troops had distinguished themselves in the conflict, and many had gained their freedom thereby. Allen had not been called upon for military service because his duties at the salt works exempted him from active combat. By driving salt wagons to Rehoboth, Maryland, he had made his contribution to the effort. When he returned to Philadelphia, along with other newly liberated men who made their way back, he knew that he was no longer the property of anyone, although what he did not know but was soon to learn was that freedom had assumed a qualitative factor and was available in varying degrees to different classes of men. Like soldiers returning from other wars, black veterans found it difficult to obtain jobs, but unlike other men they also found themselves excluded from virtually all other forms of social intercourse, including the church. The discrimination they experienced in the marketplace paralleled their treatment in the sanctuary.

Religious forms in Philadelphia were as diverse as everything else about the city. But the numerous smaller sects that flourished never attracted significant numbers of black people, nor did Quaker meetings and Lutheran services appear to interest them. It was the major denominations, the Methodists, Episcopalians, and Presbyterians, that seemed to have the greatest appeal for church-going blacks, with the Baptists at that time following some distance behind.

The most prestigious church in Allen's hometown was the Episcopal Church, composed of a union of Christ Church and St. Peters, and it had already begun to acquire some black adherents. If the possibility of recent slaves attending the same church as their former masters seemed curious to observers, it became more understandable once the particular circumstances were known.

[28] Sparks, *Writings of Washington*, VIII, 322-23; quoted in W. B. Hartgrove, "The Negro Soldier in the American Revolution," *JNH*, I (1916), 125.

The individual church had an unusual tradition that helped explain its practice of encouraging black attendance: not only had
it initiated special classes for potential black members, but unlike most other Anglican churches, it had followed the lead of its
rector, William White, and cast its lot with the patriots during
the war. Its ministry to blacks dated from 1758 when the rector
then in office had responded to the suggestion of the S.P.G. and
appointed an assistant, initially the Rev. William Sturgeon, to
catechize those who, either through their own choice or at the in-
sistence of masters, attended services there.[29] And during the war,
while most Anglican churches had to struggle to find their identity on the colonial side of the Atlantic—and many simply abandoned their futile efforts in favor of support for England—the
Philadelphia church set aside a special pew for General Washington's use and offered the services of its rector as chaplain to
the Continental Congress.[30] Black people who first came to the
church when Yorktown was just a memory may have been unaware of its interesting past, but they found the welcome acceptable and its patriotic politics agreeable. The attitude of its white
parishioners, probably consistent with the local aristocracy's mood
of passive paternalism, tested the forebearance of black worshipers. But it is not surprising that despite its best efforts the church
failed to recruit significant numbers of blacks, because basically
its low-church, but formal, services and polished sermons were
designed to meet the needs of the socially elite. And, in addition,
it placed limitations on black worshipers in terms of seating arrangements and participation. A few prominent Negroes among
Allen's contemporaries eventually became Episcopalians by joining the racially separate African Church of St. Thomas, and of
these perhaps the best known were Absalom Jones, friend to Allen
and first rector of the church, and James Forten, well-to-do sailmaker, social activist and patriarch of a family of community

29 Richard James Hooker, "The Anglican Church and the American Revolution" (unpublished Ph.D. dissertation, University of Chicago, 1943), 69.
30 William White not only served as chaplain to the Congress, but was consecrated as the first American bishop in 1787. See Walter H. Stowe (ed.), *The
Life and Letters of Bishop William White* (New York: Church Historical Society, 1937), No. 9; Sydney A. Temple, Jr., *The Common Sense Theology of
Bishop White* (New York, 1946).

leaders. The majority of black observers, however, found the Episcopal services unappealing.

The Presbyterians tried not to be outdone by the Episcopalians in their efforts to acquire black members, but they seemed to meet with no greater success. The official regional body, the Presbyterian Synod of New York and Philadelphia, recorded its corporate approval of abolition in 1787, while it also managed to add the observation that those who are "introduced from a servile state to . . . civil society, without a proper education . . . may be . . . dangerous to the community."[31] Their Calvinistic concern for education was apparent, too, in the sermons of the clergy, but comparatively few local black residents responded to them with any degree of enthusiasm. The size of the Negro membership nevertheless managed to grow slowly but steadily until, by 1801, it was thought expedient by both groups to organize a separate African Presbyterian Church. John Gloucester was subsequently called as its first minister, after which he and Allen began a competition for members in the local area.[32]

Although the Quakers had many admirers in the black community—including Allen and Absalom Jones who adopted some Friendly practices—the Society acquired few converts. The problem was that while blacks obviously supported its vigorous antislavery campaigns, they found its meetings unimpressive and occasionally unfriendly. The number of Negroes actually accepted for membership in Quaker societies was probably very small.[33]

The Baptists offered the kind of service that black people could respond to, one relatively free from the more obvious social elitism of the other groups, but they recognized their opportunity later than the other denominations, and therefore had to meet

[31] Quoted in Anson Phelps Stokes, *Church and State in the United States* (New York: Harper & Brothers, 1950), II, 137.

[32] William T. Catto, *A Semi-Centenary Discourse, Delivered in the First African Presbyterian Church, Philadelphia, May 1857* (Philadelphia: Joseph M. Wilson, 1857), 25.

[33] Henry J. Cadbury, "Negro Membership in the Society of Friends," *JNH*, XXI (1936), 151-213; Herbert Aptheker, "The Quakers and Negro Slavery," *JNH*, XXV (1940), 331-62; Thomas E. Drake, "Joseph Drinker's Plea, for the Admission of Colored People to the Society of Friends," *JNH*, XXXII (1947), 110-11. Aptheker and Drake, in particular, maintain that few Negroes were admitted to membership in Quaker meetings.

the competition of already existing programs.[34] The fact that Baptist churches relied on local initiative and direction also affected their rate of development, and unfortunately for historians, contributed to a haphazard system of record keeping.

There were black members scattered among the various other denominations and sects in the city, but they were to be found in greatest numbers among the Methodists, and particularly at St. George's Church, where they formed a sizable segment of the membership. When Allen returned to the city at the request of the Methodist elder, it seemed quite natural for him to make his church home at St. George's.

St. George's represented another of the physical, as well as cultural, changes that had occurred in Philadelphia while Allen had been away in Delaware. It had been constructed in 1763 by the Dutch Presbyterians during a period of optimism, but the Calvinists soon realized that they had overbuilt, and rather than lose everything they had invested, they sold it at auction in 1769 for less than one-third its value.[35] The building, centrally and conveniently located for colonial missionary work, became known as the Mother Church of American Methodism, or "the Cathedral of Methodism." That reputation was further enhanced when Francis Asbury preached his first sermon in America from the pulpit of St. George's on October 29, 1771. Asbury became to American Methodism what Wesley was to English Methodism: occupying a position at the peak of the organizational structure, he was the denomination's acknowledged leader and self-effacing source of inspiration for the infant group. One of the first bishops of the American church, a bachelor who spent his lifetime as an

[34] Woodson, *History of the Negro Church*. Woodson has pointed out, as many other writers have, that black membership was highest among Baptists and Methodists.

[35] Fred Pierce Corson, "St. George's Church," in *Historic Philadelphia* (Philadelphia: American Philosophical Society Transactions, 1953), XLII, 231. The Methodists apparently did not buy it directly at the auction. According to the journal kept by the Rev. Joseph Pilmoor, the Methodist minister, a gentleman's son whom he described as being "non compos mentis," made a bid on the building at the auction for £700. Rather than reveal his son's condition, the father honored his bid, but then resold the structure immediately to the Methodists for £650. The building reportedly cost the Presbyterians £2000 to construct.

itinerant, he regarded St. George's and Philadelphia as the closest approximation to a home that he could achieve. And in addition to Asbury's connection with the church, St. George's figured in the organizational history of the denomination by hosting the first three Annual Conferences of Methodism, beginning in 1773.[36]

The church continued to grow in membership just as the denomination as a whole began to expand. And when Allen worshiped at St. George's he discovered that most of the black participants seemed to appreciate the type of service being offered: they responded, just as he had, to the almost irresistible appeal of the Wesleyans. The elder in charge asked him to preach to various black groups, and he accepted the offer, in spite of the fact that he still lacked ordination and official status. This was his first formal association with a church, since up to that time he had been traveling steadily without the luxury of a settled place.

Allen's preaching career in Philadelphia began with a schedule that would have sorely taxed the energies of an older man. As it was, the routine proved to be a "great cross" even to the twenty-six year-old exhorter, who was often required to be at his assigned post at 5 o'clock on a Sunday morning. But he accepted the appointment, and was able to report that "We had a good time, and several souls were awakened"[37] (the latter obviously meant in a spiritual sense). With the early morning service completed, he was only just beginning a day that extended on through three or four more gatherings in other parts of the city until well into the evening. He adjusted to the routine with appropriate good humor, perhaps aware that the geographically scattered schedule brought him into contact with a fairly wide representation of the black population that could not be reached at St. George's alone. He noticed that few of his African brethren attended any church at all, and he may have felt that it was up to him to help to try to change the situation.

Allen had originally intended to stay in Philadelphia for only "a week or two." Since Methodist practice encouraged an itinerant ministry, it was quite in keeping with accepted conventions

36 *Ibid.,* 234.
37 Allen, *Life Experience,* 23-24.

for Allen to anticipate a lifetime on the road. But his plans changed during that fortnight, and he decided to remain in Philadelphia. During that brief period he had met more black Methodists than he had ever encountered previously in one place, and observed even more unchurched freedmen, who were all, he might have speculated, potential converts for Methodism. It was a field "ripe for the harvest," and he was going to reap the grain. He began by teaching classes for adults at St. George's, as well as conducting regular prayer meeting sessions. He also entertained the notion of creating a separate African Methodist Church because he believed that two basic ingredients were present to bring it about; a relatively large free black population and a vital interest in Methodist practice. The idea represented yet another variation on his tendency to associate Methodism with freedom and liberation.

There was, in fact, an interesting parallel between that ideological combination and the way certain events had materialized in the city. Ironically, Philadelphia had itself witnessed the simultaneous rise of Methodism and the liberation of slaves during Allen's residence out of state, an order that did not escape the attention of local black residents. The advent of Methodism alone did not determine the demise of slavery—agitation for abolition had been initiated by Quakers long before the followers of Wesley made their appearance—but the influence of its antislavery stand came at an auspicious time, when the institution was proving to be an economic liability and slaveowners were vulnerable to emancipation appeals made by social reformers.

Methodism had acquired an historic identification with Philadelphia in the public mind, even as early as 1786. The city had served as one of those centers where some of the first potential Methodists had gathered to pray and discuss their mutual concerns, and where, while the denomination was still regarded as a movement within the Anglican fold, the first three Annual Conferences met to conduct business and assign preachers. Unfortunately for Philadelphia, the most portentous event to transpire in the early life of the church—the gathering of the first General Conference—occurred not in the City of Brotherly Love, but in its neighbor to the south, Baltimore. The General Conference of

1784, known also as the Christmas Conference, provided an occasion for church leaders to look back on what they had achieved in the colonies, and to look forward to what they would like to see emerge from their efforts. As such, it served as the organizing General Conference of American Methodism, and, according to one participant, William Watters, created "a separate church" no longer tied to Anglicanism. The Baltimore meeting also worked out decisions affecting denominational discipline, polity, and structure, thereby affirming its own separate identity and incidentally impressing recent converts like Allen with its apparent commitment to principle. (Allen reported the names of some church leaders who attended the Christmas Conference, and he may have attended the meeting himself, although such a possibility seems remote.)[38] Thus, the fact that it was Baltimore rather than Philadelphia that served as the formal birthplace of American Methodism conferred on the city of the prestige attached to historic priority, while Philadelphia retained its symbolic image as the sentimental center of the denomination, particularly since Asbury, now officially recognized as Bishop, used it as his home base.

Allen was impressed by the accomplishments of the Baltimore delegates, particularly in two areas: the form of central organization which was outlined, and the platform on slavery which was adopted.

Previously aware of the denomination's stand on slavery, he subsequently became a vigorous supporter of its organizational structure. Methodist opposition to slavery seemed to be something he could almost expect to take for granted: hadn't Wesley declared himself to be an enemy of the practice, and hadn't the Discipline—the codification of church policy and polity—attacked slavetrading and slaveholders and refused church office to slaveowners? Such a policy was bound to attract new black members, if the ideas were presented in a sensitive way, and if there was an

---

[38] *Ibid.*, 22. Allen reported the names of Coke, Whatcoat, and Vassey among those in attendance. Some writers maintain that Allen attended the Christmas Conference, although there is no evidence to corroborate such a statement beyond Allen's comment concerning the presence of the church leaders. He may have been an observer or Whatcoat's guest—as a layman he would not have been permitted to participate—but even his attendance is unconfirmed.

organizational framework to contain the new adherents. He examined Methodism in both categories and found it equal to the challenge: said Allen, "[t]he reason that the Methodist is so successful in the awakening and conversion of the colored people, is the plain doctrine and having a good discipline."[39]

The organization that Allen supported was based on a tightly knit hierarchical structure rooted in the parish and directed by the General Conference. The Anglican heritage of Methodism was obvious in many respects, being noticeably apparent in this system of organization, but Wesley reinforced the already rigid superstructure by adding yet another level as a check against denominational laxity. He suggested the creation of local parish disciplinary committees whose responsibilities included listening to cases of members accused of variously identified indiscretions, then passing judgment, and issuing penalties for alleged offenses. Such an arrangement had the effect of keeping everyone, from parishioner to presiding Bishop, in a state of constant watchfulness, and served to shape the organization into an army of anxious zealots, ready to do battle with the sins of secular society. Beyond the level of the local society, the Conference was the basic unit of organization, and clerical delegates at Quarterly, Annual, or General Conferences dealt with church business while they, too, kept an eye on matters of discipline; in this case as they related to the clergy. Allen apparently discerned a way to put this type of organization and discipline to practical use to meet the needs of black converts, spiritual and otherwise.

But for Allen, Methodism was not merely the sum of its attributes—its organization, Discipline, theology and style of worship—rather it was a way of life, a wholly new regenerative and revitalizing experience. And an integral part of that experience was the emphasis on antislavery, not as a mere afterthought, but as a basic denominational doctrine. Eighteenth-century Methodism seemed no more likely to be separated from its policy on slavery than the itinerant preacher from his horse and saddlebags. So strong was denominational concern in this regard in 1784, that written into the Discipline was a plan to expel from membership all those

[39] *Ibid.*, 29.

who bought or sold slaves except for the purpose of freeing them.[40] Eventually, it is true, this policy would be challenged by those who disagreed with it—including Southern planters and Northern laborers—but when Allen accepted Methodism its official position seemed incontrovertible.

A similar situation prevailed in secular society: an apparently strong Pennsylvania law seemed bound to guarantee freedom and civil liberties to black residents. If the 1780 measure, referred to as "the first statutory action against slavery in the United States,"[41] represented a more cautious approach than the one offered by the Methodists, it was obviously more far reaching in its application. The legislation seemed to be one by-product of much of the egalitarian Revolutionary rhetoric that had circulated freely in the city at the time of its adoption, one that Quakers, Methodists, Deists, and sectarians could all support. The impact of the act was felt only gradually, since it provided that, although all children born subsequent to its passage would be free, all Negro or mulatto children born to slave mothers would remain servants until they reached the age of twenty-eight. This moderate approach, designed to give white people and institutions the opportunity to adjust slowly to the expanding free population, also afforded masters time to discover the loopholes in the act, such as the practice earlier referred to of sending women out of state to bear their children. These gaps remained open until 1788, when the legislature passed an amendment to the original measure.[42]

---

[40] Stokes, *Church and State*, II, 135. See also the Methodist Episcopal Church *Discipline* for 1784, and Donald G. Mathews, *Slavery and Methodism: A Chapter in American Morality, 1780-1845* (Princeton: Princeton University Press, 1965).

[41] Kutler, "Pennslyvania Courts, the Abolition Act, and Negro Rights," *Pennsylvania History*, XXX (1963), 14.

[42] 13 *Pennsylvania Statutes at Large*, 54; Kutler, "Pennsylvania Courts, the Abolition Act, and Negro Rights," *Pennsylvania History*, XXX (1963), 14-15. Kutler points out that masters not only sent pregnant females into slave states to bear their children, but that they also sold their other slaves into non-free states. He suggests that "the judiciary of the state played a vital role in its [slavery's] eradication."

There were other changes which the law of 1780 provided for men like Allen. They were technically accorded legal rights in the courts, except that until 1847 a slave could not testify against a freedman. And although virtually no black men voted, the state Constitutions of 1776 and 1790 did not bar them

In spite of the fact that it was a cautious measure, the 1780 act promised the possibility of a fundamental change in the existing social order. In Philadelphia, for example, at the time of the first national census in 1790, the urban population of 28,000 was 6 per cent black.[43] As the provisions of the law began to take effect, and new freedmen were joined by former Southern blacks who emigrated to the city, the pressure on social institutions to implement racial equality grew more intense. The white social structure had previously accommodated a few freedmen with relative ease, but now it seemed to lack the flexibility and willingness to cope with the new pressures created by the increase in the free population. It seemed rather ironical, but true, that the Quaker City of Brotherly Love encouraged emancipation while it simultaneously fostered a segregated social structure that was recognized, if not legitimized.

For most new freedmen, the obstacles in the way of a new life seemed formidable, and it is not surprising that some chose to remain on as hired hands in the homes of their former masters. The opportunity to strike out as independent workers, however, seemed far more attractive to the majority of free Negroes, who preferred to accept the risks and insecurities that accompanied their new status. Few were very long in encountering the limitations that that status conveyed; discriminatory practices qualified their independence and restricted their mobility in the voting booth, at the marketplace, and in the church pew.

---

from doing so, as that of 1838 later did. In theory, the law of 1780 provided that black people were to enjoy the same civil rights as whites. See Kutler, "Pennsylvania Courts," 15; John H. Fertig and Frank M. Hunter (eds.), *Constitutions of Pennsylvania* (Harrisburg, 1916); John Purdom (comp.), *A Digest of the Laws of Pennsylvania from 1700 to 1861* (9th ed.; Philadelphia: Kay and Bros., 1862), 716.

[43] Department of Commerce, Bureau of the Census, *Negro Population, 1790-1915*, 55.

There are two official population figures available for Philadelphia in 1790: 28,522 and 54,391. The former figure includes only the city itself, while the latter is a combination of city and neighboring districts. The city total of black people was 1,630; for city and suburbs 2,489. It was in the city that Negroes represented 6 per cent of the total population. See *Philadelphia in 1824*, n.a. (Philadelphia: H. C. Carey and I. Lea, 1824), 29; Edward R. Turner, *The Negro in Pennsylvania, 1639-1861* (Washington: American Historical Association, 1911).

Success in the marketplace determined the freedman's social standing and therefore influenced virtually all the rest of his social relationships. And it was in the marketplace that he found his civil rights most obviously and seriously threatened. While he might be dissuaded from voting through more subtle exercises of pressure, such as fear and intimidation, he was openly challenged in the field of job competition by rebuff and discriminatory hiring.[44] Custom and tradition had assigned a social value to virtually all jobs, and the most menial of these were reserved for recent immigrants and blacks who were thus forced into frequent competition with each other for the same positions. The black worker's limited experience and education restricted still further his employment opportunities. The charity schools in the city, which had been conducted by Benezet and the Abolition Society, met the educational needs of only a fraction of the black population.[45] Most black workers were therefore forced to accept the lowest paying jobs available, such as day laborers, chimney sweeps, house servants, woodcutters, seamen, carpenters, and baggage carriers, to mention just a few. Others were even less fortunate, and had to exist on temporary or part-time wages paid for day work at odd jobs. If there was any gradation on the black social scale, it was more obvious in this distinction between those fully employed and those underemployed, rather than between a menial working class and a professional middle class. To be sure, there were the successful men who had gambled on their future and won, and their meager ranks included not only James Forten and the physician, James Derham, but also Absalom Jones and eventually Richard Allen. But potential businessmen and shopkeepers were hindered by their inability to borrow money, and aspiring professional men were limited by their lack of access to formal train-

[44] Leon Litwack, *North of Slavery* (Chicago: University of Chicago Press, 1961), 65.

[45] As early as 1740, George Whitefield had planned to open a charity school for black students, but the effort had to be abandoned because of lack of funds. Benezet seized upon Whitefield's idea and ran a small school, which he taught himself. By 1770 his school had aroused the interest of a committee of Friends, who assumed its financial support and expanded its enrollment. The Abolition Society also supported a school for Negroes. See Turner, *The Negro in Pennsylvania*, 128; Bridenbaugh, *Rebels and Gentlemen*, 256; *The Philadelphia Register, 1819*, 199.

ing.[46] If black people hoped to improve their economic condition, they had to realize that the emancipationist sentiments of the reformers did not necessarily imply support for civil equality, that success in that struggle depended on their own efforts and those of their supporters.

Allen recognized the nucleus for black concern and activity in the small groups of Methodists he addressed around the city. Segregated in the churches and discriminated against on the job, they were pleased to have a black preacher fire their emotions and encourage their hopes. Allen thought that he saw among them the potential for creating a separate African congregation, and told the Methodist elder, whom he referred to as "The Rev. C.B.," about his idea. The elder's predictable response was negative, and the sentiments of Allen's black friends echoed his answer. But Allen remained convinced that the idea had merit, and in spite of joint opposition, he continued to lay his plans for a separate organization. He was twenty-six years old in 1786, physically free, and free from his debt to Stokeley, and if he had been warmed by the fires of Methodism and Revolutionary ardor, he had had his spirits cooled by the chill air that had a way of permeating Philadelphia social circles. He was young, enthusiastic, and ambitious; a practical man who recognized the advantage of planning for the future.

[46] Turner, *The Negro in Pennsylvania*, 123-25. The lack of credit and related financial problems failed to discourage some Negroes from buying houses. It has been estimated that before the close of the eighteenth century, nearly 100 houses in the city were owned by black people.

II

A QUESTION OF CONTROL:
BLACK METHODIST OR WHITE

We have already followed the history of the rise of the Free African Society, which was the beginning of the Negro Church in the North. We often forget that the rise of a church organization among Negroes was a curious phenomenon. The church really represented all that was left of African tribal life, and was the sole expression of the organized efforts of the slaves. It was natural that any movement among freedmen should centre about their religious life, the sole remaining element of their former tribal system.

W. E. B. Dubois
The Philadelphia Negro

WHEN BLACK PEOPLE FINALLY GOT THE CHANCE to develop their own religious interests without white interference, one of the first things they did was to negotiate for a churchyard or a segment of a Potter's Field in which to bury their dead. The move was significant, but also tragic, because it pointed to the fact that virtually all religious groups, including Quakers, refused to be buried in the same part of a cemetery that included the mortal remains of black people. It was yet another example of the kind of segregated relationships that characterized life for the Northern freedman in the new nation. More than a contradiction of Revolutionary promises, it suggested that interest in implementing claims for civil equality was practically nonexistent, and that the egalitarian mood of the war generation had changed into one that offered pity for black folks who could never make themselves white—as the celebrated Henry Moss reportedly had done.

The formation of the first African Church in the United States was both a challenge and a response to that kind of thinking. It was also a commentary on the rise of institutionalized racial segregation in Northern society. As the free black population grew in size, it threatened to disrupt the emerging peacetime white consensus, and the only way that social leaders seemed able to deal with it was to separate it and restrict it. In those places where blacks were few in number, as in New England, there was little black agitation for separate organizations; indeed, in many locations there were simply too few resident freedmen to make it feasible for them to even consider such an option. But in cities like Philadelphia, where black people could make their presence felt, they were alternately confronted with harassment and neglect. Rather than put up with that kind of situation, they chose to look for their own solutions. They began with that area of their life in which they had retained an element of self-expression, and that was the church.

Allen said he "saw a large field open in seeking and instructing my African brethren, who had been a long forgotten people . . ."[1] and decided to remain in Philadelphia, rather than move on after two weeks as he originally planned. Personal considerations were undoubtedly involved in his decision: the status of freedmen was, at best, anomalous, at worst, extremely hazardous, and the city offered the protection of a degree of anonymity along with a sense of community among local blacks. The possibility of creating some kind of financial security also existed, as it did not in rural areas, and certainly not in the itinerant ministry. Shops and stores, houses and land, described the business mentality of the area, and Allen thought he saw a chance to be a part of it.

Allen's ambition, however, tended to be of the expansive kind

[1] Allen, *Life Experience*, 24.

that rarely found sufficient satisfaction within the limits of personal security alone. Security was obviously important, but he was willing to risk it occasionally to satisfy certain drives, whether personal, professional, or racial. To him the unchurched population of urban freedmen seemed to offer the kind of challenge that his ego and intellect required. He preached whenever asked, and within a relatively short time managed to establish regular prayer meeting sessions that attracted as many as forty-two people. A group of that size could readily serve as the nucleus for a separate church, but without their active support and with the open opposition of the Methodist elder, the prospect had to be dropped temporarily. He reported that his request to the elder was refused in language that was "very degrading and insulting."[2]

Instead of forming a church, Allen and his friends devised an alternate proposal: they would organize instead a nonsectarian, benevolent Free African Society. The new Society would technically be a nonreligious body, although given the denominational inclinations of its supporters, it was perhaps inevitable that certain church practices would eventually creep in. Unlike the earlier project, this idea gradually gained momentum and support, finally culminating in a decision to create a formal organization, complete with written rules for personal conduct and a statement of purpose, described as the Preamble and Articles of Association. The official documents were drawn up, presented to a select committee of eight on May 17, 1787, and were unanimously approved, slightly more than a month after the idea first assumed written form.[3] Prominent among the signers and throughout the proceedings·were the religious co-workers, Allen and Absalom Jones.

The friendship between the two men began when Allen returned to Philadelphia and endured until Jones's death in 1818 at the age of seventy-one. Both became clergymen in Philadelphia

---

[2] *Ibid.*

[3] William Douglass, *Annals of the First African Church in the United States of America, now styled The African Episcopal Church of St. Thomas;* also, *Minutes of the Free African Society* (Philadelphia: King & Baird, 1862), 7. Douglass, a mid-nineteenth-century minister of St. Thomas's, reproduced the minutes of the Free African Society in his *Annals;* they are therefore both available in the same volume.

—serving the first two African churches in the North—and managed to cooperate effectively on numerous projects of mutual concern in spite of their differences in temperament and interest.
Some of the differences that described the two men could be
traced to age: Allen in 1787 was twenty-seven; Jones was forty-one.
But this alone was not a sufficient explanation, because there were
other personality differences separating the men that could not be
attributed simply to age. Reared in the same tradition of Middle
States slavery, Jones embarked upon a career that, while profes-
sionally similar, offered an interesting comparison with that of his
younger colleague. Jones had been born in Sussex, Delaware,
where he remained until his master sent him to work in a shop in
Philadelphia. Just as diligent as Allen, Jones worked in the store
by day and attended a Friend's school at night to learn the basic
skills he had been denied in slavery. Again like Allen, he saved
his money until he had accumulated enough to purchase his own
freedom, and also his wife's, and somehow managed to have
enough left over to buy several income-producing houses in the
city.[4] But in spite of the fact that he had bought his own freedom,
he continued to work in the store owned by his former master,
with the difference being that as a freedman he earned "good
wages." His decision to remain with his previous owner may have
been an indication of a cautious, conservative nature, or simply
the result of certain practical financial considerations. A man of
average height, with dark complexion and stocky frame, he later
acquired the powdered wig and clerical attire that Allen scorned.
He was never charged with being domineering and forceful, as
Allen was, but neither was he remembered for his preaching style.
He was reportedly a mild-mannered man, conscientious about his
pastoral duties and committed to racial and moral reform. In recognition of his usefulness to the denomination, the Methodists
licensed him, as they had Allen, as a lay preacher in the church.[5]

Jones's moderation served as an effective balance for Allen's enthusiasm in determining the direction of the Free African Society.

---

[4] Absalom Jones, *Narrative of the Life of the Rev. Absalom Jones*, n.d., n.p.
[5] Albert Cliffe, *The Glory of Our Methodist Heritage* (Nashville: Abingdon,
1958), 124. Cliffe, a mid-twentieth century minister at St. George's, wrote a
history of the church based on the historical records available.

Another interest they shared, respect for the Quaker tradition that had given them some schooling, also helped to temper the mood of the meetings. The Articles of Association that they adopted, however, which were actually guides for good conduct, were far more effective in maintaining order and a sense of purpose than either Jones's personality or Quaker influence. The guidelines clearly established the Society as a benevolent organization, concerned about the welfare of its members, their children, wives, and widows. Those who joined were required to observe the rules that included regular attendance at meetings (unless excused for reasons of health), consistent contributions to the general treasury, sobriety, and decorum. All infractions were judged by a committee of members, and those found guilty of a violation were accordingly penalized, usually with a fine but sometimes with suspension. The dues that accumulated in the treasury were available to the widows and orphans of members, as well as others in need, at the rate of three shillings nine pence per week. But the Society was more than a mutual aid organization, since it was as interested in supervising the moral life of its members as it was in providing for their physical needs. In addition to the injunction against the use of alcohol, the group encouraged thrift, propriety, and marital fidelity, and its diligent committees saw to it that the rules were respected.[6]

Allen's participation in the Society did not prevent him from carrying on with the rest of his commitments. He continued to meet his preaching and teaching obligations at St. George's while he simultaneously pursued first one and then another secular calling: among the occupations he reportedly followed were those of blacksmith, wagon driver, grocer, shoe merchant, and landlord. He was, in addition, the only black preacher in all of Philadelphia at the time (Jones's ministerial time was devoted to teaching rather than preaching at this point) and his services, much in demand, produced tangible results. Black converts began to fill the seats in St. George's until no more empty ones remained. In the future, who would stand and who would sit during Sunday worship? The answer was hardly a problem. The black Methodists

[6] Douglass, *Minutes of the Free African Society*, 16-17.

were asked to give up their seats, and, said Allen, they were "placed . . . around the wall."[7] Somehow that section of the Discipline dealing with racial policies seemed to have little practical relevance for this particular branch of Wesley's Zion.

The revised seating arrangement failed to solve the predicament at St. George's. The church was clearly overcrowded, with the only sensible solution being the addition of new facilities. In a great flurry of activity, the membership embarked on a rebuilding, refurbishing campaign, with black members contributing a significant share of muscle and money. When the project was completed, the members naturally resumed their former habits, including their old seating patterns, but black parishioners were told that the situation would henceforth be different for them: in the future they would have to sit in the new galleries above the seats they had previously occupied on the main floor.

For many of Allen's racial contemporaries, the order was not without precedent. They were beginning to recognize discriminatory treatment as inevitable in other areas of their lives, and its current appearance in their church life only served to remind them that segregated seating was becoming an integral part of a developing pattern. There were certain aspects of this situation that were different however: tempers on both sides had been raised over the issue of a separate African church, and the newly redecorated sanctuary itself was a vivid testimonial to the contributions of black members to St. George's. Further, it may have appeared to Allen that as a recognized lay preacher, he was entitled to a certain amount of respect and consideration. The tensions generated on both sides were not to be denied; Allen was convinced that church officials regarded the "colored brethren" as "a nuisance," and local leaders were suspicious of African designs for separate worship facilities. The ingredients for a confrontation were present, awaiting only the right stimulus to set them in motion.

Such a situation presented itself when the church was re-opened for worship. Allen and his friends, arriving just after the service had begun, were directed by the sexton to seats in the gallery.

---

[7] Allen, *Life Experience,* 25.

The places they occupied were apparently not the ones intended for them, for shortly after prayers had begun, and while everyone was kneeling, a trustee approached Absalom Jones and began to pull him off his knees. Jones asked the man to wait until the prayer had ended, but the impatient trustee refused to be put off a moment longer. " 'No,' " he said, " 'you must get up now, or I will call for aid and force you away.' "[8] A second request by Jones was again denied as the white man motioned to another trustee to assist him in pulling the praying Africans from their knees. Just as they were ready to act, the prayer ended, the black group walked out in a body, and, according to Allen, "they were no more plagued with us in the church."[9]

The dramatic withdrawal of the black Methodists, perhaps the most significant event that Allen witnessed in his lifetime, marked the beginning of the independent black church movement. Unlike previous Southern attempts to practice religious separatism, this move initiated a sustained effort, carried out under black direction, and frequently in opposition to white demands to desist. The withdrawal from St. George's came in November 1787, seven months after the Preamble for the Free African Society was first composed.

It was the issue of separate black worship facilities that brought tempers to the boiling point; the seating problem simply caused the emotional juices to overflow. From the Methodist elder's point of view, there was no reason for the Africans to desire or require separate church accommodations. Their spiritual needs were being met at St. George's through the standard schedule of preaching, praying, counseling, and singing that served alike for whites. Why were the black members so anxious to worship apart? Allen's perspective was necessarily quite different. Why should black people accept segregation and discrimination in the white church when they had the potential for creating a church of their own? Why should they be regarded as a "nuisance" when they asked for the opportunity to meet by themselves for prayers? And why, when the nucleus for a congregation already existed in the African Society, why then accept the insults and indignities publicly

8 *Ibid.*
9 *Ibid.*

hurled about by trustees during Sunday prayers? Allen later speculated that the white Methodists, when they reflected on the events,
"were ashamed of their conduct," but in view of their continued
harassment of the seceders, such a conclusion seems rather generous.

The events that took place in Philadelphia in the fall of 1787
bore an uncanny resemblance to similar ones that had transpired
that previous summer in Baltimore, although the evidence suggests that the two developments occurred independent of each
other. The black Methodists there had also been restricted by the
white majority, and choosing not to submit to continued indignities, seceded to form an independent group. They were forced to
improvise means at every stage in their development: they had no
internal organization, no meeting place, no funds, no minister,
and no real leadership. Still they continued, and approached
Bishop Asbury with a request for a church of their own, but were
turned down. The local white leadership reportedly regarded
them as a "body of malcontents," whose plans for separation were
dangerous and disruptive.[10] They managed to survive in this disorganized state until a later acquaintance of Allen's, Daniel Coker,
arrived on the scene around the turn of the century and eventually supervised their purchase of church property in 1817. The se-
quence of events in Baltimore suggested that as discriminatory
treatment became an ever more prominent feature of Methodist
church life, it encouraged black demands for separate facilities.

The Allenites were more fortunate than their friends to the
South in having not only competent leadership but also a previously existing organization on which to rely. During the uncer-
tain period that immediately followed the secession, Allen and
Jones kept the group together, using the meetings of the Free
African Society to develop plans for the future. And now that
they were all without a church home, the members looked increasingly toward the Society to suggest some kind of meaningful
substitute.

[10] James A. Handy, *Scraps of African Methodist Episcopal History* (Philadelphia: A. M. E. Book Concern, n.d.), 24, quoted in James M. Wright, *The
Free Negro in Maryland, 1634-1860* (New York: Columbia University Press,
1921), 217.

Under the circumstances, it was almost inevitable that the Society would modify its format somewhat, but the change it took was not to Allen's liking. A tendency toward Quakerism gradually began to pervade the group's sessions in subtle but significant ways. A simple marriage ceremony adopted for use by members was basically Quaker in background, as was the resolution to observe fifteen minutes of silence before the start of meetings. Allen, increasingly discontented with the Society's failure to form a denominational alliance, found such Friendly practices to be purposeless gestures, leading him to break with the group. It was not that Allen bore the Quakers any ill feeling—as a member of the founding committee of the Free African Society he had given his consent to a provision which said that the first and all succeeding F.A.S. clerk-treasurers should be Friends—but rather that he felt that there were other groups, notably the Methodists, whose message had greater relevance to the concerns of the black community. Quaker detachment and introspection were not without value, but they did not seem to speak to the immediate needs of black people as Allen saw them. Methodist conversion was observable, enthusiastic preaching brought results, structured organization discouraged laxity: it was such things as these that Allen enjoyed in his Methodist associations and missed in the Society.

Allen's departure from the Society probably occurred in the spring of 1789, nearly two years after the withdrawal from St. George's. A seven-man committee was appointed to deal with him, to persuade him to abandon his attempt to encourage Methodist affiliation, and to remind him that it was contrary to Society rules to convene a group of members without full membership approval, as he apparently had done. Even after several entreaties, Allen remained unmoved, refusing "to submit himself to the rules of the Society," and was "accordingly disunited until he shall come to a sense of his conduct, and request to be admitted a member according to our discipline."[11]

He held his ground, although it was obviously a frustrating position for a man with his church interests to be in. He had sat through endless meetings of the Society while supporters discussed

---

11 Douglass, *Minutes of the Free African Society,* 24.

issues that were important but nevertheless peripheral to his main concern: his long-range interests extended beyond such immediate concerns as the merits of a particular kind of wedding ceremony, or the value of promptness, or the need to buy a section of the local Potter's Field. All such conversation could be borne with if the final result was a decision to accept Methodist affiliation. But now it seemed as if these former Methodists were passing judgment on their old denomination by adopting an obvious Quaker practice, and Allen was displeased. He had not broken his ties with St. George's to become a Quaker, and he was not going to permit the Society to persuade him to do so.

With Allen gone, the leadership of the organization fell to Jones, who, though less dynamic than his young friend, was more patient and conciliatory when it came to dealing with refractory members. He sensed the feelings of the members, and accurately diagnosed their desire to form new religious ties. They voted on the issue of affiliation, and remembering their past treatment at St. George's, a majority elected to become Episcopalians. Jones was not a member of the majority, but he appreciated their sympathies, and offered to direct their efforts to gain recognition by the Episcopal hierarchy.

Allen had denied himself the right to vote on the matter when he withdrew from the Society, but he never would have agreed to an alliance with the Episcopalians in any case. Sometime later when a few members approached him with a request to follow them into the Episcopal Church, he refused. He preferred, he said, to remain with his first religious loyalty, even though Jones had decided to do otherwise. But the two men were not cut out of the same psychic cloth; while Jones was essentially a quiet, peaceful man, a committed churchman whose intuitive skill in diplomacy prevented angry confrontations, Allen was a more aggressive person, capable of exercising leadership, but lacking Jones's tact in social relationships.

Allen did manage to convince some of his friends from the Free African Society to join him in his attempt to shape a Methodist society out of the remnant of seceders. The result was that the previously harmonious mutual-aid society was divided into two camps: one group, the larger of the two, worked with Jones to gain Episcopal recognition, while the other, considerably smaller, accepted Allen's direction to return to Methodism. Jones's numerical advantage permitted him to proceed immediately with plans for a church building, while Allen had to wait until he had enough support to implement less ambitious plans.

Allen's personal resources were meager; those of his followers even less ample, which meant that funds for their own church building would have to be raised through a general public subscription. The local free black community could provide some, but by no means all, of the money they needed since the basic requirements for survival took most of their cash, and whatever the religiously inclined had set aside for church purposes had already been donated toward the building of the galleries at St. George's. Still, a public subscription was the only alternative and the black community was asked to do its part, while the gifts of interested white patrons were also quite welcome. Allen called on two friends of antislavery, both members of the Abolition Society, Dr. Benjamin Rush and Robert Ralston, to ask for their help. The two philanthropists, according to Allen, "pitied our situation, and subscribed largely towards the church, and were very friendly towards us, and advised us how to go on."[12] Both men assisted the Africans in their solicitation—Ralston by serving as treasurer, Rush by promoting their case publicly—and in the process incurred the gratitude of Allen, whose expressed hope it was that their names "will never be forgotten among us."

Rush and Ralston's civic interests involved them in a wide range of community projects, but local black residents knew them best for their work as active abolitionists. They served as leaders in the state Abolition Society, which was, in turn, a powerful force within the national organization. Their personal values and feelings therefore cast a rather long shadow. Not only were their personal convictions the reflections of the larger group, but the Abolition Society itself mirrored some of their concern for a natural-rights inspired commitment to humanitarian service. They represented the social standards of their own particular class—the liberal upper class—by serving as symbols of the ideal standards to which many of their peers publicly claimed to aspire.

12 Allen, *Life Experience,* 12.

And the national Abolition Society thought it helpful to pass on
these values to their black friends to help them improve their conduct, that is, to bring them to the standards admired by the white
philanthropists. When the Society adopted nine "Articles of Advice" to "Free Africans" in 1796, it passed on to them a list of
suggestions that had a familiar ring, including such recommendations as: attend church regularly, work diligently at "useful
trades," respect education, dress modestly, avoid "frolicking,"
"idleness," and liquor, contract legal marriages, and save money.[13]
Undoubtedly many of the black people who scanned the list saw
in it yet another example of class paternalism, to be regarded about
as seriously as empty promises of civil equality, but to the small
minority who had been members of the Free African Society there
was nothing very unusual about the list; indeed, it all seemed like
common knowledge. They could easily recall, if they took the

[13] *Minutes of the Proceedings of a Convention of Delegates from the Abolition Societies* (Philadelphia, 1796), 12-15. Turner has said of the Society that
its greatest assets were "thoroughness and persistence." Turner, *The Negro in
Pennsylvania*, 215.

The Minutes of the Society offer some insight into the change in racial attitudes that occurred during the last decade of the eighteenth and first decade
of the nineteenth centuries.

In 1794 the Abolition Society was able to affirm, "The voice of reason, and
the impulse of humanity, always at war with injustice, gradually tend to the
emancipation of slaves. . . ." *Minutes of the Proceedings of a Convention of
Delegates from the Abolition Societies* (Philadelphia, 1794), 15.

After 1800 members of the Society found their optimism dimmed and their
confidence somewhat shaken. Reports of the attempted Gabriel insurrection
in the South led them to resolve:

"In common with the rest of our fellow citizens we sincerely deplore the
late attempts at insurrection by some of the slaves of the southern states.
. . . We all revolt with horror from the anticipation of an organization on
the part of slaves. . . . An amelioration of the present situation of the
slaves, and the adoption of a system of gradual emancipation . . . would
also be an effectual security against revolt." *Minutes of the Proceedings of
a Convention of Delegates from the Abolition Societies* (Philadelphia, 1801),
38-39.

By 1804 they were forced to conclude that ". . . although the indifference and
dislike to the universal extension of the blessings of freedom, manifested by
some of our fellow citizens, would tend to excite a degree of discouragement,
yet we feel a hope that the day is approaching when the rights and preveleges
[sic] of men, will be . . . fully enjoyed by our brethren of African descent. . . ." *Minutes of the Proceedings of a Convention of Delegates from the
Abolition Societies* (Philadelphia, 1804), 11.

time to, that the Free African Society had written into its discipline similar rules that tended to suggest the same high regard for the values promoted by the white abolitionists, values not usually associated with the poor and working classes. The causes for the similarity were twofold: first, because active antislavery freedmen worked closely with white abolitionist leaders they tended to absorb some of their social and intellectual priorities; and second, the prevailing spirit of the times, that sought to improve the "natural" man, affected black people as well as white. The principles involved became part of the ideological frame of reference for men like Jones and Allen, whose work in the religious separatist movement convinced them that the ideas had value for their own congregations and the black community as a whole. But unlike the white reformers who believed that "proper" conduct had certain intrinsic worth for the "natural" man—a sort of generalized assumption that virtue was its own reward—the black preachers appreciated its more practical aspects. They freely adapted these seemingly middle-class values to meet the needs of the poor freedmen who filled their congregations.

But Methodist denominational officials were as unimpressed by the social standing and moral priorities of Allen's white patrons and black associates as they were by his plans to build an African church. They insulted him, harassed him, and threatened to read him out of the society unless he abandoned his separatist tendencies. Allen tried to make it clear to them that while he was unwilling to return to St. George's, he was still basically loyal to Methodist tenets as he understood them. But no amount of reassurance on his part could convince them that his plan had merit. And yet, in an apparently paradoxical move, St. George's indicated its approval of segregated worship facilities when it sponsored a separate African chapel, called Zoar, in 1796.[14] There was, of course, a quite obvious difference between Allen's proposal and theirs: in the former situation black members would be directing their own religious affairs, while in the latter they would simply be responding to the directions of white supervisors.

[14] Cliffe, *Glory of Our Methodist Heritage;* Asbury, *Journal,* II, 93; Records of St. George's Methodist Episcopal Church, Philadelphia, MS, Methodist Historical Society, Philadelphia.

Allen's ultimate objective was clearly contrary to white designs, which meant that whatever other help he received, he could not count on support from the denomination. Even without their help he had managed to devise a simple meeting house by hauling a blacksmith shop to an available site on a team-drawn wagon. But in spite of the fact that the shop was refitted for its new purpose, it quickly proved to be too small for the growing congregation. A bigger building required more careful planning and greater support, and it was at this point that he had approached Rush and Ralston.

While Allen developed his plans, the remainder of the original group of seceders worked with Jones to devise a public subscription campaign that would help them acquire a building. Once the money was raised, they laid plans for the new facility, and in the process, acquired some practical knowledge of economics as they negotiated with local businessmen for both money and supplies. For most of those appointed to the committee, arranging for a $2,000. loan or for the purchase of 160,000 bricks was a new experience, but they managed to cope with the situation with a minimum of confusion and outside assistance.[15] When their building was finally completed, it was dedicated as the African Episcopal Church on July 17, 1794, after which the founders and trustees drew up a Constitution which was approved on August 12 of that year.[16]

Up to the point at which they both embarked upon fund raising campaigns, Allen and Jones faced similar problems, but thereafter their situations differed, particularly in the kind of response they received from the community. Their personality differences undoubtedly contributed to their success or failure and affected their relationships: Allen was outspoken, sometimes abrasive, and always adamant; Jones was usually agreeable, occasionally accommodating, and comparatively flexible. The result was that Jones was encouraged by Episcopal leaders throughout his church building campaign, while Allen was repeatedly challenged and rebuffed by the Methodists for engaging in the same type of activity. Jones had, of course, chosen to align himself with a religious body

[15] Douglass, *Annals*, 54-55.
[16] *Ibid.*, 96-99.

that regarded tradition as a major consideration, colonial developments notwithstanding, and he recognized that he must either respect those traditions or forego Episcopal affiliation. He apparently elected to abide by traditional practices, even if it meant some personal sacrifice, for the sake of psychological equanimity and denominational support. He soon learned, for example, that Episcopal ordination through the ranks of deacon and priest required certain academic credentials that he didn't possess and couldn't easily acquire—particularly a knowledge of Greek and Latin. Bishop White, who was the local bishop responsible for accepting him for ordination, agreed with the recommendation of the state Episcopal Convention to dispense with the language requirement on the condition that the African Church be denied the right to send a clergyman or other delegates to denominational sessions *"at present."*[17] But St. Thomas's Church was repeatedly excluded by every succeeding convention until 1854, long after the church had first acquired a fully qualified clergyman who met the requirements of Greek and Latin. But Jones was ordained as promised; first as deacon in 1795, and then as priest in 1804, remaining as rector of the church until his death in 1816. The Constitution the church adopted established its racial structure by limiting membership to Africans, although a similar restriction was not applied to the office of rector. St. Thomas's, with its non-voting status, was placed in the same category as Zoar Methodist Chapel: both were assumed to be financially independent, but organizationally and doctrinally dependent, on the sponsoring denominations. Of the two, St. Thomas's was better off for having the services of Jones, since Zoar had to depend on the white preachers they paid to have sent to them from St. George's.[18] As long as Zoar and St. Thomas's respected the limits of their independence, they were free to conduct their own affairs without denominational interference.

Allen admired Zoar's independence at the same time that he

17 *Ibid.*, 106. See also *Journal of the Convention of the Episcopal Church of the State of Pennsylvania,* held in Christ Church, Philadelphia, June 2, 1795. The statement referred to St. Thomas's "peculiar circumstances *at present.*"

18 Minutes of St. George's Church, MS, Methodist Historical Society, Philadelphia.

deplored its lack of autonomous control. He continued to press his case for complete African autonomy, with the almost predictable result being "a trial that I never had to pass through before."[19] His steadfast refusal to abandon his plans served to exacerbate a problem that had much deeper roots. But he managed to recall in later life that even at the height of his difficulties with denominational leaders his affection for the church that had "awakened" him was not diminished by the uncharitable actions of its clergy; said Allen, "I feel thankful that ever I heard a Methodist preach."[20] Doctrinal loyalty was therefore not the problem, as the two parties involved seemed to realize: the issues at stake involved matters of racial autonomy and social control which somehow became submerged in the welter of words about property rights and preaching assignments. Methodist leaders could hardly challenge Allen's grounds for separate status; they had, after all, just recently covered similar territory themselves when they severed their ties with the Anglican Church. Their repeated threats to him suggested rather that they equated church control with social control, and that if they lost control over one—over African church property—they might eventually lose their authority over the other—that is, the black population generally. Their support for Zoar indicated that they did not object to blacks worshiping apart; the fact that they sponsored and encouraged Zoar seemed to imply a preference for racially separate facilities. Allen's situation presented them with a problem they had hoped to avoid: he was directly challenging conventional forms of church discipline, and indirectly threatening other forms of institutional control.

When Allen first attempted to solicit funds for his new building, he was admonished by the Methodist elder in charge, John McClaskey, with threats of being disowned along with all his supporters unless they abandoned their plans. Allen pointed out the futility of such a request: they had no present church home, and they refused to return to St. George's where they had been "so scandalously treated in the presence of all the congregation pres-

19 Allen, *Life Experience*, 27.
20 *Ibid.*, 30.

ent."[21] The denomination didn't pursue McClaskey's threat to disown them, although local leaders continued to harass them. The type of pressure applied varied from time to time, ranging from open threats and subterfuge to calculated neglect, but none of the means employed were sufficiently effective to discourage the Africans from going on. By June 29, 1794, they were able to dedicate their own church building for public worship in a service presided over by Bishop Asbury.[22] Local tensions temporarily relaxed, permitting the current Methodist elder in charge, the Rev. John Dickens, to participate in the celebration and to suggest the name of Bethel for the new building.

The successful completion of Bethel marked a temporary truce between the two factions, but the battle was by no means over. When the disputing sides regrouped, it was to wrangle over issues that had been implicitly involved in the earlier debate over the right to build, specifically, the matter of control over preaching appointments and property rights. Had the right to a separate building been denied, these tangential matters would have taken care of themselves; as it was, they now assumed new significance at the center of the controversy, prompting Allen to observe that "Our warfare and troubles now began afresh."[23]

The building itself remained a source of mutual discontent: the Africans assumed that they should control it since it was they who had largely financed it; the Methodists maintained that denominational policy required Conference control of all property. Both sides appeared unwilling to compromise on the issue. The African Methodists said that they had bought and paid for the property and meant to control it. The white Methodists argued that church policy allowed for no exceptions, and the will of the Conference would prevail. The issue involved a question of power, and the church building became the symbol both sides focused on in the debate. St. George's continuel to regard Bethel as one of its appendages—in much the same way that it regarded Zoar—and insisted on listing the African membership on its own rolls. The gain in black members was significant: in 1793 Confer-

---

21 *Ibid.*, 27.
22 *Ibid.*, 31; Asbury, *Journal and Letters*, II (June 29, 1794), 18.
23 Allen, *Life Experience*, 31.

ence records listed 354 whites and 20 blacks, figures that had changed by 1795, the year after Bethel's organization, to 311 and 121, respectively.[24] The African Church was obviously not only attracting more black worshipers, but was admitting them to membership more readily.

The assistant minister at St. George's, Ezekiel Cooper, reminded Allen of the denomination's official policy on matters relating to property control. It was Allen's duty as a Methodist, said Cooper, to sign over the church property to the Conference.[25] When Allen refused, Cooper changed his line of argument, and observed that it would be to Bethel's advantage to secure a document of incorporation, which he offered to draft in order to save the church money. Allen and the African Methodists accepted his offer, and the charter of incorporation was subsequently drawn up and later approved by the Supreme Court of Pennsylvania on September 12, 1796.[26]

The black Methodists later claimed that Cooper deceived them. He had respected his agreement to draw up incorporation papers, but in the process had signed over control of Bethel's building and property to the Conference. Allen lamented that Bethel now "belonged to the white Conference, and our property was gone."[27]

Cooper apparently never felt obligated to explain his action to the Allenites, perhaps because he saw no reason to grant Bethel an exclusive charter. The one he drew up was essentially similar in form and content to those in use in most Methodist churches, with just a few but significant exceptions made in recognition of Bethel's unique status. The charter, for example, began with the usual statement affirming denominational loyalty, and then went on to approve a degree of local church control by empowering adult male members to elect trustees who would, in turn, man-

24 *Minutes taken at the Several Conferences of the Methodist Episcopal Church in America for the Year 1793* (Philadelphia: Parry Hall, 1793), 16; *Minutes, etc. . . . for 1795* (Philadelphia: Henry Tuckness, 1795), 11. These figures list only members, not adherents, of whom there were many.

25 Allen, *Life Experience,* 31; Cliffe, *Glory of Our Methodist Heritage,* 84-85.

26 *Letter Book of Attorney,* Book No. 5, 458, State of Pennsylvania, in the Land Office of Pennsylvania. Reproduced in Richard R. Wright, *Encyclopedia of African Methodism* (Philadelphia: A. M. E. Publishing Co., 1947), 332.

27 Allen, *Life Experience,* 32.

age the temporal (that is, secular, not specifically property) affairs of the church. There were four provisions, however, which acknowledged the racial heritage of the membership and singled out the document as being significantly different from other charters. Article VI, for example, provided that "none but coloured persons shall be chosen as Trustees," and Article VII limited membership to "Africans and Descendants of the African race." Article X attempted to solve the problem of alleged discrimination in disciplinary cases by permitting dissatisfied black defendants to appeal a decision from the white elder to a jury composed of African trustees, class leaders, and preachers. Article XI, because it dealt with the determination of preaching assignments, suggested the greatest potential for divisiveness, particularly since it gave the right to nominate the preacher at Bethel to the Methodist elder in charge.[28] It was this latter issue and the one dealing with control of church property that became the central issues in the continuing controversy between the Allenites and the white Methodists. Temporarily, however, and for nearly ten years thereafter, the two parties were able to avert an open confrontation while Methodist officials dealt with some problems of their own that could not be put off, including such obvious priorities as budget requirements and fluctuating membership rolls.

The superficial harmony, the result of apathy, ambiguities, and misconceptions, that prevailed during the decade, was broken in 1805 when James Smith reopened the separatist issue. Recently appointed to the post of elder in charge at St. George's, Smith examined Bethel's charter and decided that he was entitled to preach and administer the sacraments at the African Church "at his convenience," for which services payment would be made to the white church. Allen agreed to let him officiate, perhaps because he assumed that even if Smith decided to take advantage of the opportunity—and previous experience with his predecessors had indicated that most of them preferred to ignore the Africans —his infrequent appearance at Bethel would have little effect on its case for autonomy. Because Allen was only a deacon, Bethel's members had to rely on a regularly ordained elder to administer

28 *Letter Book of Attorney,* Book No. 5, 458; quoted in Wright, *Encyclopedia of African Methodism,* 332.

the sacraments, and Smith's occasional visits would have been acceptable for that reason, if for no other. As for the other services, which usually totaled three or four a week, it seemed reasonable to expect that their conduct would go on as before under the guidance of Allen or some lay exhorter, since Smith had a full schedule of responsibilities at St. George's. But while Allen was willing to tolerate Smith's preaching, he was unwilling to give him or the Conference the right to control Bethel's property, a position in which he assumed he was supported by the charter of 1796. Smith apparently felt it was necessary to correct this misconception and point out the true nature of Bethel's legal status, which he did, said Allen, when he "waked us up by demanding the keys and books of the church, and forbid us holding any meetings except by orders from him; these propositions we told him we could not agree to."[29] Smith told them that unless they agreed to his demands, they would be disowned as Methodists. "We told him the house was ours," said Allen, "we had bought it, and paid for it. He said he would let us know it was not ours, it belonged to the Conference; we took councel [sic] on it; councel informed us we had been taken in; according to the incorporation it belonged to the white connection."[30]

Allen decided to beat the Methodists at their own game. They believed that they had been deliberately deceived by Cooper when he drew up their charter: they were aware of the tradition of Conference control of property, but they were also convinced that their unique situation entitled them to an exception from standard practice. After discussing the matter among themselves, they accepted the advice of a lawyer they had consulted, who told them that they could amend their charter if two-thirds of the membership agreed. They called for a congregational vote, and the membership, including women voters, agreed to hire legal assistance to draw up an amended document. The so-called African Supplement to the original charter was drafted, adopted, and legally recognized before the white elder was told of the change: it was now his turn to claim that he had been deceived.

The African Supplement not only widened the breach between

29 Allen, *Life Experience*, 32.
30 *Ibid.*

the two contending factions, but it also encouraged Bethel's separatist inclinations. Many of the changes incorporated in it were actually contrary to Methodist discipline and polity. For example, the issue of property control: according to the Supplement, the trustees of Bethel Church would now be the final arbiters in all matters relating to church property. And in the matter of preaching appointments, new limitations were placed on the prerogatives of the Methodist elder. In the future, if he refused or neglected his responsibility to preach and administer the sacraments at Bethel, he was to be replaced by someone whom the Africans themselves nominated.[31]

Methodist reaction to the Supplement was predictable. Allen recalled that "We . . . got it passed, before the elder knew anything about it. This raised a considerable rumpus, for the elder contended that it would not be good unless he had signed it."[32] Conference leaders tried to convince the Bethelites to repeal it, and when that failed, the new elder at St. George's decided to exercise his right to preach at the African church.

The Supplement entitled him to perform certain specific functions at the church, such as administering the sacraments, but since its adoption had revived old animosities, it seemed reasonable to expect that his presence at Bethel now would be both untimely and unwelcome. The Africans didn't openly contest his sacramental services since that was something they could not provide for themselves, but they did object to the amount and method of payment they had to make to St. George's for his sacramental assistance. They were initially required to pay $600 annually for his serves, but when the black people objected, the Methodists reduced the amount to $400. Allen maintained that even the lowered figure was a burden for his poor congregation, so the Methodists reduced it once more to $200. According to custom, this money would be paid by a "preaching station" such as Bethel directly to the supervising church, but the Bethelites, per-

---

[31] "Amended Articles, Improving, Amending and Altering the Articles of Association of the African Methodist Church, Approved by the Supreme Court of Pennsylvania, March 16, 1807." Reprinted in Wright, *Encyclopedia of African Methodism*, 332-34.

[32] Allen, *Life Experience*, 32.

haps equating their assessment with a form of tribute, preferred
to give their money directly to the visiting elder. St. George's refused to consider such an arrangement, and after a heated debate,
Bethel finally backed down and agreed to continue paying the
church.[33] Sometime later, Allen complained that the elder was
once again neglecting his responsibilities; he claimed that since
the Methodist supervisor had actually appeared at the church
only five times during the course of a year, the Bethelites were
justified in reducing their payment from $200 to $100. He may
have reasoned that since he carried the major burden of church
responsibility without any compensation, why should the elder receive $40 for each official appearance he made? Once again St.
George's refused to compromise, and when their demand for continued payment at the original level was refused, they discon-
tinued the services of the visiting elder. Bethel was deprived of
the sacraments, but it was also undisturbed by Methodist interference for over a year.[34]

The Supplement placed Bethel in an anomalous position with
the denomination and provided an obvious basis for its eventual
break with the Methodists. The document was clearly different
from those in use in white Methodist churches, although it did
contain the standard affirmation of denominational loyalty.
Bethel was in the curious position of being neither wholly independent of the denomination nor fully aligned with it, a situation somewhat akin to the predicament Allen himself was in: although a deacon since 1799, when he was ordained by Bishop
Asbury, he could neither participate in Conference sessions nor
vote at meetings. The white Bishop and clergy regarded Bethel
as an adjunct of St. George's and subject to its direction: the African Methodists seemed to consider themselves nominally Methodists yet free to control their own internal affairs.

The issue of control, which had temporarily been overlooked,
had reappeared, now supported by the props provided by two
charters and whatever legality attached to them. During the time
between the adoption of the first charter and the second, relations
between the Allenites and the white Methodists were strained but

33 *Ibid.*, 32-33.
34 *Ibid.*, 33.

tolerable, but during the period that separated the drafting of the amended charter from the final recognition of A.M.E. independence in 1815, that relationship steadily deteriorated. The change within the denomination reflected a similar shift in racial attitudes within the larger society. Few Methodist officials wanted their African members to leave the church; indeed, Bishop Asbury did what he felt he could to encourage Allen in his work. But the two charters became symbolic of the issue of control that was affecting the entire community at large. As the mushrooming free black population pressed its demands for civil equality, encouraged by men like Allen who could remember brighter days, it was repeatedly immobilized by new and increasingly repressive measures. By taking the initiative in 1807, the African Methodists may have assumed that they could effectively challenge such practices within white institutions and force a change. They soon learned that they faced formidable odds.

III

THE PASTOR OF MOTHER BETHEL

We have no purpose or intention whatever of separating ourselves from, or of making ourselves independant [*sic*] of the Methodist Conference, and the Discipline of the Methodist Episcopal Church.

Richard Allen
Letter to the Philadelphia Conference
of the Methodist Episcopal Ministers

. . . The Jews in Babylon were held against their will. So were our brethren [the Allenites]. But how, it will be asked, were your brethren bound?

1. By the deed. 2. By the charter of their church. (To whom were they bound? To the conference. For how long were they bound? Answer. It was supposed by the ecclesiastical expounders of the law, that it would be till the last trump should sound!)

The Rev. Daniel Coker
Sermon celebrating the independence
of Bethel Church

NEARLY A DECADE OF STRUGGLE separated Bethel's adoption of its African Supplement from its final legal recognition as an independent society in 1816. During that ten-year period the Allenites' demand for separate status grew more aggressive at the same time that white Methodist leaders implemented a watered down version of the denomination's official policy on slavery. To some extent, the prevailing political climate of opinion influenced the moves, although it alone failed to explain the change in attitudes on either side. In 1807, just after the Supplement was drawn up, Allen and the trustees of Bethel wrote the preceding letter to local denominational officers to assure them that despite their desire to acquire greater autonomy, they had no "intention whatever of separating" from the Methodist Episcopal Church. If the document was a true reflection of their feelings at the time, what then caused them to change their minds and demand independence by 1816? The answer to the question would have to include a description of all the racial readjustments that were taking place within the various denominations during the early national period, as white congregations tried to devise ingenious ways of keeping their black members on the rolls while also keeping them out of their corporate worship services.

Most denominations seemed to think that they could solve their dilemma by continuing the practice of providing segregated worship facilities within their churches, but they found that many of their black members were unwilling to accept that arrangement, particularly after 1800. Loosely combining in what has been referred to as a "grand united Negro movement," groups of African Protestants followed Bethel's example and organized racially separate churches that originated in many of the urban centers of the North. The movement produced independent congregations of Baptists and Zionite Methodists, as well as separate, but denominationally dependent societies of Presbyterians and Episcopalians. The appearance of a large and growing class of freedmen presented unanticipated adjustment problems for Northern whites, who were thus placed in a situation not unlike the one that existed nearly a half-century later in the South after Reconstruction, when Bourbon Democrats refused to accept the social implications of black emancipation. In both cases, the first groups of freedmen to challenge existing social conventions were blocked by barriers of legal and traditional restrictions, and whatever patterns their efforts established remained the norm for many years thereafter. Bethel's struggle with the Methodists was indicative of the kind of reaction that freedmen received when they attempted to exercise the rights attached to their free status, in this case the right to make their own religious choices. It became clear to someone like Allen that social standards and conventions had not evolved with the needs of black people in mind, and he presumably decided that he would have to devise his own, necessarily unconventional, alternatives.

The Supplement was an example of the kind of adaptation he thought their situation called for, and apparently even Bishop Asbury did not regard its separatist implications as a serious threat to denominational harmony at the time. He stayed on good terms with the Bethelites throughout the decade of struggle, visited with them, and occasionally stopped at Allen's home. When he received a copy of the Supplement that accompanied Bethel's letter announcing its intention to remain within the fold, he responded with a note that said, "provided the Supplement to your act of Incorporation which you allude to, be not contrary to the allow'd usages, customs & privileges of the Methodist Episcopal Church . . . the Conference accepts your Memorial, & entertain[s] a confidence that our Affracan [*sic*] brethren, will evince their unshaken stability & firmness as Methodist. . . . And we cordially wish you prosperity, unity, holiness and happiness. . . ."[1] Asbury may have either misunderstood the document or simply not have read it, because other denominational officials were quick to point out the places where it departed from accepted practice. This correspondence caused additional problems later, as white Methodists referred to Bethel's statement as a misrepresentation of its real position, and black Methodists claimed Asbury's letter as a sign of his support. As subsequent events were to prove, Bethel had not falsified its intentions because in the most significant portion of the letter to Asbury its objectives were stated quite clearly: "Our only design," it said, "is to secure to ourselves, our rights and privileges to regulate our affairs temporal and spiritual, the same as if we were white people, and to guard against any oppression which might possibly arise from the improper prejudices or administration of any individual having

[1] Francis Asbury to the Trustees of the African Methodist Episcopal Church called Bethel, April 9, 1807, MS, Methodist Historical Society, Philadelphia.

the exercise of Discipline over us."[2] That seems to be an uncomplicated, forthright statement in favor of self-determination.

As the only regularly ordained member of its congregation, Allen served as Bethel's pastor and chief spokesman during the negotiations with the Philadelphia Conference. By the time the Supplement was drawn up in 1807 he had acquired additional responsibilities both to his own growing family and to the secular community. In 1800 he had married a former slave named Sarah, of whom little is known except that she came from Isle of Wight County in Virginia, and that she and her husband eventually became the parents of six children. To meet their needs and provide for the childrens' future, Allen took on more secular jobs, accumulating enough extra cash to purchase several parcels of property around the city. Perhaps the wealthiest member of the church, he continued to serve as its voluntary pastor, unpaid by either the local congregation or the Conference. That the Conference contributed nothing toward his support was another source of discontent to the black Methodists, who pointed out that the denomination did provide for the maintenance of white ministers at preaching stations in the city, while Bethel had to pay for the services of the visiting elder. According to Conference policy, St. George's Church was charged with superintending the affairs of all Methodist societies in Philadelphia, of which there were then four, including the two black chapels, Zoar and Bethel. Although the African groups were assessed by St. George's for yearly contributions toward expenses, the black ministers received no compensation from the mother church while their white colleagues in other preaching stations did.[3] To be sure, no Methodist preacher in the itineracy or in a preaching station ever became wealthy on the salary he received for his work, but he was usually supplied with the basic necessities, such as a house, a horse, and

[2] Memorial of the Trustees of the African Methodist Episcopal Church, called Bethel, to the Philadelphia Conference of the Methodist Episcopal Ministers assembled, April 8, 1807, MS, Methodist Historical Society, Philadelphia. This item follows directly after Allen's statement quoted above.

[3] Minutes of Trustee Board of St. George's Church, Philadelphia, April 23, 1806 to October 21, 1819, MS, Methodist Historical Society, Philadelphia. In 1807 St. George's recorded contributions from Bethel of $75, and from Zoar, $50; the following year the figures were $100 and $25, respectively.

money for personal needs like laundry, which relieved him of the necessity of finding ways to provide for his daily keep. Allen had no such assurance and had to get by on his wits.

He was usually fortunate enough to find the kinds of jobs that allowed him to regulate his own time schedule. Unlike many of the other members of his congregation who had to report daily for work as hired shopkeepers, barbers, house-servants, and the like, he was essentially among the ranks of the self-employed, whether he was occupied as chimney sweep, grocer, blacksmith, or shoeshop proprietor. As a result, he could find time to engage in church and community activities when other black people had to be at work. Fortunately his energy seemed to keep pace with his manifold interests, and while his family may have seen little of him, the community saw him a great deal, often in positions of leadership. In 1793, the mayor had called on him and Absalom Jones to help out during the yellow fever epidemic that hit the city. They volunteered their services then, and once again during the War of 1812 when they were asked to raise black recruits in the event that Philadelphia was endangered. It was also about this time that he started a school for black children at Bethel sponsored by "the Society of Free People of Color, for Promoting the School Education of Children of African Descent."[4] The school opened in 1804, supported by a general subscription fund, but with no assistance or encouragement from the members of St. Thomas's who seemed anxious to dissociate themselves from the undertaking, even though there was no state-supported school for black children at the time, and would be none until 1822. Allen respected their decision and ran the school until his supply of funds gave out.

Much of what might be called his spare time was spent in dealing with Conference officials who were determined to get the Bethel charter Supplement repealed. But what he had to contend with was more than simply a local situation because denominational leaders in Philadelphia were also reflecting the reassessment of racial policy that was currently going on within the Methodist Church as a whole. When he joined the church as a

4 David McNeely Stauffer (ed.), *Westcott's History of Philadelphia, 1609-1829* (Philadelphia: Sunday Dispatch), XXIV (1913), 1839.

young man, its Discipline adhered to the seemingly uncompromising antislavery stand announced by John Wesley. But after 1800 that position was becoming less popular, and the Methodist Church, now grown large and respectable, was concerned about its popularity. And besides, if even the Abolition Society, one of the forerunners in the antislavery movement, saw fit to change its original stance—ostensibly due to the Gabriel Prosser slave revolt[5]—why shouldn't church officials rationalize a justification for doing likewise? It was this kind of racial attitude that encouraged leaders in church and state to consider ways in which they could restrict the mobility of free blacks at paradoxically the same time that Jeffersonian politicians, and later their Jacksonian descendants, were claiming an interest in opening new opportunities for the "common man" (and incidentally trying to secure his vote). Allen's problem with the Philadelphia Conference was one manifestation of a widely current desire to effect some control of freedmen.

The actions of the local Conference become clearer when viewed against the background of denominational decisions. The first signs of ambivalence regarding slavery on the part of the national church appeared in the General Conference of 1800. Carried along, perhaps, by the remnant of its eighteenth-century abolitionist ethic, that Conference voted to ordain their "African brethren" as local deacons, if the candidates had been recommended by white ministers and two-thirds of the men in their own society.[6] Allen, it will be remembered, had been ordained by Bishop Asbury the previous year, and was thus made the first ordained black preacher in the Methodist Church, one year before the General Conference gave its approval. Then, having dealt with the issue of ordination, the Conference considered the

[5] American Convention for Promoting the Abolition of Slavery, *Minutes of the Seventh Convention of the Abolition Societies* (1801), 37-39. The delegates insisted that their ultimate objective was total abolition, but they said they had no desire to contravene state laws nor "hazard the peace and safety of the community." They wanted to have it noted that they "deplore the late attempts at insurrection by some of the slaves of the southern states. . . ." *Minutes*, 38.

[6] *Journals of the General Conference,* I, 44; found in Donald G. Mathews, *Slavery and Methodism* (Princeton: Princeton University Press, 1965), 63.

dual problems of slaveholding and emancipation among its membership, and it was here that the delegates betrayed their own anxieties as well as those of the parishioners they represented. They were faced with a decision, described as a choice between "purity and popularity"[7] and, under pressure from their Southern constituency, they decided in favor of the latter. They seem to have concluded that if the church was to grow in the future as it had in the past in Southern states, and not become a small abolitionist sect, it would have to modify its stand on slavery. The result was equivocation and compromise. The old abolitionist sentiment was resuscitated—although not given new life—in the form of a set of instructions to the annual conferences, directing them to circulate petitions, addressed to Southern legislatures, asking for the implementation of gradual emancipation laws in all those states that were still without them.[8] The developing trend in favor of modification was revealed in the companion decision to permit a traveling preacher to hold slaves, if emancipation was not practicable in the state in which he lived.[9] The contradictory nature of the measures, which were designed to placate both North and South, indicated that Conference officials were still unsure of what course of action they and the church should pursue—should they continue to pressure the states and thereby provoke the civil authorities as well as some of their own members, or should they withdraw from the realm of politics entirely and content themselves with discussions on the immorality of slavery? The delegates in 1800 seemed to have no sure answer to what role the church should play, if any, in the matter of political involvement.

By shifting the burden of responsibility for implementing the petition appeal to annual conferences, the national body absolved itself from any direct complicity in state and local affairs. When Southern Methodists gathered in their annual sessions after this national decision had been passed down, they attacked the "Address of the General Conference" as an "incendiary broad-

[7] The quote is from Mathews, *Slavery and Methodism*, 18.

[8] Mathews, *Slavery and Methodism*, 20; H. R. Bascom, *Methodism and Slavery: A Controversy Between the North and the South* (Charleston, 1822), 14.

[9] Bascom, *Methodism and Slavery*, 14.

side," and hinted that if it became accepted policy they would keep their slaves away from church services in the future.[10] In Georgia, for example, it was reported that the state's legislative response to the "Address" was an act prohibiting any form of emancipation without the approval of the legislature.[11] In view of this kind of Southern reaction, the church re-examined its petition plan and then withdrew it, which seemed to be its only alternative in any case, since many annual conferences had simply ignored it or failed to comply with it.

Once the move in the direction of compromise was started, it began to pick up support in subsequent Conferences, until it finally produced an almost complete revision by 1808. At the meeting in 1804 it had been agreed that there would be no church censure directed toward those lay people who owned slaves in states where slavery was still legal, and by 1808 the General Conference arranged to grant annual bodies the right to establish their own regulations dealing with holding and selling slaves. Whatever pressure or vision the national church had been able to exert in the past was thus weakened by this decision to permit the annual conferences to reflect undiluted local passions on the issue of slavery.

It is not surprising in view of this state of denominational affairs that Bethel's Supplement, with its implied demand for autonomy, would appear to Conference leaders as a threat to the delicate factional harmony that was just being negotiated. And forces at work in the secular community indicated that the church was not alone in redefining its racial objectives. In secular circles colonization was being discussed by white politicians and social leaders as one possible way in which they could deal with the advent of a growing class of freedmen, whose removal to Africa would make it possible for them to retain the racial status quo in society. That idea, too, gradually gained support, until by 1816 it was gathered into a national movement to sponsor the emigration of free blacks to Africa.

The struggle between the two groups of Philadelphia Methodists over the charter Supplement, an example of this new direc-

10 Mathews, *Slavery and Methodism,* 21.
11 Bascom, *Methodism and Slavery,* 14.

tion in racial matters, all too frequently involved a contest of wills rather than a debate over issues. The white Methodists would accept nothing less than its repeal, the Africans demanded its complete acceptance. As the chief black spokesman, Allen made it clear that they would not be intimidated by repeated threats to disown the Bethelites from Methodist society. He realized that he was dealing with a fairly wide spectrum of white opinion when he took on the Conference, but he also knew that he had a broader base of black support than just his membership at Bethel. His congregation was, in fact, growing so rapidly that it temporarily discouraged a local black Presbyterian minister, John Gloucester, from going ahead with plans for a church of his own because he was told that "the people in heart were Methodist, and would finally all be received into Methodist Churches."[12] The actual size of Bethel's membership was irrelevant (and figures tend to vary with the sources); the important consideration was the fact that it created the impression that people were drawn by Allen's preaching like a magnet, and, in the words of one observer, they were "flocking by thousands" to the church.[13] One look at the membership roll at St. George's, where the black seceders were still listed, would have bolstered such observations: in 1807 there were over 700 black Methodists out of a citywide total of something over 1800.[14] That kind of information may have provided Allen with a comforting source of moral support during his trials with Conference leaders.

At the heart of the debate was the issue of control, or stated another way, who was to govern Bethel's internal affairs, the Africans or the Conference. From the time that its building was completed until 1805, Bethel enjoyed a limited degree of self-government simply by default, because white officials, who were occupied with other problems, concluded that there were too few separatist sympathizers for them to be seriously concerned about. And except for the brief intrusion by the Rev. James Smith in

---

[12] William T. Catto, *A Semi-Centenary Discourse, delivered in the First African Presbyterian Church, Philadelphia, May, 1857,* 27.

[13] *Ibid.,* 82.

[14] *Minutes of the Conference of the Methodist Episcopal Church* (Philadelphia: Ezekiel Cooper & John Wilson, 1806), 13.

1805, when he demanded his right to preach at Bethel, the Africans continued to enjoy a virtually autonomous society. But things began to change after 1811 as Bethel gained new members and St. George's acquired a series of more aggressive elders—most of whom followed the Methodist tendency of remaining in a post only one year—who seemed anxious to assert the limits of their own authority at the same time that they restricted Bethel's independence.

Stephen Roszel, a native of Virginia,[15] was the first of this later group of elders to renew the issue of the Supplement, and like his predecessors he reminded the Africans that their refusal to repeal it made it impossible for him or any other white preacher to serve them or administer the sacraments. The Bethelites had heard such threats before, and as before, continued to disregard them, because except for the denial of the sacraments, they preferred to be free of all white intervention. And so they were ignored once again until the ministers of the Academy Church, a white group that had also seceded from St. George's, approached them with the offer of preaching help. That arrangement lasted about a year, terminating when the white preachers demanded a payment of $150, which was refused. An additional consideration may have been the fact that the Academy preachers were reportedly threatened with expulsion from the denomination if they continued to serve Bethel.[16]

Roszel's successors were even more determined to force Bethel to accept a relationship that was consistent with standard denominational practice. John Emory, who eventually became a bishop, was appointed as an associate at St. George's in 1813, and he, along with two others who served at the church—first Robert R. Roberts and then later Robert Burch—actually precipitated the series of events that led to Bethel's final independence, by pursuing more obviously aggressive tactics. Emory's efforts began with the publication of a circular letter disowning the Africans as Methodists, a scheme that had been tried before to no avail. When that proved to be ineffective, he attempted to open a Con-

---

15 Allen calls him "Samuel Royal" in his memoirs. See *Life Experience,* 35.

16 Daniel A. Payne, *History of the African Methodist Episcopal Church* (1st reprinting; New York: Johnson Reprint Corp., 1968), I, 6.

ference-sponsored church close to Bethel to attract those people he
suspected might prefer to remain loyal to the denomination
rather than to Allen. That plan died as quickly as the first when
he discovered that few Africans could be persuaded to leave
Bethel.[17]

Roberts decided to follow a different tack, but one equally direct. He went to meet with a few of the Bethelites and told them
that he intended to preach to them the following Sunday. They
opposed his demand, and could point to some specific provisions
in their Supplement to support their stand. Article V, for example, stated that:

> . . . in case the said Elder [of St. George's] shall refuse or neglect to
> preach and exhort in the said Church [Bethel] . . . once on every
> Sunday, and once during the course of the week . . . or shall neglect
> or refuse to attend therein to administer the ordinances of baptism
> and the Lord's supper, in that case a majority of the said Trustees or
> their Successors, may appoint any other person duly qualified . . .
> to officiate in the place and stead of the Elder so refusing or neglect-
> ing. . . .

Article VI restricted white involvement still further:

> It is hereby further agreed and declared, that the Elder of the
> Methodist Episcopal Church for the time being, of the city of Phila-
> delphia, shall in no case nominate any person to preach in Bethel
> Church . . . unless with the concurrence of a majority of the Trustees
> of said Church. . . .[18]

They were therefore prepared to act on the assumption that their
own document, which had received court approval, reinforced
their position on two counts: first, since the white elders had repeatedly ignored them in the past, they were entitled to appoint

[17] Allen, *Life Experience,* 34. At the time, Emory was serving at St. George's,
although Allen described him as the elder of the Academy. It is possible that
part of his responsibilities included serving the Academy. See also Emory's
statement of April 6, 1815 (MS., Historical Society of Pennsylvania), in which
he said that to his knowledge the Conference never saw a copy of the African
Supplement before it was adopted. He concluded that the amended version of
the charter which Bethel acquired was "inconsistent with the Discipline &
Usages of the Church. . . ."

[18] The Supplement is contained in Richard R. Wright, *Encyclopedia of
African Methodism,* 333.

a replacement; and secondly, since Roberts did not have the approval of a majority of Bethel's trustees, he was not authorized to preach to them. But Roberts would not be put off by their objections, and insisted on his right to use the pulpit. He underestimated the intensity of their opposition as well as their ingenuity: when he arrived at Bethel the next Sunday he discovered that the pulpit was already occupied by one of the exhorters in the congregation. As he began to approach the front of the sanctuary to challenge the black preacher's right to speak, the Bethelites moved into the aisles and blocked his passage at the center of the church.[19] Angered and surprised, he turned to the witnesses who had accompanied him and pointed out that "that man" in the pulpit had usurped his right to preach. Frustrated in his futile attempt, Roberts withdrew, and never visited Bethel again during his tenure in office.

Roberts left his post to Robert Burch, a native of Ireland, who may have thought that some Gaelic pluck could succeed where other measures had failed. He knew that the Bethelites had had a trying year during Roberts's ministry, barely surviving an attempt to take their building away, and he may have concluded that they would be vulnerable to a fresh appeal to occupy their pulpit. He was also aware that two local lawyers, Joseph Hopkinson and one S. Shoemaker, had passed judgment on their Supplement, deciding that the document was "not binding upon the Methodist Episcopal Church"[20] because, among other reasons, it "was fraudently obtained by a false representation to the Court."[21] But Burch's assessment of the situation was as bad as his timing: Bethel had saved its building only through Allen's intervention and they were more determined than ever to protect their holdings. The church had been put up for auction—reputedly at the suggestion of the Conference—and was retained by the Africans when Allen outbid a competitor and purchased it

---

[19] Letter of Robert Burch, December 16, 1815, MS, Historical Society of Pennsylvania. Burch refers to Roberts's treatment in his letter, as does Bishop Payne in his *History of the A.M.E. Church*, 6, 7.

[20] Letter of S. Shoemaker, April 7, 1815, MS, Historical Society of Pennsylvania.

[21] Letter of Joseph Hopkinson, April 24, 1815, MS, Historical Society of Pennsylvania.

back for $10,125.[22] Burch made his first blunder when he accepted an invitation to preach at Bethel from one Robert Green. Green was a disaffected member of the congregation, in poor standing with his brethren because he had attempted to bring suit against another member, a violation of church Discipline. In addition, he may have been Allen's competitor at the auction.[23] Burch, of course, quickly accepted his invitation, and as he made his plans to appear, news of his impending arrival spread among the members of the congregation. Word reached Burch that the Bethelites planned to use "deadly weapons"[24] to keep him from their pulpit. He decided to verify the reports and visited Allen, who was then indisposed, only to find that the black preacher corroborated the story. It was the white elder's turn to be intimidated, and, alarmed by what he heard, he decided not to keep his appointment. He reported his experience to the Conference, including in his statement a reference to Bethel's claim that "the council of Nine lawyers" whom the trustees had consulted, supported their stand.[25] Burch then abandoned his plan to preach to them "untill [sic] they would be convinced by some legal process that they were acting contrary to the peace and happiness of Society."[26]

Burch, with Conference backing, took the case to court for a decision regarding the legality of the African Supplement. On January 1, 1816, he applied to the Supreme Court of Pennsylvania for a writ of *mandamus,* giving him the right to preach at Bethel. After hearing the lawyers for both sides, the judges, Yeates and Breckenridge, denied the writ, saying that nothing would be gained by forcing the Bethelites to listen to a preacher whom they opposed. Bethel took that decision to mean that they had been

[22] Notice of Sheriff's Sale, June 12, 1815, Copy, Historical Society of Pennsylvania; and Statement of Jacob Fitler, Sheriff, to Judges, June 22, 1815, MS, Historical Society of Pennsylvania. Payne, in *History of AME Church,* says that Allen paid $10,500. Payne, 8.

[23] Benjamin Grant (comp.), *Reports of Cases Argued and Adjusted in the Supreme Court of Pennsylvania,* I, 67; Green vs. A.M.E. Church, January term, 1815. In his *History of the A.M.E. Church,* Payne says that Green bid against Allen at the sale. Payne, 8.

[24] Letter of Robert Burch, Philadelphia, December 16, 1815, MS, Historical Society of Pennsylvania.

[25] *Ibid.*

[26] *Ibid.*

granted official, legal recognition as an independent body:[27] St. George's was no longer their mother church, and they were now free to control their own religious affairs.

It was a momentous occasion for Northern freedmen, and the event was celebrated in a sermon by the Rev. Daniel Coker, another black Methodist preacher who knew from personal experience what the Bethelites had had to contend with to reach that point. Ordained a deacon by Bishop Asbury, Coker had been working in Baltimore since the turn of the century, trying to keep alive an African School as well as a church, both the by-products of the African response to segregation in local white Methodist churches. He had been born in Maryland to an English indentured serving woman and an African slave, and had only escaped slavery himself by running away to New York, where he had accepted Methodism and met Asbury. When he returned to his native state, he remained in hiding until he could raise the money to purchase his freedom from his former master, and then joined the local congregation of African Methodists shortly after, serving as their pastor and spokesman during their uphill struggle for self-government.[28] Now that the Allenites had reached that goal, he could share their success by identifying it with his own, commemorating the event as evidence that "God seems to be answering [our] prayers. . . ."[29] In his address he compared their former situation with that of the Jews in Babylon, an analogy that had become fairly common in black sermons. Just

[27] The testimony of participants serves as the only evidence to corroborate the decision, since official court records do not list it. Charles Wesley, in *Richard Allen, Apostle of Freedom* (Washington: Associated Publishers, 1935), 141, cites a letter of Richard Allen to Daniel Coker, dated February 18, 1816, as additional proof. See also Daniel Coker, *Sermon delivered extempore in the African Methodist Episcopal Church in the city of Baltimore, on the 21st of January, 1816, to a numerous concourse of people, on account of the coloured people gaining their church (Bethel) in the Supreme Ct. of the State of Pennsylvania;* . . . taken from Herbert Aptheker (ed.), *A Documentary History of the Negro People in the United States* (New York: Citadel Press, 1951), 67-69. See also Allen, *Life Experience,* 34, 35.

[28] James A. Handy, *Scraps of African Methodist Episcopal History* (Philadelphia: A.M.E. Book Concern, n.d.), 35, 36; Payne, *History of the A.M.E. Church,* 88-90.

[29] Coker, *Sermon,* cited in Aptheker, *Documentary History of Negro People,* 68.

as the Jews had been, so were they bound, and now they were free, with "none to make us afraid."[30] God had promised freedom to the Jews and had now made it available to these Africans; God was indeed the God of the oppressed. A brief reference in his sermon to the history of Bethel's development offered perhaps the best contemporary account of how the Africans viewed their experience:

> The conference . . . [had] said repeatedly, that the coloured socie-
> ties was nothing but an unprofitable trouble; and yet, when the society
> of Bethel Church unanimously requested to go free, it was not
> granted, until the supreme court of Pa [sic] said, it should be so. But
> again, it will be asked, who could stop them, if they were determined
> to go. None—Provided they had left their church property behind; to
> purchase which, perhaps many of them had deprived their children
> of bread. —And this in my opinion, would have been about equal to
> captivity.[31]

Their own religious captivity now a thing of the past, the black Methodists in Baltimore decided that it would be in the best interests of racial unity if they pooled their resources with those of their Methodist brothers and sisters in Philadelphia. Coker, Allen, and their respective congregations decided to gather a general meeting of all concerned black Methodists in Philadelphia on April 9, 1816. That meeting proved to be the first General Conference of a racially distinct denomination, the African Methodist Episcopal Church.

Five separate congregations of African Methodists were represented at that first session, and all could testify to similar discriminatory treatment in the past when they were members of white societies. In addition to the delegates from the Mother Church in Philadelphia and Coker's group in Baltimore, there were other representatives from Pennsylvania; Salem, New Jersey; and Wilmington, Delaware. The exact number of members these men represented is difficult to determine because the system of record keeping varied among them—in some cases adherents were counted as members and in other cases they were not —but if Bethel, Philadelphia accounted for approximately 1,500

30 *Ibid.*
31 *Ibid.*

and Bethel, Baltimore, 633, as one author suggests,[32] then the total was probably around 2,500.[33] The previous year the Philadelphia Conference had listed 1,371 black Methodists and 1,208 white; after the separation in 1816 St. George's total membership dropped from 2,579 to 1,271 since all but 75 Africans left, and presumably most of those who remained were to be found at Zoar.[34] The Allenites were therefore the largest congregation in the denomination, and they represented what was to become known as the Mother Church.

It was probably a very moving event for the participants, but since no one kept any minutes of the meeting, its history has been preserved only through the recorded memories of some of the observers who were present. According to their account, one of the first things the sixteen delegates agreed upon was an official name, the African Methodist Episcopal Church. After that, they moved to adopt, virtually intact, the Discipline of the Methodist Episcopal Church, the only exception having to do with the role of the presiding elder. It apparently made little difference to these founding fathers that the Discipline they adopted was the same one used by the white Methodists; they were confident that in their hands it would be interpreted to meet the needs of black people.

That, after all, was what the struggle over the Supplement was really all about. The debate symbolized the inflexibility of the white institutional structure when it came to dealing with the needs of black people. From the perspective of white denominational officials, the black Methodists were engaging in illegal and unconventional behavior by demanding the right to control their

32 Wright, *The Free Negro in Maryland, 1634-1860,* 218.

33 This figure is approximate and probably open to question. See, for example, Wright, *Encyclopedia of African Methodism,* 464, where the author cites Bishop Payne's claim that Philadelphia alone had 4,000 members in that year.

34 Two splits within St. George's affected the size of the membership. In 1801 a group of about 50 seceded from the church and established the Union, or Academy, Church. In 1809 a group of approximately 18 left Zoar Chapel to create a separate church, which in 1817 became Union A.M.E. Church. See Wright, *Encyclopedia of African Methodism,* 476; Albert Cliffe, *The Glory of Our Methodist Heritage,* 94; and also *Methodist Episcopal Church Conference Minutes,* Philadelphia, 1815.

own property and affairs, an offense that they compounded by drafting their own charter supplement without denominational approval. The Africans respected the need to conform to certain legal formalities, in this as on other matters, and did so to their own satisfaction although not to that of current judicial and ecclesiastical opinion. The difference in interpretation was typified by the decision offered by Joseph Hopkinson, one of the lawyers who reviewed the Supplement. Hopkinson talked in terms of the traditional rights of corporations as opposed to those of individuals, and concluded that "what may or may not be done by a corporation is to be ascertained by its charter which is the source of its power as well as its existence."[35] What Hopkinson failed to consider was that corporate life had been dominated by white interests and not black.

The African Methodists planned to remedy that situation, at least as much as they were able to, through their separate religious organization with its unique approach to the Discipline and an organizational structure that limited conference participation to black people. With only five congregations represented, it may have seemed like wishful thinking for the delegates to talk about annual conferences, but they outlined two—one in Philadelphia and one in Baltimore—and planned to add more as membership growth warranted it. The high point of the meeting came near the close of the session when the delegates agreed to elect a bishop to preside over the new denomination. Their first choice was Daniel Coker, the amiable minister from Baltimore, but for reasons never fully revealed, he declined the nomination.[36] Their

[35] Letter of Joseph Hopkinson, April 24, 1815, MS, Historical Society of Pennsylvania.

[36] The reasons given for Coker's refusal have been variously blamed on scandal and his light skin color. David Smith, an A.M.E. Church historian, has said that Coker's extremely light complexion was considered to be a handicap for an African bishop by his contemporaries. In addition, Coker's interest in the American Colonization Society may have been a factor. See David Smith, *Biography of David Smith of the African Methodist Episcopal Church* (Xenia, Ohio, printed at the *Xenia Gazette* office, 1881), 17. Bishop Payne said that a tendency developed in the church later to alterate light-skinned bishops with dark-skinned ones.

There has been some concern among A.M.E. Church historians to establish which congregation achieved independence first; Bethel, Philadelphia, or Bethel, Baltimore. According to Bishop Payne, a letter from Richard Allen

second candidate was Richard Allen, and on the following day he was elected unanimously.[37] In keeping with Methodist tradition, he was first ordained an elder, and the next day, April 11, 1816, he was consecrated as Bishop with the laying on of hands by five local clergymen, one of whom was probably his old friend, Absalom Jones, in a ceremony that, too, has passed by unrecorded. The pastor of Mother Bethel and the architect of religious separatism for freedmen, Allen claimed that he and his associates had developed an alternative to "that spiritual despotism which [they] recently experienced."[38] The meeting ended when the delegates rose and sang, "Praise God from Whom All Blessings Flow."

Much work still had to be done before their ambitious plans could approach any semblance of reality. They could claim existence as a separate denomination and could boast a few thousand members, but their liabilities were formidable; their financial resources were very limited, their members were generally poor and inexperienced, and their activities were subject to community opposition and political reaction. In addition, if the emigration program of the American Colonization Society worked, much of their membership potential in the free black population would be scooped up in the ships sailing for Africa. A broad effort was called for, one that would simultaneously enlist new members and raise money through domestic missionary work while it also battled the Colonization Society. The new Bishop seemed convinced that the success of the plan would depend on the members' willingness to accept a disciplined approach to moral reform and a commitment to black unity. During the rest of his ministry at Mother Bethel, he directed his energies toward implementing these objectives in the community as well as the church.

---

dated February 18, 1816, suggests that the Baltimore group separated from the Methodist Episcopal Church three weeks before the decision in Philadelphia freed the Allenites. The Allenites had, of course, been meeting separately for a longer period of time than their friends in Baltimore. See Payne, *History of the A.M.E. Church,* 3.

[37] For references to the consecration, see Benjamin T. Tanner, *An Apology for African Methodism* (Baltimore: n.p., 1867), 66; Anson Phelps Stokes, *Church and State in the United States* (New York: Harper & Bros., 1950), I, 776.

[38] Allen, *Life Experience,* 35.

IV

AMERICA'S FIRST BLACK BISHOP

The African Methodist Episcopal Church of America has exerted a wider and better influence upon the Negro race than any other organization created and managed by Negroes.

. . . it became the most powerful organization of Colored men on the continent.

George Washington Williams
A History of the Negro Race in America

Ye ministers that are called to preaching,
Teachers and exhorters too,
Awake! behold your harvest wasting;
Arise! there is no rest for you.

Richard Allen
Life Experience and Gospel Labors

JUST HOW MUCH REST ALLEN ENJOYED following his election as bishop is questionable. At the same time that he retained his pastoral office at Bethel and tended a boot and shoe shop, he also supervised the growing pains of not only the new denomination but of his own six children as well. And remarkably, he maintained an active interest in all but one of these four roles—as bishop, pastor, father, and storekeeper—up until the time of his death; he saw to it that his children had an adequate education, he supervised Bethel's growth and expanding membership, he helped the African Methodist denomination extend its work into Haiti, Canada, and West Africa, and he sacrificed only the shoe shop as a concession to his advancing years. Community organizations took up whatever free time remained in his schedule.

In the early years following his consecration, Allen's dual responsibilities as pastor and bishop frequently overlapped, the new denomination being so small at the time that decisions made at Bethel tended to affect the life of the whole church. Added to that was the fact that his strong, sometimes domineering, personality had almost as much impact on the denominational level as it had on his local church. His political interests also served to tie his responsibilities together because he realized that if an organization like the American Colonization Society ever became sufficiently popular and powerful it could effectively undermine all voluntary associations in the black community, Bethel Church as well as his wider constituency. Secular developments thus became as important to him as his ministry and episcopacy, which seemed to be the way he preferred it in any case. His own relationship with the church was on a very personal level; he worked at basically the same kind of weekday job as the other members of his congregation with the result that he was in touch with their routine problems and not just their religious concerns. And he brought his own interest in moral reform to bear on the whole denomination, just as he did at Bethel, on the assumption that it would be beneficial to the individual and the race, by offering a visible rebuke to those people who stereotyped all blacks as potential threats on the basis of color alone.

The hierarchical structure of the denomination made it easier for him to extend his personal priorities to all the churches in the connection than would have been possible with a different form of organization. That structure was basically pyramidal in shape, with Allen and the General Conference at the apex supervising the whole. Below them were the annual conferences and then the quarterly conferences, which served as intermediaries between the Bishop and those at the top, and the local churches that formed the base. Even within the local church the same order was preserved, with boards of deacons, trustees, and disciplinary councils working to maintain the standards of the Discipline. At all levels adequate provisions were built in to assure that decisions would be reached democratically—and for black people who were denied a voice and vote in secular affairs this was a welcome change—but on some occasions Allen's own opinions prevailed.

He had a chance to experiment with his ideas at Bethel, where he knew people better, and he seemed to conclude that what worked well for Bethel would be equally good for the whole denomination. He was conscientious about his work at Bethel, despite the fact that his new office brought with it additional commitments, and its growth in membership indicated one measure of his success: by 1818, Philadelphia accounted for 3,311 members, which was nearly half of the denominational total of 6,748.[1] And if some of his parishioners enjoyed having a bishop serve them, others may have preferred to be out from under his watchful eye some of the time, because he was a vigorous disciplinarian whose attention to issues of moral reform was constant.

The fact that he kept his home in Philadelphia also strengthened his association with Bethel since it meant that they all shared the same urban environment. The denomination itself was basically an urban organization—of the 6,748 members listed in 1818, 6,225 were to be found in three major cities, Philadelphia, Baltimore, and Charleston—but Philadelphia had a particular appeal because of its location and history. The early home of abolition societies and antislavery agitation, the city's social make-up began to change shortly after Allen's consecration due to the arrival of Southern freedmen and European immigrants. Between 1820 and 1830 the white population rose from 123,746 to 173,173, while the number of black inhabitants increased from 11,891 to 15,624, and white racial attitudes reflected this growth. The "better" families in the area regarded both groups of new arrivals suspiciously, fearful that their traditional influence might now be dissipated, while the immigrants themselves directed their anger, born of economic frustration, at local blacks. Statistics-watchers fed such fears by pointing out that there was a disproportionate number of black inmates to be found in Philadelphia

[1] Payne, *History of the African Methodist Episcopal Church,* 26, 27.

jails.[2] As the familiar social patterns began to change in response to this influx of new arrivals, white people found it increasingly easy to identify their preconceived notions of black behavior with all that was wrong with the city. Freedmen, from the white point of view, were a menace to order and stability and must either be controlled or sent away—colonized—some other place. Allen was only too aware of the popularity of such ideas—the columns of the newspapers served as regular reminders—and he realized what they could mean for the free black community if they ever gained legal acceptance. He seemed to conclude that adequate attention to matters of moral reform could, among other things, serve a socially useful purpose by demonstrating that black churchmen were temperate, hard working and self-reliant.

Bethel had chosen to adopt its own standards of moral behavior, or rather Allen had persuaded it to accept certain standards, and it set itself the task of seeing to it that the membership conformed to them. The church kept a Journal of Proceedings for the period 1822 through 1831, and if its entries provide a reasonably adequate guide to what actually took place, then it appears that attention to matters of conduct and behavior took up a significant part of church time. The handwritten Journal contains an assorted collection of reports of trustees' meetings, conference sessions, and disciplinary councils, and serves as one of the few available records of early black church life.[3] And apart from occasional references in conference minutes and his own memoirs, it is the only account of Allen's ministry at Bethel. It may be that what happened at Bethel was typical of what occurred in other black churches of the period, both those within and those outside the denomination, but until additional evidence comes to light, it is something that will have to remain conjectural. During Allen's lifetime, black church record-keeping was limited by two factors: the lack of experience and educational opportunities of

2 *Philadelphia in 1824: Or, a Brief Account of the Various Institutions and Public Objects in this Metropolis* (Philadelphia: H. C. Carey and I. Lea, 1824), 144.

3 Journal of Proceedings of Bethel Church, Philadelphia, August, 1822-January 1831, MS, Bethel Church, Philadelphia. At last account, the Journal remained in the possession of Bethel Church. It may have been copied from other sources and collected into one volume.

those assigned to the task, and the desire to maintain secrecy as a means of self-protection.[4] That Bethel's early records were preserved says something about the interests of its members and the significance they attached to its history.

The Journal describes discussions and debates over issues that were common concerns among church groups: maintaining property, raising money, securing new members, planning new programs; but it also recounts in minute detail the proceedings of disciplinary councils called to judge the conduct of supposedly wayward members. The disciplinary system appears to have had its practical side as well as its social and theological value insofar as it penalized members who failed to carry out a church job they were appointed to do. Bethel's trustees realized that planning for programs and services would be meaningless if the people who were supposed to execute them neglected their obligations. Some jobs, such as caring for the burial ground, simply could not be put off: if the person assigned to that task chose to ignore it, especially in the hot summer months, the foul odor of a decaying corpse in the middle of Philadelphia would be reason enough for city officials to close the church. It is little wonder then that an unreliable gravedigger was fined by the church. But the majority of cases dealt with infractions of the social and moral code to which Bethel and Allen subscribed, and a judicial mechanism was set up to ensure that those accused of violating it would be judged impartially. Bethel's Journal therefore sheds some light on the values of its members, and also its pastor, since he initiated the custom of the disciplinary councils in the church, and served as one of the judges at most hearings, where his opinions commanded the respect and accord of his colleagues.

The system operated at Bethel in much the same way that it did in other Methodist churches. Allen had, after all, first come in contact with it at St. George's where, he later complained, it operated to the disadvantage of black members who were inevitably judged by all-white councils. Defendants who were dissatisfied with the decisions they received at Bethel could appeal

---

[4] Those churches that made a systematic effort to keep records sometimes had their work go up in smoke when fires gutted the buildings and sometimes lost their documents when they were borrowed or misplaced.

their cases to the Quarterly Conference. At the white John Street Methodist Church in New York City, for example, members were tried for such offenses as drunkenness, "reproachful language," quarreling, and "disorderly walking."[5] All such alleged misconduct, if proved, led to dismissal from the church. The Bethelites conducted similar trials for similar offenses, the most common being domestic feuds, sexual misbehavior, stealing, and indebtedness.[6] Punishment for someone found guilty naturally depended upon the seriousness of the offense: at Bethel, a minor disturbance of domestic harmony could produce a three-month suspension, whereas conviction on a more serious charge, such as adultery, led to the automatic expulsion of the offender, who was thereby "disowned." But if the systems were virtually identical at both John Street and Bethel, there was a significant difference in the complexion of the council members, which Bethel considered to be one of the fundamental advantages it enjoyed as a result of its separation. They believed that they were often judged unfairly in the white church and they intended to guard against partiality in their own hearings.

The evidence indicates that Bethel's jurors took their responsibility seriously, apparently even discounting such things as the influence or social standing of the defendant. Sexual offenses seemed to be fairly common charges in both black and white Methodist societies, and they usually invoked the ultimate punishment of expulsion. A few fairly typical cases selected from the Journal can reveal just how the system worked. One man, for example, a trustee of Bethel and a leading figure in the congregation, was found guilty of adultery and was expelled as readily as an inconspicuous member who had made himself conspicuous by visiting "Dame houses."[7] In cases where the testimony of witnesses made the accusations appear questionable, however, a measure of justice, and perhaps charity, was displayed. One Hannah Harris, accused of being pregnant, murdering the child, and then having her uncle take "the Chamber pot to the privey House

---

[5] Records of John Street Methodist Episcopal Church, Book Ia (1787, *passim*.); Book Ib, 28, MS, New York Public Library.

[6] Journal of Proceedings of Bethel A. M. E. Church.

[7] *Ibid.*, 79, 118, *passim*.

for her," was acquitted after several female witnesses testified that she was an "upright person."[8] In another case, a man was charged with slander for claiming that the wife of a member had been "in bed with a whiteman." He was found guilty and expelled, although the same woman was later accused of another sexual offense and was suspended for three months.[9]

The jurors paid particular attention to cases that dealt with threats to family stability, perhaps because many of them still held painful memories of what had happened when slave families were separated through sale. One woman was "disowned" from the society because she would not "Submit to her husband as a dutiful wife."[10] And in the family of the Morris Dublins, the husband was removed from his official church office and placed on probation, referred to as "trial" membership status, for six months because he sold the household goods to pay the rent; the unfortunate Dublin actually paid twice for his crime, since his wife had already hit him on the head with a "Brick Bat" when she discovered the sale. In an unusual decision, both a husband and his wife were placed on trial status for six months because he pushed her out of bed when she attempted to retire late in the evening, thus provoking a heated family argument.[11]

Allen and his fellow committee members also listened to grievances that were concerned with such financial matters as contractual obligations, stealing, individual fiscal responsibility, and personal property rights. In Isaac Gilmore's case, the man was expelled because he refused to give his business partner, James Gibson, his $20-share of the partnership money.[12] Charles Pierce was silenced "until the quarterly Conference" for "waging money and not paying according to promise."[13] And a female member was disowned for "taking a shawl pair of stockings and a Peticoat."[14]

Not all cases ended in stern penalties. Although most hearings resulted from an accumulation of evidence prejudicial to the de-

8 *Ibid.*, 105.
9 *Ibid.*, 9.
10 *Ibid.*, 82.
11 *Ibid.*, 86.
12 *Ibid.*, 91.
13 *Ibid.*, 84.
14 *Ibid.*

fendant, some ended with relatively mild decisions, and a few with acquittal. Isaac Cook was one who was "bore with" after he confessed his actions and repented; he had been accused of excessive drinking and saying that the "Trustees and Church might all go to hell."[15] For two women involved in a name calling match on the street, the judgments varied: the first woman was suspended for striking her neighbor and calling her "a black infernall beach," while the second was simply suspended from class meetings for three months with an admonition that if she "brings froth [sic] fruit . . . She may be bore with," only because in fighting back, she called her assailant "a Black infernall hornery Negor."[16] Just how many marriages were saved or how many people were deterred from becoming hopeless drunkards because of the decisions of some church council will never be known, although it is necessarily true that conviction by a disciplinary committee was not the way for a Methodist to improve his standing in the community.

The Journal, as well as other sources, revealed another side of Allen's ministry at Bethel, one that was as important to him as moral reform, and that was his missionary effort to gain new members. In this area particularly, it is difficult to separate his pastoral role from his episcopal one, a distinction that was probably never clear even in his own mind, because when Bethel added new members or occasionally a new branch, it was a gain for the whole denomination. Some of his community activities, in what might now be called public relations work, probably encouraged some of the unchurched to become members, although that form of outreach—such as the Masonic lodge that he helped to organize[17]—could be expected to produce only limited returns. He preferred to add groups of people when he had a chance, who would then serve as either a missionary extension of Bethel or a branch of the denomination; sometimes he was successful and sometimes he was not. His efforts to secure the support of Wesley (sometimes called Wesleyan) Church, Philadelphia, was one of his less successful ventures.

15 *Ibid.*, 110, 112.
16 *Ibid.*, 108.
17 Wesley, *Richard Allen*, 93, 94.

Wesley Church had been formed by a group of disgruntled Bethelites, who, unhappy with Allen's leadership, started their own society only "90 feet" away from the Mother Church. They had learned from Allen that, among other things, it was helpful to have the support provided by denominational ties, and they proceeded to arrange for them with the African Methodist Episcopal Zion group in New York City. The Zionites, as they were called, were an offshoot of Methodism in New York, just as the Bethelites were in Philadelphia, and the two groups were at that time essentially similar in most respects. Bishop Allen and the Zionites were in the process of trying to negotiate a merger, with some unfortunate consequences that will be discussed later, so that he could only regard Wesley's friendly overtures to the New Yorkers as a personal affront. But while Wesley's arrangements with the Zionites were still in progress, its situation changed: it acquired a resident minister when a member, Simon Murray, was ordained by the Zionites, but it also piled up an unwieldy debt even before it could obtain a charter of incorporation. As a result, the negotiations with the Zionites were broken off and redirected toward Bethel with the intention of forming a merger between the two churches. Trutees from the two groups, meeting at Allen's home, drew up Articles of Agreement that permitted the members to choose their place of worship, while they also granted Allen, as senior minister, the right to take his turn preaching at Wesley. A joint congregational vote on the union showed that all but three people, all from Wesley, approved of the action. Shortly after, Allen announced that he intended to preach at Wesley Chapel as soon as possible, accompanied by some of Bethel's trustees. In the interim, however, the opposition faction at the chapel secretly secured a new charter of incorporation to continue the separate life of their group.[18]

When Allen and his associates arrived at Wesley on the appointed day, they were stopped at the steps by some of the dissidents, led by the Rev. Murray and one William Perkins. After a considerable amount of pushing and shoving, Allen succeeded in reaching the pulpit and began to speak, although not without

18 Journal of Proceedings, 76, 77.

interruption. Perkins reportedly ran up into the gallery and "jumped out of the gallery into the pulpit and sit upon the pulpitt along of Rev. Richard Allen during the time of worship and disturbed the congregation very much. He spit several times on the Rev. Allen while preaching."[19] It was certainly an unusual reception for a visiting Bishop.

The Wesley separatists, seeking to avoid another embarrassing performance, brought suit against Allen and some of the trustees, charging them with an attempt to seize their property and for engaging in assault and battery on Murray and Perkins, details that are noticeably missing from Bethel's account of the affair. Bethel hired a lawyer to defend their men, and assessed the members of the corporation twenty-five cents each per week to help meet the $300 court fee. Wesley won the case in the Supreme Court of Pennsylvania in January, 1824.[20] Eventually it reopened negotiations with the Zionites, and after it joined the fold, it became an active and vocal member of the denomination, chiding the group on its failure to take a stronger stand in its dealings with the white Methodists. In sum, Allen's missionary activity only ninety feet from his front door was a dismal failure.

He had one other unfortunate experience as a missionary, and that quite obviously in his role as bishop rather than local pastor, before he came to terms with his own limitations and left the field to those whose personalities were better suited to the work. His episcopal failure as a missionary was actually a sequel to the Wesley affair since it involved a proposed merger with the African Methodist Episcopal Zion group (A.M.E.Z.). To appreciate the issues which complicated that controversy, it is first necessary to understand something of the history of Zion and how it evolved.

The Zion Methodists withdrew from the John Street Methodist Church in New York City because they had experienced the same kind of segregated treatment there that the Allenites had received in Philadelphia. From 1800 until 1819 they existed as a separate black congregation within the Methodist denomination, but by the latter date they began to resent the limitations of their semi-independent status and started to look for other options. Their

19 *Ibid.,* 78.
20 *Ibid.;* Wesley, *Richard Allen,* 147, 148.

most serious liability at the time was the lack of an ordained clergyman, a need that Allen offered to fill. The Bishop agreed to ordain one of Zion's members, William Lambert, in the fall of 1819, ostensibly for the purpose of supplying them with a resident minister. But when Lambert returned to New York following his ordination, he surprised and dismayed the Zionites by opening a new church rather than serving them.[21] The move antagonized the New Yorkers who became suspicious of Allen's motives, believing that he had encouraged Lambert in his course of action. They assumed that the Bishop was more interested in consolidating his own power than in uniting black Methodism, which was not really the case. He may have alienated some of their leaders by his aggressive personality, but they were also very sensitive when it came to anything affecting their own independence.

Allen's contacts with Zion continued even after the Lambert affair, since some members still thought that his offer to ordain one or more of their men would be a solution, if only a temporary one, to their problem of clerical leadership. But the pro-Allen faction was overruled, and the church had to remain in its quasi-independent condition, ministered to by William Stillwell or Stilwell), a white clergyman who had guided its secession from the Methodist Church.[22]

According to the later testimony of one of Zion's early bishops, Christopher Rush, the Zionites eventually called a meeting to determine their future course of action. Two "grand questions" were put to the participants: "Shall we join Bishop Allen? Answer, no. Shall we return to the white people? Answer, No. . . ."[23] The unanimity of opinion was more apparent than real, however, because one of the patricians of the society, Abraham Thompson, continued to press his demand for ordination at the hands of Allen. Thompson was "much displeased" by the suggestion that

21 Payne, *History of the A. M. E. Church,* 34, 35.

22 Stillwell and some other white Methodists had seceded from the denomination themselves over the issue of property control. They were afraid that if certain Conference proposals were adopted that they would have the net effect of reducing lay control over property.

23 Christopher Rush, *A Short Account of the Rise and Progress of the African Methodist Episcopal Church Zion in America* (New York: Marks Printer, 1843), 43.

the white Episcopal bishop, John Henry Hobart, ordain Zion's leaders when the black bishop was in the city and willing to do it.[24] Before the meeting adjourned, the members appointed two separate committees, one to visit Hobart, and the other to see Allen.

The committees did their jobs and reported back to the Zionites, who seemed to find in their accounts confirmation of their opinions of Allen. The Hobart delegation had said that since the Bishop was out of the city, they were referred to his representative, the "Rev. Thomas Lyel" [*sic*] whose personal observation it was that the Africans would be better served by having Stillwell ordain their men rather than Hobart, although he ventured the opinion that the Bishop would be willing to do it. The report from the Allen contingent was somewhat less encouraging. They said that "after some conversation with the old man . . . [he] let them know that he 'was not a child, that he knew his business' (as he said) and that he had no intention to assist in ordination, except we put ourselves under his charge."[25] They believed that his response was uncharitable and resulted from "selfish motives on his part. . . ."

The matter did not end there because, although a majority of Zion's members seemed to find Allen's manner and methods offensive, a remnant continued to favor the "old man." The latter group was impressed by his ability to attract new black-separatist societies into the ranks of his denomination, which he was doing with some success even on Zion's home grounds. But most of Zion's trustees seemed to think that they were entitled to prior claim on any separatist groups that were organized in their vicinity, and they resented the intrusion of Allen and his missionaries, who nevertheless pursued the contest for converts. Lambert's pro-Allen group grew, but hardly spectacularly, from seven in 1819 to twenty in 1820, which was also the same year that the A.M.E. acquired the more substantial support of black Methodist seceders in Brooklyn.[26] Much to Zion's distress, other groups soon fol-

[24] *Ibid.*, 44.
[25] *Ibid.*, 45.
[26] Payne, *History of the A. M. E. Church*, 35, 36. The Zionites had also hoped to entice the one hundred members in Brooklyn to join with them.

lowed the example of the Brooklynites, as A.M.E. missionary activity spread north of the city into White Plains and on into New Bedford, Massachusetts, with the result that by 1822 the Allenites were able to establish the New York district as a separate conference.[27]

Zion's Abraham Thompson respected Allen's visible signs of missionary success, and according to Bishop Rush, attempted to "hold up the old man as a proper source for the organization of our church in preference to [the] white man [presumably William Stillwell]."[28] But Rush was not moved, and neither was James Varick, another leader who subsequently became the first bishop of Zion Church. Both men continued to argue against a merger with the Allenites, even though the alternative was ordination by white churchmen. At their suggestion, the Zionites appealed to the white Methodist Conference of Philadelphia in a note that described the state of their dilemma:

> . . . we have not the least expectation that African or coloured Preachers will be admitted to a seat and vote in the Conferences of their white brethren, let them be how much soever qualified for the work of the ministry; nor do we desire to unite with our brother Richard Allen's connexion, being dissatisfied with their general manner of proceedings; (for our brethren, the members of the Wesleyan Church, in Philadelphia, withdrew from them . . .).[29]

When the white Methodists responded, they confirmed Zion's opinions about voting in conferences and suggested that they might consider the possibility of Methodist ordination as an alternative to Allen.[30] But that suggestion failed to materialize because the New York Conference of white Methodists refused to consider it as long as Zion insisted on remaining independent. At that point, the Zionites seemed convinced that they had exhausted their possibilities and finally—perhaps reluctantly—turned to Stillwell to help them end their impasse. Stillwell did what he had promised to do, and assisted in the ordination of their leaders. Zion's independence was assured, but Allen had missed the chance

---

[27] Handy, *Scraps of African Methodist Episcopal History*, 64, 65. A. M. E. tradition suggests that a meeting of the New York Conference was held in 1821, but no records of such a meeting exist.

[28] Rush, *A Short Account of the A.M.E.Z.*, 46.

[29] *Ibid.*, 62.

[30] *Ibid.*, 66, 67.

to unite two groups of black Methodists, apparently due to the fact that at some point during the negotiations he had antagonized Zion's leaders by his dogmatic approach. It was not the only time that a church politician overplayed his hand, but the failure of this bid for unity unfortunately came at a time when pro-colonization forces were trying to stack the cards against the freedmen. A unified black Methodist opposition might have been more effective than a divided one.

As Allen matured in his role as bishop, he learned from these mistakes and mellowed considerably. He still felt the need to develop a black community of interest, which he described in missionary terms, but he was now content to dispatch other men into the field while he remained at home soliciting contributions for their support. Before his career ended, he had helped the A.M.E. Church establish missionary outposts in such widely scattered places as Canada, Haiti, and West Africa. His part in that operation consisted of finding people willing to serve, and then finding money to assist in their support.

The lack of money was one of the constant concerns of his professional life, a problem most other clergymen could appreciate. But in his case, the situation seemed to assume a rather poignant dimension because the needs of his members were so great and the resources available to him so meager. Black Methodists, like all freedmen generally, were forced into the kinds of jobs that were most vulnerable to fluctuations in the labor market, and the insecurity of their personal incomes was reflected in their church giving. And with no income from other sources to draw on, Bethel and the A.M.E. Church had to rely for their support solely on the voluntary contributions of the membership. In spite of these limitations, however, the church managed to survive, due largely to the ingenuity of its leaders and parishioners who had had personal experience in learning how to make ends meet, and who seemed to have developed a mutual understanding of what could and could not be done in the way of program, services, and salaries. As W. E. B. DuBois has pointed out, a study of economic cooperation among black people must begin with the church.[31]

The matter of clerical salaries was a fair indication of the kind

[31] W. E. B. DuBois, *Economic Cooperation Among American Negroes* (Atlanta: Atlanta University Press, 1907), 54.

of working relationship that congregations and preachers developed. Allen, for example, seemed to take it for granted that his
members could not support him and also maintain the church
buildings, so he assumed the full burden of providing for his
family himself, just as most other black clergymen did. In his
case, the situation was actually reversed: since he enjoyed greater
financial security than most of his members, and also his clerical
colleagues for that matter, he was able to make sizable donations
to the church, rather than having the trustees pay him. Once in a
while he would meet with the trustees to "settle the books" between them, but since he never demanded payment on the church
mortgage which he had assumed, it was never paid off. One of his
associates claimed that the total amount of money Allen received
from church sources during his entire ministry was $80.[32] As he
got older and the demands of the denomination increased, he felt
the need to have other clergymen brought in to assist him with
the work at Bethel, and since the younger men had no independent incomes, they had to be partially subsidized by the church.
When Morris Brown came to work at Bethel, and before he was
elected as Allen's assistant bishop, he was reimbursed for his
board by the trustees, who also helped another aide, William Cornish, with his laundry bills and medical expenses.[33]

But token payments would not suffice when it came to meeting
the costs involved in maintaining church property. Such things as
the stoves that were used for heating had to be looked after, and
because fire was a constant hazard, Bethel at one time appointed
a committee to "take charge of the Stoves on men [sic] side," there
presumably being a similar group or person to take care of the
womens' side.[34] Vandalism was also a problem, perhaps more so
at Bethel than elsewhere because of its urban location, and as a
precaution, the church posted a watchman and "peace officers" to
guard the building on Saturday and Sunday evenings.[35] Keeping
up the churchyard was a time-consuming and expensive proposi-

[32] Payne, History of A. M. E. Church, 84.
[33] Journal of Proceedings, 116. By 1829, the trustees had paid Allen $1,898.21
toward the mortgage he had acquired in 1815.
[34] Ibid., 78, 81.
[35] Ibid., 99, 113.

tion, but since other burial grounds were restricted, it was a service that Bethel felt it owed its members. Sometimes the graves would sink due to heavy rains, and when that happened, it became necessary to hire someone to repair the damage. When expenses such as these arose and there was no money to cover them, the trustees resorted to other expedients, such as selling unused stoves, or even selling some church property. In better times they were able to create an interest-producing reserve fund as a check against additional property loss. The church treasurer noted all of these financial transactions and made a quarterly report on them to the congregation.[36]

Bethel's program, its service to its members and to those in the community at large, depended on matching needs with available resources. The voluntary groups so characteristic of American church life appeared at Bethel in the form of the United Sons of Bethel and the United Daughters of Bethel, organizations that not only met certain social needs for their members, but also produced additional income for the church through annual contributions that originally averaged around $20.[37] The various types of schools and educational activities that Bethel sponsored from time to time were usually abandoned when the supply of funds was exhausted. But the more traditional kinds of "religious" societies, such as prayer groups and Sunday classes, remained an integral part of church life. Organizations of this type performed a social function for their members at the same time that they provided them with some of the few opportunities they had for self-expression.

The services the church offered to individuals from the community revealed one aspect of its social conscience. For black people in the city, the church was the only social agency, other than fraternal groups, to which they could turn for help, and they came to depend on it. Money was too scarce for Bethel to give away, but it did offer goods and services. Perhaps one of the most valuable services it performed was assisting runaway slaves, many of whom were given protection by Sarah Allen or one of the other members until any immediate danger passed, and then she would

---

[36] *Ibid.,* 98.
[37] *Ibid.,* 96.

often give them money to get them on to Canada, if that was their destination. The church helped individuals in other ways, less spectacular and certainly less dangerous than hiding fugitives, but still important to the person being helped. Bethel bought a suit and a pair of shoes for one Beryn Clark, who pitched the tunes for singing during services.[38] The church provided a new roof for the home of a disciplined member, Peter Lux, before he strayed from the path of righteousness, and gave him "assistance" when he was sick.[39] And it assumed the expenses involved when an indigent member, Florah Griffith, was buried in the churchyard.[40] Cases similar to these became fairly commonplace at Bethel, and there is no evidence to suggest that anyone ever complained of being turned away without help.

Bethel's program, directed by a man whose ministry was more of a priestly than a prophetic type, offered service and continuity to the local black community. The church was important to him as a means for promoting racial responsibility and he encouraged members to look beyond their own needs to those of the slaves. In one appeal he told them:

> Much depends upon us for the help of our color—more than many are aware. . . . He who knows how bitter the cup is of which the salve hath to drink, . . . ought . . . to feel for those who yet remain in bondage. Will even our friends excuse—will God pardon us—for the part we act in making strong the hands of the enemies of our color?[41]

It was an appeal for compassion rather than specific action, a reminder to those more fortunate that there were brothers and sisters still enslaved. It indicated further that the black Methodists were not planning any revolutionary social change although, paradoxically, the existence of their own program was itself a revolutionary form of social change. While it did not include any broad-based drive for emancipation, it did promote individual emancipation of a different sort, not only by sheltering fugitives, but by offering freedmen the chance to liberate them-

38 *Ibid.*, 81.
39 *Ibid.*, 93.
40 *Ibid.*, 81.
41 Allen, "To the People of Color," *Life Experience,* 73.

selves from the kind of psychological dependence that slave life had created. Allen was therefore able to consider his service to the free people as his primary responsibility, and through them could hopefully keep alive the cause of the slave. The only other help he felt he could offer slaves was a message of hope and concern that promised them that:

> [The] love of God dwelling in your heart . . . will be a consolation in the worst condition you can be in, and no Master can deprive you of it . . . I wish you to think of this more than anything else; then you will have a view of that freedom which the sons of God enjoy. . . .[42]

Bethel's own members wanted a different kind of commitment from him, one that included respect for their freedom to choose what was best for the future of the church.

The members wanted to be consulted, and were, whenever the hierarchical structure of Methodism allowed for congregational expression on issues. Voting was taken seriously, and Bethel evolved an elaborate procedure to make sure that elections followed a democratic process. When a vote was to be taken, polls opened at the church one hour during the morning of the election day, after which an officially appointed "judge" counted the secret ballots.[43] Few people neglected the opportunity to vote; anyone who could not sign his name marked his ballot with an "X." Members were entitled to vote for their representatives on the board of trustees, who were responsible for dealing with most policy questions and problems relating to church maintenance. The minister appointed the board of stewards and only male members voted for delegates to the General Conference, while the entire congregation was consulted on matters dealing with the sale or alteration of church property.

The way policy was determined at Bethel was essentially similar to the way it was done in other churches of the denomination, if only on a smaller scale. Bethel, in fact, offered a representative view of the whole church, a parallel fostered by Allen's dual roles. He brought the same set of values and priorities to bear on the

---

[42] *Ibid.,* 72, 73.

[43] Journal of Proceedings, 93. The announcement for an upcoming election was usually made the previous Sunday.

denomination as on his local church, with the result that the similarity that existed in the area of policy making was extended to include such concerns as moral reform, missionary activity, and racial responsibility. The denomination seemed to do well under his leadership—if membership figures are regarded as criteria, having reached nearly 10,000 members by 1826. Most of these were to be found in the Middle States area, although some were the products of missionary activity in western Ohio, and others were located in a branch in South Carolina, which was officially defunct in 1826.[44] If he had succeeded in effecting a merger with the Zionites, the figure would obviously have been much higher, although given the fissiparous tendencies of American Protestantism, it is surprising that he attracted and held as many separatist congregations as he did. Denominational growth during this period was achieved despite the efforts of colonizationists to undermine the fabric of the free black community, and despite the efforts of two state legislatures, Ohio and South Carolina, to curtail A.M.E. activity. The enforcement of Black Codes in Ohio and the restrictions placed on religious gatherings and speakers in South Carolina set up new obstacles in the way of A.M.E. growth.

In those two states, public opinion supported the moves against the A.M.E., with the result that the congregation in Charleston had its very existence snuffed out, and the groups in Ohio were seriously threatened. White churchmen in the North had become seemingly content with religious separatism and no longer challenged the separatist objectives of black ministers, but they undermined the life of the churches in ways that included support for colonization and restrictive legislation. In the South, however, some white clergymen were less reluctant to express their personal racial attitudes. To them, black preachers were simply "blind leaders of the blind," and they "entertain[ed] very low opinions of the intellectual capacity of the Negroes."[45] As public figures, their ideas carried considerable weight in the community,

44 Payne, *History of the A.M.E. Church*, 38, 44. The figure includes the 1,500 to 2,000 members of the church in Charleston, who still considered themselves Methodists even though the church was closed after the Denmark Vesey affair.

45 Charles Colcock Jones, *The Religious Instruction of the Negroes: A Sermon* (4th ed.; Princeton: D'Hart & Connally, 1832), 12, 13.

although often they were reflecting public opinion as much as they were creating it, and public opinion, both North and South, was alarmed by the growth in the free black population. Allen and A.M.E. leaders appreciated the vulnerability of their situation, but they seemed convinced that the addition of new branches would strengthen their defenses, even in potentially dangerous areas, like South Carolina.

The denomination had been so successful in extending its influence from its Philadelphia-Baltimore axis that its leaders were tempted to enlist the support of interested groups of freedmen in the Deep South. There was a sizable free black population in Charleston, South Carolina, that seemed to offer the potential for becoming another A.M.E. branch. Morris and Marcus Brown, two former Methodists, had initiated black Methodist activity in the city, and their efforts produced a congregation in 1816 anxious to be identified with the A.M.E. The Charleston group had considered sending delegates to the organizing conference held in Philadelphia that year, but they decided against it, partly because of the cost of the trip, and partly because of the host of legal and personal problems free blacks faced when traveling in the South. Instead, they sent their good wishes and sympathies for the undertaking, which the founding leaders acknowledged, thus making it possible for them to be recognized as the second largest conference in the denomination in 1820, with over 1,500 members.[46] But white public opinion forced the church to restrict its activities and eventually to end them, supposedly because of its complicity in the Denmark Vesey affair of 1822.

The A.M.E. Church may have been involved in the so-called Vesey plot, although any direct participation is difficult to trace.[47]

[46] Tanner, *An Apology for African Methodism*, 366.

[47] See Richard C. Wade, "The Vesey Plot: A Reconsideration," *Journal of Southern History*, XXX (1964), 150. Wade maintains that the plot existed only in the fear-gripped minds of Southern whites.

See also William S. Plumer, D.D., *Thoughts on the Religious Instruction of the Negroes of This Country* (Savannah: Edward J. Purse, 1848), 4, 5. Plumer quotes the report of the plot given by the Lieutnant Governor of South Carolina, Charles Cotesworth Pinckney:

"On investigation it appeared that all concerned in that transaction [the Vesey affair], except one, had seceded from the regular Methodist Church in 1817, and formed a separate establishment, in connection with the African

Denmark Vesey was a literate man of many talents and wide experience, who reportedly preached in the A.M.E. Church, as well as others, utilizing the isolation that the meetings afforded to outline his plan for black emancipation. Morris Brown, preacher to the group, allegedly served also as secret counselor to the plotters.[48] When their plan was discovered, Vesey was hanged, the church was closed, and Brown was forced to look for sanctuary in Philadelphia. Shortly after his arrival in the North, Brown was elected to serve as assistant bishop to Allen in 1828, and later became his successor.[49] The experience of the Charleston congregation demonstrated that under certain circumstances imposed by local conditions the church was capable of nourishing and harboring militant black protest, and to white observers, that justified closing it down. The A.M.E. Church did not resume its activities in that region until after the Civil War.

The situation in Ohio involved a different set of circumstances, although it had the same net effect, that is, of curtailing the program of the church. The denomination had grown slowly but steadily in the area during the 1820's as freedmen migrated to the state looking for work or a temporary haven before continuing on to Canada. Only a few congregations had been organized when the state decided to revive its dormant Black Code in 1828, requiring a $500 bond as a guarantee of good behavior.[50] Since freedmen and fugitives required all their resources just to get by, most of them were unable to comply with the demands of the so-called "expulsory" law and had to leave, which was just what its planners had intended. Many of those exiled from Ohio settled in West Canada where they provided the nucleus for other A.M.E.

Methodist Society in Philadelphia; whose Bishop [is] a coloured man, named Allen. . . ."

See also Herbert Aptheker, *Negro Slave Revolts* (7th ed.; New York: International Publishers, 1968), 268-76.

[48] Archibald H. Grimké, "Right on the Scaffold or The Martyrs of 1822," *American Negro Academy Occasional Papers* (Washington: American Negro Academy, 1901), No. 7, 11-12.

[49] Handy, *Scraps of A. M. E. History*, 22, 69.

[50] Litwack, *North of Slavery*, 72-74; George Washington Williams, *A History of the Negro Race in America* (New York: G. P. Putnam's Sons, 1883), II, 70, 71, 111-14.

missions. It seemed that it was only in the Middle States that the church was able to carry on its program without the threat of imminent dissolution, and there the ominous cloud of exportation to Africa hung over all its activities.

The knowledge of these external threats put church leaders on their guard, and encouraged them to strengthen the internal unity of the denomination. With a certain amount of foresight, as well as theological conviction, Allen had helped to compile a book of Discipline in 1817. It represented the official statement of what the denomniation stood for, and served as well as a ready reference for questions of theology and policy.[51] Its vigorous anti-slavery position and determination to limit office holding to Africans and their descendants were all that set it apart from the Methodist Episcopal Church; everything else, including Wesley's 25 articles of religion, was taken from the parent body. Allen, as zealous a supporter of discipline as ever the English Wesleyans were, urged his clerical colleagues to carry on their work "as Methodists . . . that love discipline. . . ."[52] And so, to prevent any confusion over just what the church should be doing to maintain discipline and encourage internal unity, Allen saw to it that the denomination adopted some very specific guidelines.

The basic organization of the church, and the General Conference specifically, established the parameters within which issues of denominational concern could be resolved. The General Conference met every four years after 1816, and delegates to its sessions settled on future objectives and also passed on advice to the two lower conferences, the annual and quarterly ones. In 1820 the delegates adopted a series of very pointed suggestions for all clergy that seemed designed to make the preachers aware of what the denomination included in its definition of discipline, at the same time that it hoped to promote clerical conformity to certain standards of conduct. Some of these recommendations pertained to the delegates themselves: Conference representatives were cautioned, for example, not to fall asleep during sessions, or to contradict speakers on the floor—failure to comply meant a fine of

[51] Richard Allen and Jacob Tapsico, *Doctrines and Discipline of the A. M. E. Church* (Philadelphia: Cunningham, 1817).
[52] Payne, *History of the A. M. E. Church,* 48.

12½ cents in the one case, and 5 cents in the other. And necessarily mindful of the insecurity of their situation, they advised
the clergy to keep their activities secret during conference sessions, away from the public spotlight, and to avoid writing any
letters or documents that could lead to dissension.[53] They also
agreed on some specific suggestions for the rest of the clergy, who
were instructed not to swear, bear tales, or accumulate debt.[54]
Local ministers were further advised to begin services on time,
pronounce carefully, choose plain texts and stay with them, instruct children faithfully, and limit extemporaneous prayers to
ten minutes.[55] These guidelines were meant to be observed, and
denominational leaders were as willing to discipline offenders as
Bethel's councils, regardless of the offender's standing in the
church. In fact, Daniel Coker, one of the founders and a former
candidate for the office of bishop, was subjected to a hearing and
subsequently expelled for a year in 1818 for an undisclosed offense, after which he was reinstated and subsequently migrated to
Africa.[56] In spite of these built-in safeguards, or perhaps because
of them, Allen and the General Conference spent a considerable
amount of time over the years settling cases involving "discord,
schisms, tattling and tale-bearing."[57] Conference problems often
appeared as enlarged reflections of local issues.

One of the more onerous tasks that the General Conference set
for itself involved supervising the financial activities of the denomination, a centralization of responsibility that served as another means for promoting unity. The board was charged with
sponsoring missionary work and for seeing to it that preachers
who served the connection received some compensation for their
efforts. The Conference itself tried to arrange to contribute something toward the Bishop's traveling expenses, by requesting each
of the three district conferences—which in 1822 were Philadelphia, Baltimore, and New York—to contribute $25 annually to-
ward his costs, but it was a rare year in which he collected any

53 *Ibid.*, 28.
54 *Ibid.*, 27, 28, 60.
55 Handy, *Scraps of A. M. E. History,* 49.
56 Payne, *History of the A. M. E. Church,* 28.
57 *Ibid.*, 20.

stipend.[58] Other men who served the connection were paid something for their work, though scarcely enough to support their families. The General Conference directed the annual conferences to pay the men out of the monies the district organizations received from the churches, and it was usually done on the basis of the size and importance of the charges they served. The Baltimore Conference in 1825 allocated the lion's share of its clerical disbursements to the minister at Bethel, Baltimore, who received $98.25. That same year the traveling preacher of the rural Easton circuit, W. Richardson, received $14.50.[59] Because the salaries were so small, it meant that the preachers had to work in shops alongside their members, thus preventing a gap between pulpit and pew, but also eliminating the chance for them to have the kind of leisure needed to develop polished sermons and refined theological arguments. Sermons did, of course, have other rather unique qualities, although in terms of content, they were, at their best, the hasty compilations of a week's experience and impressions. As their Bishop, Allen was chief pastor to the clergy, a task made more complicated by their dual occupational interests and limited educational opportunities. Nevertheless, he seems to have been fortunate enough to have had in his care men whose abilities equalled their responsibilities, whose level of achievement was probably generally higher than that of the average person in the pew.[60]

As the denomination grew, the services it offered to the churches increased. Allen felt that the A.M.E. Church should have its own hymnal, and he directed that one be compiled, adapted, as the Discipline had been, from Methodist sources. In 1818 the church created the post of book steward and appointed a leading Baltimore layman, Don Carlos Hall, whose job it was to arrange

58 *Ibid.*, 32.

59 *Ibid.*, 46.

60 As one criterion of achievement, it can be noted that a higher proportion of the men from Bethel Church, Philadelphia, who were accepted for clerical offices in the denomination, could write their names than the general congregation. None had been disciplined by the local church and most had served on at least one committee. Journal of Proceedings, Bethel Church, 102, 103, *passim.* It may be true that a similar distinction existed between churched and unchurched blacks.

for the publication and distribution of literature to the churches in the connection.[61] Later, as the denomination established new branches in the western territories, resident book agents performed a similar function there.[62] The addition of these projects strained Allen's already heavy work schedule, and he welcomed Morris Brown's help when Brown joined him in the episcopacy. Growth also brought with it the Conference equivalent of local volunteer groups such as the Daughters of Bethel, who were known on the national church level as the Daughters of Conference.[63] But growth also produced some problems unforeseen at the founding conference when only sixteen delegates were present: as the number of those eligible to participate in conference sessions increased, the Baltimore Conference decided in 1826 to restrict future participation in its proceedings to licensed clergymen, while still giving laymen and unlicensed preachers the right to attend but not to vote.[64]

The internal problems that developed as a result of membership growth were clearly much easier to deal with than the external community pressures that built up as denominational rolls expanded. In the minutes of almost every conference that convened during the period of Allen's lifetime, there is some reference either to specific community complaints or to precautionary measures that were adopted to avert such developments. When the Baltimore Conference was confronted with criticism about its late night meetings in 1823, it passed a resolution directing the churches to begin their meetings at one "regular hour," which was set at 7 P.M. in the winter, and 8 P.M. in the summer. The measure was adopted, the delegates said, not only as a helpful example for children, but also "for the safeguard and welfare of our brethren and sisters that are in servitude."[65] Allen himself urged ex-slave preachers who lacked freedom papers to limit their activities to

[61] Handy, *Scraps of A. M. E. History,* 27; Payne, *History of the A. M. E. Church,* 18.

[62] Payne, *History of the A. M. E. Church,* 61.

[63] *Ibid.,* 56.

[64] *Ibid.,* 46, 47; Wright, *Free Negro in Maryland,* 228, 229. Lay participation in conference sessions remained a characteristic of Zion Methodism. See also DuBois, *The Negro Church,* 45.

[65] Payne, *History of the A. M. E. Church,* 40, 41.

the area north of Maryland.[66] He knew from his own experience
with the slave catcher in Philadelphia that the black Methodists
were all too vulnerable to various kinds of threats and intimidation, and that their independent status increased their visibility.
But at least within their own society, they had the freedom to determine their own options and their own responses to community
pressures.

And Allen enjoyed certain other advantages by being recognized as the first black bishop. It was certainly an ego-satisfying
role. It offered him greater freedom of expression and flexibility
than would have been the case if he had remained attached to the
white denomination, as his black colleagues in Presbyterian and
Episcopal churches were learning. He probably had a closer rap-
port with his members than most white bishops, drawn to them
as he was by the adversity they shared and the work they did to
earn their daily bread. And they seemed to respect his leadership
on social issues as well as religious matters; in fact, much of the
black community in Philadelphia, church people and non-church
people alike, looked to him, as they did to James Forten, as someone who would fight to protect their interests. His work in the
community defined him as a political spokesman as well as a religious leader, but the desire to win converts was still a compelling
motive behind many of his activities.

66 *Ibid.*, 23.

V

"WHO IS MY BROTHER?":
SERVING THE WIDER COMMUNITY

Have you dedicated any portion of your labors to God,
who blessed them, by doing good to any besides your own?
Has the stranger, the widow or the fatherless ever tasted of
your bounty? If you have never done things of this kind,
. . . your talent is as yet hid in a napkin. . . . And consider further, that the real poor and needy are Christ's
representatives.

> Richard Allen
> *Life Experience*

I do hereby openly affirm it to the world, that he [Richard
Allen] has done more in a spiritual sense for his ignorant
and wretched brethren than any other man of colour has,
since the world began.

> David Walker
> *Appeal*

DAVID WALKER WAS NOT THE SORT OF MAN given to praising the
works of churchmen. Something of a religious mystic himself, he
suspected the organized church and its white clergy of using the
institution as a means for perpetuating, if not actually promoting,
black oppression. But he thought he recognized a very different
quality in Allen's ministry, one which from Walker's point of

view was revealed at its best in the Bishop's response to the program of the American Colonization Society. In that fight, the Bishop drew together all the members of the black community who wanted to enter the struggle, church members and non-church members alike, and to Walker that seemed to be a welcome indication that Allen was willing to deal with the totality of black needs and not just confine himself to the requirements of his own religious constituency.

Allen was, in fact, part of a small group of leaders in Northern black society who helped to develop community objectives, people who served also as spokesmen in matters of racial concern. Although the political and social restrictions of the period served to limit the size of the group, clergymen were nevertheless noticeably well represented. As soon after Allen's death as the decade of the 1830's, this situation changed somewhat as laymen came to assume more visible roles, and even during his own day there were notable exceptions to the dominant pattern of clerical leadership, including men like James Forten, John Russwurm, Paul Cuffe, and even Walker himself. But generally it was the clergyman who commanded the local scene in the black community. Most preachers recognized their unique position and addressed themselves to a wide range of interests, without distinguishing between activities that were of a religious nature and those that were not.

Allen himself seemed to look at his community and denominational work as simply two different aspects of the same vocation, a view that was essential if he was to minister successfully to the comprehensive needs of his members. Their problems were often more than those of just a religious nature, and if he expected to deal with them, as, for example, in the case of a fugitive slave, he had to be prepared to consider the total situation—physical, psychological, political, as well as spiritual—and all of this when he was not involved in his own weekday job. After he was elected bishop, his participation in community activities increased, although his interest remained fairly constant throughout his career. There were three different areas in the civic sector that seemed to concern him particularly, and they included A.M.E. missionary programs, political activity, and moral reform. Denominational missionary work, per se, might be more specifically "religious" than the others.

Why should the bishop of a relatively small group of Northern freedmen, politically and financially insecure, be interested in missions? Since his congregational resources were so meager, it would be logical to expect him to concentrate them on a more limited area at home, rather than diminish their effectiveness by spreading them around. His missionary motivation was little tainted by the fiery altruism of other sectarian missionaries who almost seemed to relish the physical privations associated with serving in some remote jungle outpost or primitive village; he was far too pragmatic about his missionary objectives to be swept off his feet by that kind of ideological impulse. He was, of course, eager to enroll new black Methodists in his denomination wherever and whenever he had the chance—and that was one of his motives— but he also viewed missions in political and social, or cultural, terms. Some black people, notably from Ohio, had been forced to become exiles in Canada, and there were others, too, who had removed to Haiti, and these emigrants needed to hear the message of liberation that African Methodism offered as much as they also required the racial ties it provided. It was one of the few props he could offer to help them sustain their loss and the kind of life they had known. His interest in African missionary activity was of a qualitatively different sort from his support for work elsewhere. Ideally, black people should have been free to choose where they would like to settle—Canada, Haiti, or wherever—but these were far from ideal times for freedmen, and political pressures helped to determine their choice of these two areas. Few had or would elect to go to Africa during his lifetime. Allen's concern for African expansion was therefore only indirectly related to political developments, but seems instead to have been inspired by a kind of nostalgic respect for a cultural homeland, a feeling that many other freedmen appeared to share. Unlike Daniel Coker, he expressed no consistent desire to go there himself, although he did feel a need to evangelize the "homeland" in whatever way he could. Basically that meant sending A.M.E. missionaries, a very expensive proposition, and one which, without the kind of subsidy that Coker accepted from the Maryland auxiliary of the

American Colonization Society, made it difficult for the denomination to undertake alone.

Since the Colonization Society offered to sponsor black emigration to Africa, it might appear to have been a matter of self-defeating foolish pride on Allen's part to have rejected their help. After all, if some black people felt a real urge to go there, why shouldn't they accept free passage from the white organization? Allen's sentimental regard for the place hadn't blurred his vision of the realities of colonization, which he saw to be basically coercive and antithetical to black interests. If colonization was accepted on the terms suggested by the A.C.S., it could encourage state legislatures to adopt even more repressive measures to force free people to leave, and with the free population gone, could result in perpetual slavery for those who remained behind. From Allen's point of view, when black people decided to develop colonies of emigrants in Africa, they would be better served by doing it on their own terms, which seemed to be his way of defining self-determination. Evangelization of the brothers and sisters who lived there also had to be considered from this perspective.

The fact that Coker embarked on his African missionary adventure fairly soon after he had been expelled from the denomination for undisclosed reasons leaves his motivation open to question. But the fact is that he had been reinstated a year before he left, and probably could have chosen to remain in Baltimore if he had preferred. Instead he sailed for Africa in 1820, the year before a black Baptist missionary, Lott Cary, left with the support of the Richmond Baptist Missionary Society and the approval of the Baptist General Convention.[1] Coker's subsidy from the Maryland Colonization Society didn't prevent Allen from pronouncing a benediction on his work, which was about all that Coker did take with him to guide him on a very indefinite project in an unfamiliar country. He did have access to the information that Paul Cuffe had made available after his earlier pilgrimage to Africa,

---

[1] Miles Fisher, "Lott Cary, the Colonizing Missionary," *JNH*, VII (1922), 381, 388. Cary went to Liberia. He and his associate, Colin Teague, received partial support from Benjamin Lundy and The American Convention for Promoting the Abolition of Slavery. See Lundy's *Genius of Universal Emancipation*, I, No. 1 (April 1822), 161.

but that was precious little to go on when he himself embarked with 88 other black Americans. Although he was a representative of the A.M.E. Church, he thought of his mission as something broader than an exclusively denominational venture. It was, he said, rather "a united effort among christians," to see that "darkness is driven from this land. . . ."[2] He had grandiose expectations: he planned to convert "Thousands, and thousands . . . from Paganism and Mahometanism [sic] to the religion of Jesus."[3] He kept a journal in which he recorded his impressions of the place, his own successes and disappointments, and while he occasionally referred to the obstacles he faced in the land that was to be his last home, he seemed generally satisfied with his decision, convinced that emigration had produced certain unexpected compensations. He noted with some pleasure that there was no denominational squabbling in Africa. Allen claimed A.M.E. credit for Coker's missionary gains in Africa, even though Coker himself described his work in more ecumenical terms.

The Bishop's concern for the Haitian field was stimulated by the combination of conditions that had sparked his interest in Canada and Africa. As in the Canadian effort, there were political implications involved insofar as the emigrants to the island demonstrated by their departure their rejection of mainland intolerance. And black Americans retained a certain historical identification with Haiti, as with Africa, that had been strengthened in part by the 1801 slave revolt of Toussaint L'Ouverture. Allen began planning for a mission station in Haiti as early as November 1824, when he called local leaders and preachers to a meeting in Philadelphia to sketch his proposal.[4] The group liked his idea, and after agreeing to ordain a local carpenter, "Brother Thomas Roberson" [Robertson], as a missionary, they arranged an appointment with the Haitian agent, M. Granville, to explain their intentions. They didn't go ahead with the work at the time, primarily because Robertson reconsidered his decision to go, but

2 *Journal of Daniel Coker* (Baltimore: John D. Fay, 1820), 43. See also Ephraim Bacon, *Abstract of a Journal* (3rd. ed.; Philadelphia: Clark and Raser, 1824), 4.
Leone.

3 Coker, *Journal*, 42. Coker settled first in Liberia, then moved to Sierra
4 Journal of Proceedings, Bethel Church, 94.

they were able to renew their plans three years later when Scipio Beanes presented himself as an eager candidate. Within the course of a week, the Baltimore Conference ordained Beanes as deacon, then elder, and commissioned him to serve in Haiti.[5] Although he didn't stay there very long—about a year—he was reasonably successful in organizing Methodist societies on the island. When he left, the several congregations had to fend for themselves, until in 1830 two groups, one in Samana and the other in Santo Domingo, petitioned the Baltimore Conference to ordain two of their men as elders. The Haitians appeared optimistic about their future despite their small membership, but they believed that ordained help would make it easier to spread their religion in a land where it was protected by "Church and State," and where "soldiers is plenty, but Christians is few."[6] Of the two men, presumably Isaac Miller and Jacob Roberts, the first was licensed to return as an elder and the second as a deacon.[7]

Much of this overseas work was, however, like the star on the Christmas tree, an embellishment on something much more basic. The real foundation of the church rested on domestic missionary work. Prior to 1816 there were officially no African Methodists, so that most additions had to be gained through a process of sustained, evangelistic efforts directed at unchurched or sympathetic members of the community. There were some exceptions, as in Canada, Charleston, and a few other places, where ready-made congregations applied for A.M.E. affiliation, but more often than not, new groups had to be convinced to join, if only because they were previously unaware that such an organization existed. The typical pattern of expansion called for sending a preacher, or lay exhorter, from one of the two original conferences to serve a small group of worshiping freedmen in an outlying community. Sometimes there were no more than a dozen or so people in a particular congregation—sometimes there were fewer—and the preacher would have to enlarge his circuit by either forming or serving additional groups in nearby towns. When informally organized congregations like the Brooklyn seceders or the Canadian exiles

[5] Payne, *History of the A. M. E. Church,* 55.
[6] *Ibid.,* 65.
[7] *Ibid.,* 66-68.

asked to be admitted, it saved the church this kind of grassroots missionary work and allowed it to concentrate instead on offering the kind of help that the groups had in mind when they applied for affiliation.

The Brooklyn Methodists wanted clerical help to assist them to become a viable congregation; the Ohio exiles in West Canada wanted a preacher to supply them with the kind of ties they had left behind. Allen ministered to both groups, although he clearly felt that the needs of the exiles were more pressing. At the time that they appealed to him for a preacher, they were just beginning to recover from a harrowing ordeal: forced out of their homes in and around Cincinnati by the revitalized Black Codes, many of them had been unable to leave the city before being terrorized by white mobs.[8] Many, but not all, had been African Methodists in Ohio, having joined when that state was included in the western missionary district in 1827. Although the district theoretically served all the land west of the Alleghenies, it actually ministered to only the black communities in the immediate environs of Pittsburgh and Cincinnati.[9] When the Ohio contingent of between 1,100 and 2,200 black residents emigrated, they joined other emigrés, fugitives, and colonists who had taken up residence in Canada, in an area where the denomination soon recognized the potential for forming new branches.[10] Allen did more than respond to their request for a preacher; he convened a special meeting in 1830 to consider their plight, the first session of what was to become the National Negro Convention movement.

Political considerations of one kind or another were involved in virtually all of the denomination's expansive efforts to reach unchurched members of the black community; some were the re-

8 See Litwack, *North of Slavery*, 73; the editor of the Cincinnati *Gazette* is quoted as saying he regretted the haste with which the Black Laws had been enforced, since the end result was that the "industrious" were driven away, while the "profligate" remained behind.

9 The Ohio or Western Conference was not formally organized until 1830, although an A. M. E. Church had functioned in Cincinnati since 1824. Payne, *History of the A. M. E. Church*, 62, 97.

10 Payne, *History of the A. M. E. Church*, 34, 51, 61-63, 126-30. Payne says of the expansion into Canada, ". . . the Canadian Societies multiplied till every important town in Canada West was marked by one of our churches. . . ." There were also churches in Steubenville, Zanesville, and Chillicothe, Ohio.

sult of direct legislative pressure, as in Ohio, and others the in-
direct product of social prejudice, the stimulus that had provoked
the move toward religious separatism. As the free black population in the North attempted to work out a place for itself within
a society that was implementing new patterns of segregated organization, it looked increasingly toward the church as a source
of identity and racial expression. Their sympathies fostered
A.M.E. growth, and made it possible for the denomination to
open up new traveling circuits in the city of Washington, along
the Eastern Shore in Maryland, and in 1828, in western New
York as far as Buffalo.[11]

They came to expect community spokesmen like Allen to protect their interests and look out for their needs. It was a job not
easily done, as any civic leader could verify. Allen and his friends
were put in the almost untenable position of trying to assert black
claims for social justice at the same time that they had to deal
with representatives of white vested interests. Local politicians
and social leaders looked to them as the representatives of the
black community, just as their own constituency did, but each
group expected something different from them. When the Mayor
of Philadelphia needed black help during the yellow fever epidemic in 1793 and again in 1814 when the city seemed threatened
by the possibility of a British invasion, he knew whom to call on—
Allen, Forten, and Jones. The men volunteered their assistance
as a form of civic responsibility, and it was, in general, gratefully
received. But when they engaged in work on behalf of the black
population, they were considered irresponsible by those same people who were willing to solicit their help when it seemed necessary to them. White observers were quick to criticize such things
as the antislave trade petition the black men drafted to Congress
in 1800, their rumored support for fugitive slaves, and their efforts to defeat the Colonization Society. The 1800 memorial to
Congress was, like most petition appeals, a symbolic gesture intended to exert pressure rather than a demand that the petitioners
expected to have satisfied. Not only did it go unfilled, but it was
alternately ridiculed and rejected by the legislators when it was

---

11 *Ibid.,* 34, 40, 57.

brought up for consideration.[12] Their suspected willingness to harbor runaways was something the politicians took more seriously because, from their point of view, it promoted disobedience to the law; some may even have entertained secret hopes that the slavecatcher's claim on Allen would have sufficiently intimidated the preacher to convince him to quit the work. And they were equally suspicious of black efforts to organize opinion against colonization.

Black community leaders gained a wider audience for their views with the advent of *Freedom's Journal* in 1827. The *Journal,* a black enterprise originating in New York City, supported positions that men like the Bishop had held for some time and made them appear fresh and novel to people who hadn't heard about them before. Some of those ideas were as old as the Free African Society, others were as recent as the latest ploy developed to confuse the colonizationists. Allen was a popular figure in the pages of the *Journal;* his views were entirely compatible with its editorial stance, a similarity that held true for other black spokesmen as well. The paper attacked colonization, and supported temperance, education, racial unity, and a host of other causes that Allen had been identified with over the years, until it ceased publication in 1829, due, rather ironically, to the acceptance of colonization by one of its editors, John Russwurm, and his subsequent departure for Liberia.

During its brief existence, the *Journal* applauded the attempts that churches, like Bethel, Philadelphia, made to serve the needs of local residents. Schools for people of all ages was one of its priorities, and whenever a church introduced some new program, such as a nursery school, or musical instruction, or night classes, the paper made sure that an announcement of it reached the readers. Bethel had a rather spotty record as an educational institution, having opened a series of schools only to see them close, one after the other, when money ran out. But past failures seemed to have no bearing on its willingness to try again: at one time it took on an ambitious instructional project that involved maintaining two separate programs simultaneously, one for children that was

---

[12] *Annals of Congress,* 6th Cong., 1st Sess., 232, 239-46. The petition was presented to Congress by Robert Waln on January 2, 1800.

conducted during the day, and one for adults that ran during the evenings and Sunday afternoons.[13] The schools were open to any member of the community who wanted to attend, since church membership was not a criteria for enrollment. The *Journal* seemed to think that these church-sponsored schools were especially commendable because they reserved for black people "the privilege of educating their own children according to their respective views."[14] In an editorial that sounded like one of the Bishop's appeals, the paper said that the African's three objectives should be "education, economy and union. . . ."[15]

All three of those goals were probably combined in a community service group that Bethel organized called the Bethel Benevolent Society. Designed to offer help to needy local residents on a regular basis, the Benevolent Society became a model for similar groups in other churches, until by 1828 *Freedom's Journal* was able to report the existence of forty such organizations. It followed in the reform tradition of offering words of advice along with its goods to those who came looking for assistance: a man who asked for shoes or a warm coat might receive the articles along with a sermon on morality, or the need for church attendance.[16] Although a project of church women, it generally served the needs of the community more than those of Bethelites, since destitute members were more inclined to present their cases directly to the board of trustees.

Allen probably inspired the creation of the Benevolent Society, but even if he did not, he assuredly gave it his seal of approval. It represented the kind of community involvement that he believed the church should be engaged in. It combined the essential ingredients of his religious outlook; individual salvation—which he usually defined in terms of moral reform—and social responsibility. Like most of his fellow Methodists, he was more concerned with experiential religion than he was with systematic theology, and for him as well as for them that implied constant striving to-

---

13 *Freedom's Journal*, August 29, 1828; October 3, 1828.

14 *Ibid.*, February 15, 1828. On June 11, 1827, the *Journal* reported that it knew of the existence of twelve African Free Schools in the North. There were others, however, which the paper failed to list.

15 *Ibid.*, November 23, 1827.

16 *Ibid.*, March 14, 1828.

ward moral improvement or perfectibility in everyday activities. He was not a Christian perfectionist in the sense that he believed that it was a condition that mortal man could attain; he seemed rather to regard it as a goal toward which imperfect beings could aspire. The result was that, in the first instance, he could recognize life's imperfections, and, in the second, determine to do battle against them. On a more practical level, it meant that he could regard total perfection and total freedom as eschatological hopes rather than present realities, while at the same time encouraging freedmen to remember their responsibility to work on behalf of the slaves. He advised free people to engage in acts of "mercy and charity," advice that he also applied to himself.

In addition, he urged them to accept the need for moral reform as one of the conditions vital to racial improvement. To promote the issue, he participated in community projects that were concerned with promoting civic morality, and he talked about it and wrote about it whenever he had the chance—including it even when it did not seem germane to the topic under consideration. On those public occasions when he could give it his undivided attention, he really warmed to his subject. An "Address to the People of Colour" in 1808, following the conviction of some young men for a local murder, offered just such an opportunity. After discussing the circumstances of the murder, he gave some direct advice:

> Labour with thy hands and thou will provide things that are honest, and with a good conscience enjoy them. Fly for thy life from the chambers of the harlot. Know, O young man, that her steps take hold of hell. Secret crimes shall be dragged to light and seen by the eye of the world in their horrid forms. The solemn record is standing: 'Whoremongers and adulterers, God will judge.' Go not to the tavern; the song of the drunkard will soon be changed to weeping and wailing and gnashing of teeth. Drunkenness hurls reason from the throne, and when she has fallen, Vice stands ready to ascend it. Break off, O young man your impious companions. If you still grasp there hands they will drag you down to everlasting fire.[17]

Probably also incorporated into a sermon he preached at Bethel Church, the Address touched on all those issues he had supported

---

[17] Richard Allen, *Address to the Public and People of Colour* (Philadelphia, n.p., 1808).

from the time he had been a member of the Free African Society, and perhaps even before. The themes had been fairly common among the early members of the Abolition Societies and were ones generally accepted by most social reformers; temperance, marital fidelity, thrift, industry, and abolition. Abolition was not dealt with directly in this message, but his readers and listeners understood it to be implicit in what he said. Moral reform had to include emancipation, an equation that also worked in reverse. From Allen's lips, these ideas took on special relevance for black people, although he was willing to preach them to anyone who would listen. His access to the pulpit gave him the chance he needed to reach the people at Bethel, but he had to find other ways to get his message to the people in the wider community. In 1809 he helped James Forten and Absalom Jones create the Society for the Suppression of Vice and Immorality, an organization whose members pledged to supervise morals in the black community.[18] The leaders of the new group singled out the use of liquor as a particularly loathsome and harmful practice, and championed the cause of total abstinence. The three men, who presumably felt as strongly about the matter as the white men who organized the American Temperance Society in 1826, had succeeded in sponsoring a Black predecessor to that group. Allen enjoined his members from using alcoholic beverages and Forten forbade the presence of liquor on his business premises.[19] One aspect of the temperance campaign unique to the black reformers was their opinion that alcoholism might be used as an argument to deny freedmen their political rights, in a way that white alcoholic imbibers were not similarly denied, and they intended to refute that argument by example. By applying that same logic, they hoped to eliminate the other white objections raised against black social equality.

Allen's interest in social equality also led him to join Forten in

---

[18] George F. Bragg, *A History of the Afro-American Group of the Episcopal Church* (Baltimore: Church Advocate Press, 1922), 70; William C. Nell, *The Colored Patriots of the American Revolution* (Boston: Robert F. Wallcut, 1855), 180; Charlotte L. Forten, *Journal of Charlotte Forten*, ed. by R. A. Billington (New York: Collier, 1961), 13-14; Douglass, *Annals of St. Thomas Church*, 11.

[19] Nell, *The Colored Patriots of the American Revolution*, 180.

supporting woman's rights, at a time when most secular reformers had not yet included it in their list of concerns. The issue was not particularly popular even among their black contemporaries, who seemed to find it difficult to view discrimination in jobs and voting from the point of view of sex rather than race. Among the religiously oriented reformers sex discrimination was a matter they were obliged to contend with, since a woman was as apt to be "moved" by the Spirit as a man, and her right to speak, pray, and preach was difficult to deny.

Allen had two encounters with female preachers; in one case he denied her request to preach, and in the second he approved. The first occurred in 1803, when he was theoretically still identified with the Methodist Church, which may help to account for his negative response. Dorothy Ripley was an English visitor to Philadelphia who asked for the right to address the congregation at Bethel. Allen told her that the board of trustees turned down her request because it was "diametrically opposite to the letter and spirit of the rules of society . . . and the discipline . . . of the Methodist Episcopalian Church. . . ."[20] She nevertheless found a chance to speak at Bethel, rather spontaneously, when she stood and addressed the congregation following a sermon by Allen. It was an unsettling experience for her and for the Bethelites, not because of any overt signs of discrimination on their part, but because a drunken white soldier unexpectedly appeared and disrupted the crowd.[21] Ms. Ripley left for home with some kind words from Absalom Jones and some lasting impressions of American church life.

His second association with a woman preacher involved a different set of circumstances. Jarena Lee was a black woman, a member of the A.M.E. Church, and the widow of an African preacher.[22] At the time of her request, Bishop Allen was free to determine his own policy, unhampered by the restrictions of his former Methodist ties, and he agreed to her appeal. It may also

---

[20] "Letter of Richard Allen to Dorothy Ripley, May 11, 1803," *JNH*, I (1916), 436-37.

[21] *Ibid.*, 437-38.

[22] Jarena Lee, *Religious Experience and Journal of Mrs. Jarena Lee, Giving an Account of her Call to Preach the Gospel* (Philadelphia: Printed and Published for the author, 1836), 13, 32-33.

be true that during the interval that separated her case from Ms. Ripley's, Allen had personally modified his views on woman's rights. Women were an integral part of the organization at Bethel Church, supporting its activities with their contributions, and voting on many, although by no means all, issues of concern to the congregation. But his decision to refuse the British woman could have been prompted by his consideration that to let her speak would have been an open violation of Methodist Discipline, and he already had troubles enough with denominational officials without taking on more.

That Ms. Lee was an extraordinary woman Allen seemed to recognize. A pietistic Methodist, she was willing to walk twenty miles in a day to deliver a sermon to a rural congregation. Allen apparently appreciated her talents and created numerous opportunities for her to address A.M.E. gatherings. She sometimes spoke to racially mixed groups, and on at least one occasion received the prestigious assignment of preaching at Mother Bethel, the chance Ms. Ripley had been officially denied. She also traveled with the Bishop and his local associates as an unofficial member of their delegation to conference sessions in New York and Baltimore.[23] But her reception was generally less than enthusiastic wherever she appeared, and she was repeatedly called upon to defend her right to speak in public. The Bishop seemed unmoved by the protests of those members of his church who challenged what they regarded to be an unjustified privilege, and he continued to promote her interests.

The impressions he gained every day from watching his wife, Sarah—a woman of no mean talents herself—may have helped to change his views on the matter of woman's place in the church. Like virtually all others born into slavery, the facts of her early life passed unrecorded, although A.M.E. Church sources speculate that sometime during her childhood, probably around the age of eight, she moved from the slavery of Virginia to the relative freedom of Philadelphia. Whether she was emancipated, escaped, or had her freedom purchased by her family is unknown, but whatever the case, she was acknowledged in her adult life as

[23] *Ibid.*, 29, 34. Although she reported that she went with the clergy "to attend" the conference, she did not participate in it.

a friend to fugitives who came in the area. Harboring runaways, a dangerous and illegal activity, jeopardized the security of her family and her husband's position, but she continued to do it, donating her time, money, and the protection of her home to help them reach "the land of liberty. . . ."[24] Her husband was also involved in her deception—which necessarily had to be a cooperative venture if she was to hide runaways in their home—and played his part in different ways, interceding, at one time, with the Mayor of Philadelphia on behalf of children suspected of being kidnapped.[25]

Aid to runaways qualified as one of those acts of "mercy and charity" that Allen urged on all freedmen. The work had no direct bearing on his clerical role, nor did it provide the church with any tangible benefits—although some fugitives may have decided that they could safely remain in the city, and at Bethel, when any immediate danger had passed. But that was not considered as a factor when they asked for help; the Bethelites seemed unwilling to bargain with a man's freedom for the sake of an additional member. Too many of them had once been in a similar situation themselves.

The kind of personal help that Allen gave to fugitives was comparatively less direct when it came to the problems of slaves. His pragmatic sense of what was possible may have supported this approach: he could be effective in working in the free community; given his location and personal orientation, he could be less effective in ministering to slaves. His ministry to slaves consisted of offering them words of encouragement and reminding them that their free brothers were working on their behalf. It is an approach that some today might regard as a conservative, inadequate adjustment, but such a conclusion is an oversimplification that requires removing the man from his historical setting. Allen was a reformer, and he employed the tactics that are usually associated with that approach to social change. Within his own life he had accomplished a radical transformation, from slave to Bishop, and the experience strengthened his assumptions about the nature of

24 Payne, *History of the A. M. E. Church,* 87.
25 Letter from Pennel Beale to Richard Allen, April 5, 1825, MS, Historical Society of Pennsylvania. The letter requested Allen's intercessory assistance.

social change. Whether he sympathized with those who advocated
more militant measures is open to question: the Denmark Vesey
slave conspiracy was reportedly planned in an A.M.E. Church
while Allen was Bishop, but he left no record of his impressions
of that affair. He did address a statement to slaveowners to correct their assumptions regarding slave contentment, and in it he
referred to certain unspecified "instruments" of God. He said in
part:

> . . . the dreadful insurrection they [the slaves] have made when op-
> portunity is offered, is enough to convince a reasonable man that great
> uneasiness and not contentment is the inhabitant of their hearts. God
> himself hath pleaded their cause; He hath from time to time raised up
> instruments for that purpose, sometimes mean and contemptible in
> your sight, at other times He hath used such as it hath pleased him,
> with whom you have not thought it beneath your dignity to contend.
> Many have been convinced of their error, condemned their former
> conduct, and become zealous advocates for the cause of those whom
> you will not suffer to plead for themselves.[26]

His reference to God's "instruments" was sufficiently vague to allow any slaveowner who happened to read it to interpret its
meaning for himself. To support openly the actions of a militant
slave—if that was what he was doing—was to court public censure,
with all that that could imply for the Bishop and his church. He
seemed to think that in matters related to fugitives or slaves it
was better to be devious.

The circumstances were different when it came to dealing with
Northern freedmen. He was willing to participate openly in activities that affected their future, although even that involved assuming a calculated risk. And one of the organizations that attracted his attention during the later part of his life was the Free
Cotton Society, the creation of abolitionist Benjamin Lundy.
Lundy had patterned his Society after a British model that he
felt had effectively aroused public sentiment to boycott slave-
produced goods. Allen joined when he recognized its potential to
strike an economic blow at slavery if men in his position could

[26] Allen, "An Address to Those Who Keep Slaves and Approve the Practice,"
Life Experience, 71.

help to convince even a small percentage of the free black population to support its objectives. The parent body of the organization, the Free Produce Society—which wanted to boycott all
slave-produced goods—helped Lundy to purchase "free" cotton
from non-slaveholding growers in North Carolina.[27] Once the
processed cotton arrived in the North, it had to be made into
goods that would hopefully be sold to those people who were
willing to register their opposition to the peculiar institution by
buying a product that was often inferior. Allen urged freedmen
to support the boycott and *Freedom's Journal* added its approval,
even suggesting that the boycott be extended to include such com-
modities as sugar and coffee.[28] The temptation to purchase the
prohibited articles was great, primarily because they were available in greater quantity and were easier to get. People had to be
reminded repeatedly of the purpose of the boycott, and that was
a service that Allen and the *Journal* performed. Allen assisted in
another way, as a kind of labor supplier. When the cotton arrived
in the city, someone had to find people willing to manufacture it
into salable articles, and he was usually able to secure black
women to work as seamstresses. The most popular items they
made were dresses and bonnets, which their owners presumably
wore as a sign of protest.

The boycott itself was not very successful, due, in part, to the
difficulty involved in securing "free" cotton, but it did serve another and perhaps ultimately more useful function by focusing
black attention on a common economic interest. It provided a
healthy counterpart to the growing independent black church
movement which respected racial identity in religious affairs, but
then often proceeded to place denominational loyalty above racial unity. The boycott could capitalize on the racial awareness
that the church movement stimulated and promote racial solidar-
ity around an issue that had few, if any, detractors in the black
community. Allen called for "union among ourselves and a stead-

[27] *Genius of Universal Emancipation,* April 1830, 9. "Free" cotton, pro-
duced by free labor, was supplied primarily by farmers in the vicinity of
Washington, North Carolina, who experimented with growing Mexican cotton.
See *Minutes of the American Convention for Promoting the Abolition of
Slavery,* 1829, 58.

[28] *Freedom's Journal,* March 14, 1828.

fastness in the African cause,"[29] and the boycott seemed to suggest a step in that direction.

It could be argued that Allen's participation in so many diverse "causes" diluted his influence and prevented him from making an effective challenge in any specific area. When combined with his various other Sunday and weekday jobs, his community activities made for an extremely heavy work schedule. But like most reformers, he was not selective about his causes; his perception of social injustice seemed as comprehensive as his sense of mission. According to his definition of mission, the exiled freedmen in Canada were as much his concern as the fugitives in Philadelphia, the destitute A.M.E. members as much in need of his advice as the Southern slaves. His successors in the reform movement of the 1830's and '40's had an equally comprehensive list of concerns that included abolition, temperance, women's rights, pacifism, as well as a host of other, sometimes more esoteric, issues. Because ideas of what constitutes social injustice can be very personal, they, too, were criticized, not only by the openly hostile, but also by those who thought their concern was misguided—in their case for neglecting the immigrant and the laborer.

Allen can be measured against a similar yardstick of reform. He spread his interests around among a host of community projects, dividing his energy, and perhaps his impact among those issues that affected freedmen directly and slaves only indirectly. Even among his own contemporaries outside the A.M.E. Church, there was no consensus of agreement regarding the effectiveness of his ministry: the mystical, militant David Walker thought he was a kind of black savior; the middle-class Bishop of Zion Methodism, Christopher Rush, regarded him as an inordinately ambitious man.

But Rush himself admitted later, perhaps enviously, that Allen was able to exert a strong influence over people. He reported a visit that Allen made to New York City sometime after the Zionites and Bethelites ended their dispute over the possibility of creating a merger. The purpose of the visit was to dedicate one of his A.M.E. churches, and on that occasion a group of Zionites, led by

[29] This was part of his speech to the New York Conference of the A. M. E. Church in 1822. Payne, *History of the A. M. E. Church,* 37.

James Varick, flocked to the meeting. "[H]is presence," said Rush, "seemed very soon to alter the minds of our preachers."[30] His physical appearance—plumpish, and medium-sized—was not particularly impressive; it was his personal magnetism that drew people to him and enhanced his stature in the black community.

His most ambitious foray into community affairs came in 1816, when he joined the attack on the American Colonization Society, a venture that acquired greater political significance as it developed. Up to that time, except for his petition to Congress in 1800, Allen had been essentially a moral reformer, but now with his independent denominational status assured, he cooperated in what was actually a political struggle. He was among the first group of black reformers to gain a hearing, and because he was a preacher, he established a clear identification of the black church with reform efforts. The crowded pews of Bethel Church were for Allen's program of reform what the fields of Southampton County became for Nat Turner's vision of revolution: a source of inspiration on how best to deal with racial injustice.

[30] Rush, *Short Account of the A. M. E. Z. Church*, 35-36.

VI

MOBILIZING THE CHURCHES:
THE ATTACK ON COLONIZATION

> Can we not discern the project of sending the free people
> of colour away from their country: Is it not for the interest
> of the slave-holders to select the free people of colour out of
> the different states, and send them to Liberia?
>
> Letter of Richard Allen,
> Freedom's Journal

> The Colonization Society may plot your removal to a for-
> eign land—to Africa—but they will not succeed. I believe, as
> firmly as I do my own existence, that the time is not far
> distant, when you and the trampled slaves will all be free
> . . . and enjoy the same rights in this country as other
> citizens.
>
> William Lloyd Garrison,
> An Address, delivered before the Free People of Color. . . .

As an old man looking back on some of the more significant developments that occurred during his lifetime, Richard Allen may
have secretly realized that in some ways he owed the American
Colonization Society more than he cared to admit. Not that he
was any more in favor of the Society then than he had been when
it was organized in 1816, but rather that it had been more successful in accomplishing something that he had been attempting all

his professional life, and that was to give the free black community a sense of cohesiveness. More effectively than African Methodism, the Free Cotton Society, Masonry, and the numerous other
reform groups he worked in, the A.C.S. had inadvertently united
free black opinion behind a common concern, anticolonization.
Church people from the various denominations joined with abolitionists to discuss alternatives to the Society's program for sending free black "volunteers" back to Africa, temporarily setting
aside their parochial differences to deal with an issue that posed
a real threat to their continued presence in the United States.
Between 1816 and 1831, the period during which the A.C.S. enjoyed its greatest popularity, the growth of organized black protest kept pace with that of the Society, until it finally assumed a
semi-permanent form in 1830 in the National Negro Convention
movement. This was also, coincidentally, the period during which
the independent black church drive gained in strength, and the
two programs, colonization and religious separatism, were related
to a common source; the growth in size of the free black population and white reaction to that growth.

The increase in the Northern population of freedmen is simple
to trace; it resulted from the combination of gradual emancipation laws in Northern states with the attraction those free states
held for Southern emigrants and fugitives. This rather sudden
rise, unanticipated by Northern whites, disrupted their traditional social arrangements and forced them to recognize their own
racial anxieties. Unwilling and seemingly unable to deal with
their racial "dilemma," they came up with only two options, and
they were not mutually exclusive; colonization and domestic restriction. The American Colonization Society represented their
collective anxieties, just as black separatist churches were, in some
respects, another manifestation of their unwillingness to accept
religious integration. Colonization and religious separatism were
therefore two different ways of describing the same problem,
namely the freedmens' demands for social equality. Allen, whose
episcopacy coincided with the heyday of colonization, brought the
two issues together in his ministry.

He was first introduced to the colonizing scheme in 1816, but
the idea itself was not new: it had previously been endorsed by

Washington, Jefferson, and Madison.[1] Nothing came of it until 1815 when Paul Cuffe transported a small band of freedmen from Boston to Sierra Leone.[2] On his return, Cuffe was publicized in the press and sought out by those interested in his impressions of the venture.[3] One of those who questioned him was the Rev. Robert Finley, an "enthusiastic" Presbyterian preacher from New York.[4] Finley and his zealous, missionary-minded young friend, the Rev. Samuel Mills, provided the initial inspiration for organizing the A.C.S.

Finley and Mills were the kind of well-intentioned humanitarians who could impress even the skeptical David Walker—an ardent anticolonizationist—with the basic integrity of their motives.[5] But once the Society took shape, the politicians took over from them, seeing in it a politically useful issue. Finley, elected to serve the group as one of its thirteen vice presidents, died in 1818, and Mills, commissioned as an A.C.S. agent, embarked for Africa.

The politicians who replaced them in the Society came generally from those Middle and Border states where the population of freedmen was proportionately greatest. Henry Clay, a slaveholder from Kentucky, chaired the first public meeting of the organization in Washington on December 21, 1816, and like all good politicians, he used the opportunity to make a speech. Anxious to

[1] "What the Framers of the Federal Constitution Thought of the Negro," *JNH*, III (1918), 381-382; "James Madison's Attitude Toward the Negro," *JNH*, VI (1921), 74-77. An interesting discussion of Jefferson's attitude toward black people can be found in Winthrop Jordan's book, *White Over Black*, 429-75; 546-51.

[2] Letter of Paul Cuffe to Perry Sachs of the African Society, February 4, 1813, MS, Historical Society of Pennsylvania. Cuffe had circulated an appeal for passengers among the various African Societies.

[3] H. N. Sherwood, "The Formation of the American Colonization Society," *JNH*, II (1917), 218.

[4] The Rev. Isaac Van Arsdale Brown, *Biography of the Rev. Robert Finley* (Philadelphia: John W. Moore, 1857), 51.

[5] David Walker, *An Appeal*, ed. by Charles M. Wiltse (New York: Hill and Wang, 1965), 78. Sherwood, in "The Formation of the American Colonization Society," says "It seems . . . safe to conclude that the colonization movement of 1816-17 was at that time sincere in its purpose and straightforward in its aims," *JNH*, II, 226. See also G. B. Stebbins, *Facts and Opinions Touching the Real Origin, Character and Influence of the American Colonization Society* (Boston: John P. Jewett & Co., 1853), 20-21.

gain a broad base of support for the Society, he appealed to the various shades of opinion he thought might be represented; he spoke of free blacks as being a "useless and pernicious, if not a dangerous portion of [our] population," but then went on to point out the social injustices that prevented them from enjoying the "immunities of free men," a problem that could be overcome if the members accepted the "moral fitness, of restoring them to the land of their fathers. . . ."[6] When the speechmaking ended, the group approved the adoption of Articles and agreed to meet formally as a Society on January 1, 1817. At the January meeting they selected their officers, and if there had been any doubt about what direction the Society would take in the future, a glance at the slate of those elected would have ended all speculation. The president was Bushrod Washington, nephew to the General and former President, and among the thirteen vice presidents elected along with Finley were Andrew Jackson of Tennessee, William H. Crawford of Georgia, and Henry Rutgers of New York: only Crawford and William Phillips of Massachusetts came from areas outside the Middle or Border States.[7] Clearly, the racial preferences of that section would predominate.

The kind of support the Society would pick up was, therefore, almost predictable. Prior to 1832, most of the state legislatures in the area best represented in the organization had given it their official approval, and the list included Virginia, Maryland, Tennessee, Ohio, New Jersey, Connecticut, Rhode Island, Indiana, Vermont, Kentucky, Pennsylvania, Massachusetts, New York, and Delaware. Although states of the deep South were reluctant to join the vanguard, ex-President Monroe and even the King of France were not.[8] Neither were church bodies: between 1818 and 1830 national conventions of the Presbyterian, Methodist, Baptist, and Dutch Reformed Churches gave their endorsement, as well as regional conferences of Congregationalists, Quakers, and Epis-

---

6 Brown, *Biography of Finley,* 104.

7 *First Annual Report of the American Colonization Society* (Washington: Davis and Force, 1818), 11.

8 House of Representatives, *Report of Mr. Kennedy of Maryland on the Memorial of the Friends of African Colonization assembled in convention in the City of Washington, May, 1842* (Washington: Gales and Seaton, 1843), 426.

copalians.[9] It was an impressive array of church and state that had combined, ostensibly in the best interests of the freedman, to arrange for his removal to his proper "homeland." As William Lloyd Garrison later pointed out, it amounted to a white public confession, of sorts, that debased the moral integrity of the white man as well as the black. It served as an announcement that white people were unable to overcome their racial anxieties, and that black people could not expect equal justice in America.[10]

Black people tried to size up what their future would be like if the Society gained enough support to mandate political action on colonization, and it looked like a frightening prospect. The free population could ultimately be forced to leave, on the basis of some questionable explanation—such as their potential danger to the continued control of slaves—slaves themselves would be consigned to a life of perpetual bondage along with their heirs, and the colonized freedmen would be dropped into an unknown and uncultivated land with no provision made for even their basic needs. They responded to the threat as to the sound of a fire bell. Three thousand free blacks reportedly assembled at Bethel Church, Philadelphia in mid-January 1817, little more than two weeks after the first formal meeting of the A.C.S. Word of the creation of the Society had traveled quickly from Washington to Philadelphia, and within that brief span of time, Allen, Absalom Jones, John Gloucester, and James Forten had successfully promoted the mass meeting.

The leadership of the Philadelphia protest was characteristic of similar gatherings elsewhere; clergymen and lay church leaders became generally responsible for organizing anticolonization feelings. And they brought to it the necessarily diverse influences that had shaped their particular religious backgrounds. The Philadelphia group offered a good example; Allen was the recently

[9] Early Lee Fox, *The American Colonization Society*, Series XXXVII, No. 3, of *Johns Hopkins University Studies in Historical and Political Science* (Baltimore: The Johns Hopkins Press, 1919), 78-79; H. R., *Report of Mr. Kennedy of Maryland*, 927 ff.

[10] William Lloyd Garrison, *An Address to Free People of Color* (Boston: Stephen Foster, 1831), 22; Archibald H. Grimké, *William Lloyd Garrison, The Abolitionist*, American Reformer Series, ed. by Carlos Martyn (New York: Funk and Wagnalls, 1891), 146-147.

elected Bishop of an African Methodist denomination, Jones was the rector of a black Episcopal Church, Gloucester served as the minister of a black Presbyterian congregation, and James Forten was an Episcopal layman, a vestryman in Jones's parish. The anti-colonization effort brought these interdenominational representatives together, not only in Philadelphia, but in other cities in the North where their colleagues were busily engaged in similar work. It was the first concerted action by freedmen to protect and improve their lot in life, and it developed out of the churches as one of the products of their emphasis on moral reform. The transition took place so smoothly that it was scarcely noticed; it seemed a logical step to move from concern for moral improvement and self-help to action to secure self-determination. And it established a pattern for the type of future political activism that came to be associated with the churches, in most cases, irrespective of their actual denominational ties.

Although the drive toward religious separatism had begun in the eighteenth century, it didn't pick up momentum until the second decade of the nineteenth, when its growth was related, if indirectly, to the degree of public approval the A.C.S. received. It is coincidental, but not insignificant, that the courts granted Allen's request for African religious independence in 1816, the same year in which the Colonization Society was born. There was an interesting, and perhaps suggestive, parallel that existed between the three types of black church groups that developed, and the three degrees of social separation that white people supported. Among church-going blacks there were, for instance, a few who remained within predominantly white congregations, many who attended black branches of white denominations (and these included the Baptists, a group that was usually identified with the parent body in name only), and some who joined African-controlled separatist societies like the A.M.E. or A.M.E.Z. Its social equivalent followed along similar lines: it consisted of those whites who supported integration, those who favored domestic segregation, and those who wanted colonization. There may have been a cause-and-effect relationship that explained the similarity, but it was lost in the miasma of social strife.

The anticolonization movement was strongest in those cities that sustained a black community of interest built around the churches, particularly in the major urban centers of Philadelphia, New York, Baltimore, and later Boston, a relative latecomer to the campaign. The increasingly segregated population of those cities had nurtured their loyalties to their own local religious and social groups, and only occasionally did they set them aside in favor of certain broader interests, such as Allen's A.M.E. organization. That the colonization scheme was able to arouse the interests of so many freedmen in a wider effort suggests several things: it says that those agencies that shaped black public opinion, particularly the church and later *Freedom's Journal,* enjoyed a fairly high degree of respect, and that the freedman's unspoken fears of dislocation suddenly became poignantly real to him.

The effectiveness of a particular church as a social agency, in this case as a medium for expressing anticolonization feeling, depended on a combination of factors that included its local environment, its own historical development, and where it stood on the integration-segregation-separation scale. A few examples from the four cities serve to place Allen's case in proper perspective.

The African Methodist Zionites in New York City were the group most like the Allenites, but unlike their fellow Methodists in Philadelphia, they were able to contribute little to the early stages of the protest effort. Until they resolved their leadership crisis in 1823 with the election of James Varick as bishop, they were too involved with their own local problems to give much attention to colonization. In fact, during the time that they were leaderless, they barely survived disintegration as various splinter groups threatened to abandon the effort out of sheer frustration. One of the stabilizing influences that kept them together was the personality of Peter Williams, the popular sexton of John Street Methodist Church, the white parent-body of the Zionite seceders. Williams was a black layman, with a circle of friends almost as wide as his interests. He and his wife Molly opened the doors of their home to visiting clergymen and local black friends on a regular basis. Still, for all his friends and interests, he was not a community activist, at least there is no record to indicate that he was. He never even joined Zion Church, although he was obviously sympathetic to the separatist impulse and was willing to offer direction when it was needed. He had a personal reason for keeping his membership at John Street Church that had to do with his

earliest associations with the place. Born a slave, he had been
purchased by the church, which intended to give him his freedom.
He refused the gift, and insisted on repaying the church out of
his earnings as sexton, finally adding his own gold watch to complete the total purchase price.[11] Whatever other impressions the
event left him with, it apparently persuaded him that his place
was at John Street Church. His sympathy was with the Zionites,
his sense of responsibility to the white Methodists. He was a layman, in any case, and even if he had decided to join with Zion
he could not have filled the role for which an ordained minister
was required. Varick's selection ended the leadership crisis, and
when he died a few years after his election, his successor, Christopher Rush, gave the church the kind of direction it had needed
for so long. Rush finally managed Zion's identification with the
anticolonization movement and subsequently with the abolition
campaign, serving himself as one of the original directors of the
American and Foreign Anti-Slavery Society.

There were more freedmen in New York City than in Philadelphia in 1801 when the Zionites built their first church, but fewer
black Methodists, and that fact was less a reflection on the religious inclinations of Africans than a commentary on the social
milieu of the city.[12] New York was noted more for its industry
than its piety, and black residents had early been introduced to
the competitive process through the practice of hiring out.[13] The
result was that, after the adoption of a gradual emancipation law

---

[11] The Rev. J. B. Wakeley, *Lost Chapters Recovered from the Early History
of American Methodism* (New York: Carlton & Porter, 1858), 461, 463, 464,
469. See also John Street Methodist Episcopal Church Records, 1A, April 8,
1787, MS, New York Public Library.

[12] See *Negro Population*, 51.
The Methodist membership figures for 1801 to 1806 were:

	1801		1803		1806	
	whites	blacks	whites	blacks	whites	blacks
N.Y.C.	685	150	747	248	691	365
Phil.	707	448	773	552	1073	711

Minutes of Conference of Methodist Episcopal Church, Philadelphia. See also
John Street Methodist Episcopal Church Records, 1B, MS, New York Public
Library.

[13] Edgar J. McManus, *A History of Negro Slavery in New York* (Syracuse:
Syracuse University Press, 1966), 47.

in 1799. New York freedmen, reportedly "boldly self-assertive."[14] tended to concentrate their energies more on jobs than religious affairs.

Two other black churches that appeared in New York prior to 1820, one Baptist and one Episcopal, suggested yet another approach to religious separatism. Although the organization of the Baptist Church preceded the Episcopal, the latter had a more direct connection with the Zionites through the person of its rector.

The son of the sexton of John Street Church, Peter Williams, Jr., officially became the minister of St. Philips Episcopal Church in 1819 when Bishop Hobart dedicated the building. Williams had left the Methodist denomination of his parents in favor of the Episcopal Church while still a young man. After finishing a course of study outlined by the Bishop and supervised by a local rector, he followed the pattern marked out earlier by Absalom Jones, and became the denomination's second black deacon on October 20, 1820. On July 10, 1826, he was advanced to the priesthood.[15]

Unlike Allen, Williams did not initiate separate worship for black churchmen; they had been meeting apart from the white congregation since sometime after the Revolution, when Trinity Episcopal Church in the city reserved separate facilities in the building for them. But as their numbers increased, they outgrew the space provided for them and began meeting in the African Free School; it was there that Williams joined them.[16]

Williams supervised the transformation of the group from an organization within Trinity Church into a congregation that was separate from, but not independent of, the parent Episcopal Church. His membership, smaller than that of the local black

[14] *Ibid.*, 191.

[15] B. F. DeCosta, *Three Score and Ten: The Story of St. Philips' Church, New York City* (New York, 1889), 23; *Journal of the General Convention of the Protestant Episcopal Church*, 1820, 534. *The New York Commercial Advertiser* of October 21, 1820, commented that Williams was a man who had "improved his intellectual faculties by intense study and application," and that he was a person of "exceptionable morals. . . ." For his ordination to the priesthood, see *Journal of the General Convention of the Protestant Episcopal Church*, 1826, 208.

[16] DeCosta, *St. Philips' Church*, 14.

Methodists, may have been comparatively wealthier.[17] And his ministry differed from Allen's too, insofar as his work was encouraged rather than hampered by the white denomination. In fact, Trinity parish and two wealthy benefactors, Jacob Sherred and George Lorillard, made sizable donations to the building fund of St. Philips Church.[18]

Williams's ministry and the progress of the church were closely observed by the Bishop, press, and local clergy, all of whom seemed to agree that the congregation was "orderly and devout."[19] But such close attention implied certain hazards, namely censure for activities the observers considered unacceptable, and the almost inevitable rebuke under such circumstances came in the form of a warning from the new bishop consecrated in 1830, Benjamin Onderdonk. Williams had been closely connected with the anticolonization protest, serving with Allen as one of the promoters of the Negro Convention movement. From that, he moved into active participation with the American Anti-Slavery Society during the 1830's and made public statements condemning slavery and the deplorable conditions of freedmen, one of which so irritated the Bishop of New York that the black priest was told that

[17] There is unfortunately no way the incomes of the members of any of the churches discussed in this study can be gauged accurately, except in a general way, by the kinds of jobs they performed. The building that housed St. Philips, a structure that Bishop Hobart said revealed judgment and taste, was constructed largely by church members, who must have been fairly skilled mechanics. But members participated in the construction of other church buildings, too; the African Baptists in Boston and the African Methodists in Philadelphia when they were at St. George's were only some of the groups that worked on that type of construction. Another factor that may set St. Philips apart from the rest was its interest in education. Williams himself, an only child, received a fair amount of schooling and attention. He looked after the educational needs of the parish by running a day school on a regular basis, supplementing it occasionally by special music classes and concerts.

Since St. Philips' early records were destroyed by fire, its original membership can only be estimated; it was probably somewhere between 150 and 200. The building constructed in 1819 had pews to accommodate 144. See DeCosta, *St. Philips' Church*, 21; for Hobart's report to the General Convention, see *Journal of General Convention*, October, 1819; *Christian Journal*, August, 1818.

[18] DeCosta, *St. Philips' Church*, 18-20; *Christian Journal*, August, 1818.

[19] DeCosta, *St. Philips' Church*, 21-22; report of Bishop Hobart to General Convention, *Journal of the General Convention*, October, 1819; *New York Commercial Advertiser*, October 21, 1820.

he would either have to remain silent on the issue in the future or leave the church. Williams chose to accept silence in order to continue serving his congregation.[20] Prior to that time he had been as active in the anticolonization campaign as his denominational ties would allow, but he had strained the limits of white tolerance on the issue and it broke under the strain.

The Baptists who created Abyssinian Church in 1809 suffered none of the restrictions of denominational ties that bothered Williams and the Episcopalians, but neither did they have any clerical leadership to offer the anticolonization protest. A small group of dissatisfied blacks had withdrawn from the First Baptist Church when the Rev. Thomas Paul, the minister of the African Baptist Church in Boston, visited New York in 1809, two years after their first request for separate facilities had been ignored. Paul was able to stay with them for only three months because of the demands of his own charge in Boston, but it was long enough for him to help them secure a building and get on their feet. After he left, the church struggled along for a time without any minister, until finally one and then another in a series of preachers came to serve them. Added to its difficulties was its relatively small original membership, a fact which may challenge the assumption that black population growth encouraged religious separatism. But before the idea is dismissed as being irrelevant in the case of Abyssinian Baptist Church, it is essential to note that although only sixteen (or possibly nineteen) freedmen withdrew from the white church to form their own, congregational segregation could still have been a factor for even those few. Forced to sit together, they may have appeared to be a larger group than they actually were; more than one white churchman testified that his members accepted the presence of a few blacks scattered about the congregation, but grew uneasy when they appeared in a group. The records of the Abyssinian Church unfortunately suffered the same incendiary fate as those of St. Philips so that its early history has had to be reconstructed here, as in other cases, on the basis of oral tradition, and that was necessarily vague when it came to remembering details like the size of the original membership or the forces that motivated the founders to leave the white

---

[20] The immediate cause for the action was the Bishop's objection to Williams's sermon on "Slavery and Colonization."

society.[21] It seems fairly clear, however, that the Abyssinian Church experienced the same advantages and liabilities common to others in the Baptist tradition; that is, the congregation enjoyed the freedom to make its own decisions without the restraints imposed by denominational ties, but it also suffered from the lack of support, and also direction, that such ties could provide. The result was that in its early years it was too disorganized internally to contribute much to the anticolonization movement. By 1832, however, it had gathered sufficient strength to sponsor another branch, Zion Baptist Church.

But Abyssinian's loss, in the person of Thomas Paul, was Boston's gain. Born in Exeter, New Hampshire, on September 3, 1773, to "respectable colored parents," he was reportedly a very gifted preacher.[22] He was ordained in the Baptist Church at the age of twenty-eight and moved to Boston, where in 1805 he organized the first black church in the city, known successively as the African Baptist Church, and Joy Street Baptist.[23] Its local membership of freedmen included some who worked as barbers, mechanics, trades people, and seamen, as well as those involved in other crafts. Many participated in the commerce of the port city, a place in which the black population was relatively small as compared to New York, amounting in 1810 to 1,468, or 4.3 per cent of the total.[24] During Paul's ministry of approximately twenty-

[21] John Dowling, "Sketches of New-York Baptists," *Baptist Monthly Record,* IV (1849), 297. The minister who compiled a history of the church sometime after 1847, the Rev. J. T. Raymond, said that the Africans desired to leave the First Baptist Church "for reasons unnecessary now to mention." Quoted in Dowling, 297.

[22] *Ibid.,* 295. His parents may have been free rather than slave.

[23] Moses King, ed., *Handbook of Boston* (Cambridge: M. King, 1879), 184; Francis Jackson Garrison, *Address on The One Hundredth Anniversary of the Birthday of William Lloyd Garrison,* given at the Joy Street African Baptist Church, December 10, 1905 (Boston, n.p., 1906?).

[24] King's *Handbook of Boston,* Appendix, 457.

These are the figures for the period 1790 to 1830:

	blacks	Total Population	Percent of blacks in total
1790	766	18,320	4
1800	1174	24,937	4.7
1810	1468	33,787	4.3
1820	1690	43,298	3.9
1830	1875	61,392	3

five years, the congregation acquired a building, and conducted a school for black children in the basement, taught, at various times, by the minister's wife and his two daughters. The original membership was drawn in this case, as in New York, from the segregated blacks who had worshiped in the First Baptist Church of the city.

Boston's situation was unique among the four cities in that its black population experienced a scarcely perceptible increase during the time that anticolonization interest was on the rise. But the relatively limited size of Boston's black population didn't prevent social segregation from taking over; schools and churches were still segregated there as elsewhere, although there may have been more opportunity for flexibility in enforcing it. The change from more open seating arrangements in churches to a fairly restricted one took place gradually after the state first outlawed slaveholding in 1783 and before the colonization idea had attracted attention. After that time the black population grew slowly, actually declining in relation to white growth as immigrants from abroad began to settle in the area. Black interest in anticolonization was therefore related to other causes besides population increase alone. And one of those factors was the quality of local black leadership; there were those men, like Thomas Paul himself, and Prince Saunders, once a teacher at Joy Street Church, whose rather extensive travels contributed a cosmopolitan flavor to the community. Paul's preaching engagements had taken him on speaking tours around the Northeast—the reason for his being in New York when the Abyssinian Church was started—but there were other men, including Saunders, whose travels had taken them abroad. And when people like David Walker settled in the city, they added yet another quality to the atmosphere of the place. The other factor that stimulated black political awareness was the widespread influence of abolitionist opinion in Boston; taken together, informed black leaders and abolitionist advocates, they generated considerable support for anticolonization and abolition. In fact, William Lloyd Garrison organized Boston's first Anti-Slavery Society in the schoolroom basement of Joy Street Church on the cold, wintery night of January 6, 1832, and members of the congregation participated in that historic event as they had in earlier sessions that had considered colonization.[25]

Just how significant a part community leaders played in shaping black public opinion was evidenced in Baltimore, the spiritual home of Allen's associate, Daniel Coker. Allen actually owed his episcopacy indirectly to Coker, for if Coker had accepted the vote of the 1816 organizing convention of African Methodism, Allen might not have had the chance to serve. As it was, after Coker declined election, he returned to Bethel Church in his home city, and served the growing church he helped organize until he was expelled. When he returned to the fold, and offered to go to Liberia as a missionary, his decision to accept partial support from the Maryland Colonization Society[26] caused both friends and foes of colonization to re-examine their positions.

Coker had been a conspicuous figure in the black community of Baltimore, running a school and preaching at Bethel, and his decision to support colonization served as a striking example to his friends. Other local black Methodists, viewing the deterioration of their opportunities—to vote, find jobs, and move freely about—as the free population expanded, considered the merits of following his lead. During the next few years, interest in colonization gradually increased, prompting supporters of the idea to call a meeting at Bethel Church in the city in 1826 to discuss the feasibility of emigrating. It was, the participants said, the sorry state of their affairs that had led a "respectable number" of freedmen to gather, and they adopted a memorial which declared; "We reside among you, and yet are strangers—natives, and yet not citizens. . . ." They said that their removal to Africa would help to eliminate "the stain and evil of slavery . . . and result in the extension of civilization and the gospel. . . ."[27] The A.M.E. minister who chaired the meeting, the Rev. William Cornish, once served as an assistant to Allen in Philadelphia, but he evidently didn't share the Bishop's strong feelings about the disadvantages of colonization.

25 F. J. Garrison, *Address;* Lee M. Friedman, "A Beacon Hill Synagogue," *Old Time New England,* XXXIII (July, 1942), 1-5. The building that originally housed Joy Street Church was subsequently sold to a Jewish congregation.

26 *Journal of Daniel Coker,* 43.

27 H.R., *Report of Mr. Kennedy of Maryland,* 415-18.

The climate of opinion in Baltimore was an additional incentive for black residents to consider colonization. Even without a state emancipation law, the free population of the city grew dramatically, as emigrants to the area recognized that there was a greater chance of escaping enforcement of Black Laws in the city as opposed to rural areas.[28] But even though local enforcement agencies might wink at the laws, interracial cooperation was minimal; in the churches, "relations between races soon became . . . like their relations in the state generally,"[29] and that relationship was poor and uneasy. The atmosphere of Baltimore was tinged with a Southern flavor, the result, in part, of the presence of agents and dealers in the internal slave trade whose activities linked the city with the cotton kingdom of the lower South, and in that kind of environment it was difficult for the anticolonizationists to make much headway. Still, latent sympathy for Allen's approach did exist, and he capitalized on it as much as he could through his denominational ties with African Methodists in the area.

Coker's conversion impressed A.C.S. agents and they redoubled their efforts to win over urban leaders, temporarily singling out Philadelphia as the strategic center of their opposition. Supported by Henry Clay's observation that potential emigrants "would be drawn principally from the cities,"[30] one of the agents employed various techniques to try to persuade James Forten that the A.C.S. was not a coercive agency. He was promised that in Africa he would become "the Lord Mansfield of their 'Heaven-born republic,' "[31] but the appeal evidently fell on deaf ears. Forten stayed, but not John Russwurm, an editor of *Freedom's Journal,* who

[28] Between 1790 and 1860 the black population of Baltimore City increased 24.1 per cent. See Wright, *Free Negro in Maryland,* 86, 87.

[29] *Ibid.,* 215.

[30] The excerpt is taken from Clay's statement to the board of managers of the A. C. S., *First Annual Report of the American Colonization Society,* 1818, 9.

[31] Nell, *Colored Patriots of the American Revolution,* 177. Forten reportedly replied to the appeal by saying, " 'That he would rather remain as James Forten, sailmaker, in Philadelphia, than enjoy the highest offices in the gift of their society.' " See also *Journal of Charlotte Forten,* 14, 15; Phillip Staudenraus, *The African Colonization Movement* (New York: Columbia University Press, 1961), 190.

found the offer of a similar position in Africa too enticing to re-
sist, and whose departure was regarded more as a defection by
A.C.S. antagonists.[32] Forten had long been a favorite target for
A.C.S. agents, beginning with a visit in 1817 that the Rev. Finley
had paid him, Allen, and other members of the local clergy, and
they appreciated what his conversion to a procolonization position would mean for the success of their program. But he
wouldn't cooperate.

The Society continued to ply the Philadelphia area with a
steady stream of speakers, hoping to win some converts. The results must have seemed disheartening. Their gains were small
and insignificant: in 1829 a group of fifty-eight sailed from the
city, forty-nine of whom were liberated slaves.[33] The black residents of the area told the A.C.S. what they thought of its program
by supporting the stand taken by their local leaders, a position
which they knew had required a fair amount of courage on the
part of some of those who were most active.

The case of the Rev. John Gloucester was one of those they
could cite. In 1816 he was part of the local clerical triumverate
that included Allen and Jones; there were other black preachers
resident in the area—an African Baptist Church had been started
in 1809—but their roles tended to be less public. The three
preachers had helped to organize the first city protest meeting,
and after that tried to keep local interest alive by speaking out on
the issue in their churches and at public gatherings. Gloucester's
personal fortunes, less secure than those of the other two men,
might well have been placed on the line if the leaders of his denomination had taken umbrage at his actions. He was a Presbyterian, and the Presbyterian Church subsequently endorsed the
A.C.S.; when Peter Williams later failed to conform to denomina-

[32] William M. Brewer, "John B. Russwurm," *JNH*, XIII (1929), 415. Brewer
maintains that Russwurm's decision was motivated by "vision and statesman-
ship" as well as an awareness of the problems of racial adjustment in America,
and not by selfish ambition. See also Letter from John B. Russwurm to the
Rev. R. R. Gurley (of the A.C.S.), February 26, 1827, in *JNH*, X (1926), 156.
In the letter, written in response to the Society's first appeal to him—which
he rejected—Russwurm said that he decided "it would not be advisable to accept the liberal offer of your Board of Managers."

[33] *New York State Colonization Society Report*, 1834, 7. The New York
Report referred to the Philadelphia departure.

tional guidelines, he was rebuked. Allen and Jones were spared that kind of risk because the Bishop was his own denominational master, limited only by the extent of his own energy, and Jones died in 1818 before he could be put to the test of denominational conformity.

What made Gloucester's situation so vulnerable were the personal problems he and his family had experienced. He had been born a slave in Kentucky and was given his freedom by his Presbyterian master, the Rev. Gideon Blackburn, in order to work as a missionary to the African Presbyterians in Philadelphia.[34] Blackburn supervised his education, his ordination in 1810, and sent him North to preach, but without his wife and four children, who were left behind. Gloucester had first taken up his work in Philadelphia in 1807 with a small congregation of twenty-two people, a group that by 1810 had grown large enough to require its own building.[35] His membership, which was made up primarily of those who had been crowded out of other Presbyterian churches as their numbers increased, knew that his family was still in the South and tried to help him raise the money to purchase their freedom. But their meager resources alone were not enough to pay for the freedom of five people, so Gloucester went on an extensive preaching tour that took him as far as England before he could accumulate the remainder of their purchase price. His family was eventually reunited, but the memory of their long separation must have lingered on as a reminder of the kind of personal insecurity that threatened the lives of all black people.

He had not tried to disguise his interests; he had been one of the original members of the local steering committee appointed after the 1817 protest meeting, a group whose activities were conspicuous enough to draw the attention of the A.C.S. and prompt it to send the Rev. Finley around to meet with its members.[36] That session took place just a few weeks after the public meeting, and Finley's mission was to try and talk the leaders out of their

---

34 Catto, *A Semi-Centenary Discourse delivered in the First African Presbyterian Church, Philadelphia, May, 1857,* 20-21, 25.

35 "Address of John Gloucester to the First African Church, 1811"; quoted in Catto, *African Presbyterian Church,* 48, 56-57.

36 William Lloyd Garrison, *Thoughts on African Colonization* (Boston: Garrison & Knapp, 1832), 10.

plans for going on with the opposition. Finley's biographer reported the encounter with the eleven member committee—on the
basis of what he admitted was secondhand information—and according to his account this is what took place: after consulting
with Gloucester, Finley directed his conversation to two other
members, referred to in one place as "J.F. and R.A." and in another as "John Foster and Richard Allen," who were the most
outspoken supporters of colonization.[37] The two men, obviously
Forten and Allen, reportedly disagreed with other members of the
committee who favored resettling free blacks on unoccupied land
in the United States: their personal preferences were for Africa
and possibly Haiti. Forten allegedly said that he believed his people were destined to become a great nation, and that Africa offered the best opportunity for realizing that goal. And Bishop
Allen, then aged fifty-seven, is supposed to have told Finley that if
he were a younger man he would go to Africa himself. Both men,
according to this report, seemed to believe that colonization offered black people the only hope of escape from white oppression.[38]

Finley's account of the meeting, assuming it is reasonably ac-
curate, offers a revealing commentary on the attitudes of these
free black leaders toward colonization. His personal assessment of
the conversation—that the black men supported the A.C.S—resulted from misinterpreting their answers, something that may
not have been entirely his fault. In view of the subsequent statements of Forten and Allen, it became clear that what they ob-
jected to was the coercive aspect they recognized in the A.C.S. program, and not the idea of colonization. Both men were interested
in voluntary emigration, through missionary work and group
projects such as the one Paul Cuffe had organized, but they were
strongly opposed to the program of the A.C.S., which they were
convinced could only produce unfortunate consequences for all
black people, both free and slave. Their fight against the A.C.S.
was based on resistance, not to colonization, but to what they regarded as another example of white coercive efforts. If Finley

37 Brown, *Biography of Finley*, 80-81, 123-24.

38 *Ibid.*, 123-34. Brown concluded his report of Finley's interview as follows:
"The committee of whom I speak were of the most respectable class of blacks.
So far as I recollect, this is the substance of what Dr. Finley told me. As far as
I have gone, you may rely on the facts." Brown, 124.

misinterpreted their answers, it was understandable, since they may have been responding to that part of his appeal which they supported. It was not unusual for A.C.S. agents to tailor their messages to meet what they assumed were the particular concerns of a given audience: in the South they talked about the inviolability of private property, in the North they emphasized the possibility of liberated slaves becoming potentially free emigrants, and to blacks everywhere they pointed out the advantages of being in a free "homeland," and the dire state of racial affairs in America.

Such appeals produced some converts; in 1832, 796 Afro-Americans left for their "homeland," the largest group up to that time, thus bringing the total number of emigrants up to 2,638.[39] Since the free Northern black population in 1830 totaled 166,757, it was obvious that only a small percentage were listening to the Society's message.

From the time of that meeting, Allen and Forten remained publicly opposed to colonization. They wrote letters and held meetings, convening a second public gathering on August 10, 1817, to follow up on the ideas generated at the first session held seven months earlier. The participants in the summer protest drew up a memorial that seemed to describe the feelings most free blacks shared about colonization. Their statement reduced their arguments to two basic objections: the project was wrong because it produced separation—from families, homes, and Southern "brethren"; and it was poorly conceived because it intended to take freedmen out of their present communities where they had churches, fraternal groups, and schools, and place them in a colony that had none of these. The inevitable result, they said, would be that the colony would become "the abode of every vice, and the home of every misery."[40] Facing that kind of situation,

[39] "Table of Annual Receipts and Colonists Sent to Liberia by the American Colonization Society"; quoted in Staudenraus, *The African Colonization Movement*, Appendix.

[40] Woodson, *Negro Orators and Their Orations* (Washington: Associated Publishers, 1925), 54; Garrison, *Thoughts on African Colonization*, 10-13. The "Address of the Free People of Colour in Philadelphia, August 10, 1817," from the meeting referred to, is included in *Minutes of the American Convention for Promoting the Abolition of Slavery*, 1818, i-iv.

they had no desire to go. Allen, Forten, and the rest of the local leaders did their best to encourage such feelings, but it was not an easy task in the midst of a society that seemed determined to place new restrictions on the freedman.

Their work was made a little easier when William Lloyd Garrison and some of his close supporters announced their decision to back the black attack on colonization. They had previously been defenders of the plan, but after hearing the black arguments against it, the white reformers became valuable and vocal converts. In any case, they had more in common with the black clergymen than just colonization; they seemed as interested in moral reform, self-improvement, and black unity as the people who had organized the Free African Society in the late eighteenth century. The similar interests of the two groups of reformers made it easier for them to develop a cooperative alliance, a relationship reinforced by Garrison's open renunciation of the A.C.S. on the front page of *The Liberator* in its first issue in 1831.[41] Freedmen acknowledged his support by becoming the main subscribers to his paper.

Freedom's Journal served the black reformers the same way *The Liberator* served the white, as a medium for popularizing their particular ideas. Allen understood its value to the anticolonization campaign, and directed a letter to the paper outlining his position. It appeared on November 2, 1827, and said in part:

> We are an unlettered people, brought up in ignorance . . . is there any fitness for such to be sent into a far country? . . . See the great bulk of the poor, ignorant Africans in this country, exposed to every temptation before them: all for the want of their morals being refined by education and proper attendance paid unto them by their owners, or those who had the charge of them.

He concluded with the following declaration:

> This land which we have watered with our tears and our blood, is now our mother country, and we are well satisfied to stay where wisdom abounds and the gospel is free.[42]

Allen was nearing the end of his life when he wrote the letter,

---

[41] *The Liberator,* January 1, 1831.
[42] *Freedom's Journal,* November 2, 1827.

and whatever vestiges of his youthful Methodist idealism still survived might have disappeared completely had it not been for the inkling of hope that the Garrisonians and younger black preachers seemed to offer. For in spite of the best efforts of the black churchmen of his generation, they seemed to be losing out in the battle against the white anxieties that were given a corporate existence in the A.C.S. Not that the Society had made any significant progress; it was, in fact, barely holding its own, but the racial attitudes that had created it were now being manifested in other equally devastating ways. The white religious organizations that had endorsed it did so because of certain practical considerations: the Society, they believed, could dislocate the slave trade, promote missionary expansion and realize some patriotic responsibilities, at the same time that it removed a community "evil."[43] That black church people understood the reality that sometimes hid behind the altruism was indicated in a resolution that was adopted at a meeting in Wesley Methodist Church in Philadelphia in 1830, which said: "That we view with charity the national policy of the American Colonization Society; as one necessary to the interests of the white inhabitants of this country."[44]

But colonization had not served white interests as its promotors had intended; it had failed to remove their community "evil" and other measures were now being called upon to supplement or replace it. The repressive legislation adopted in Ohio that forced local freedmen to look for refuge in Canada, a move which came two years after Allen's letter to *Freedom's Journal,* offered a striking example of just how far a state was willing to go to rid itself of its black inhabitants. Even in Allen's own state of Pennsylvania the story was not much different: the state legislature endorsed the A.C.S. in 1829,[45] and set in motion a drive to restrict the franchise to whites, an effort that culminated in the constitutional

---

[43] The ideas were expressed in statements from the following church groups: Synod of Tennessee, October 3, 1817; General Assembly of the Presbyterian Church, May 31, 1819; Presbytery of North Carolina, April 18, 1818; Synod of Virginia, November 18, 1819; General Association [Congregational] of Massachusetts, June 22, 1819. Quoted in H.R., *Report of Mr. Kennedy of Maryland,* 420-25.

[44] *Hazard's Register,* V (1830), 143.

[45] H.R., *Report of Mr. Kennedy of Maryland,* 928.

convention of 1837.[46] In other states also, like New York, New Jersey, and Connecticut, property and residence requirements were taking the vote from black men in places where they once enjoyed it.[47] Such measures struck at all blacks equally, whether they were churchmen and moral reformers or not, and that realization must have been a painful one for Allen, who had identified his youthful hopes with the liberating value of Methodism.

But its basic message still seemed relevant for him, even though it appeared to have suffered badly against overwhelming opposition. It required retelling, but more than that, it needed greater support in the black community, more than his A.M.E. organization alone had been able to give it. In a slightly different form—as secularized moral reform and self-help—it emerged in the National Negro Convention movement.

The Ohio exodus of 1829 was the immediate cause for convening the First National Negro Convention. Allen and Peter Williams both knew that political reaction had forced the freedmen out of the state on virtually a moment's notice, and they wanted to let their exiled brothers know that they were not forgotten. It was obvious, too, that some changes had to be made in the anticolonization program to deal with the new legal and political restrictions that were threatening to make exiles of other freedmen: a national body with a continuing existence could convene a meeting to deal with whatever exigencies might arise. The two clergymen apparently recognized such a need simultaneously, and while Williams was considering the possibility of summoning delegates to New York, Allen anticipated his move, and invited them instead to Philadelphia, where the meeting finally assembled on September 15, 1830. The conditions that had motivated their actions were ones that black preachers involved in the campaign against colonization in other cities could well understand because they, too, sensed the political reaction. There were men like Thomas Paul and Hosea Easton in Boston, William Douglass in Baltimore, and Peter Spencer in Wilmington;[48] they, as well as

46 Turner, *The Negro in Pennsylvania*, 151-54.

47 Litwack, *North of Slavery*, 72-75.

48 *Minutes of the Second Convention for the Improvement of the Free People of Color*, 1832, 16, 24-25; L. R. Mehlinger, "Attitudes of the Free Negro Toward African Colonization," *JNH*, I (1916), 283-287.

others, would have agreed that a unified effort would help them in their individual situations.

Forty delegates came to the organizing convention at Bethel Church in Philadelphia to discuss the events related to the crisis in Ohio. Before they got to that, however, they elected Allen as their president and then adopted as their official name "The American Society of Free Persons of Colour, for Improving their Condition in the United States; for Purchasing Lands; and for the Establishing of a Settlement in Upper Canada."[49] With those details taken care of, they took up the developments in Ohio that had "awakened public feelings," and had made it necessary for them "to be prepared for future emergencies, and to extend the system of benevolence still further to those who should remove to Upper Canada. . . ."[50] They composed an "Address to the Free People of Color" which summarized their conclusions and outlined their intentions. The Address began with a reference to that portion of the Declaration of Independence which affirms the equality of all men, and then went on to explain the delegates' opposition to the A.C.S. and to the "laws [that] have been enacted in some of the states of this great republic, to compel . . . our brethren to leave their homes and seek an asylum in foreign climes. . . ."[51] It concluded with a recommendation that the proceedings in Philadelphia be publicized through local chapters, which could continue to function as auxiliaries of the national convention. The auxiliaries could also collect money at the local level which would then be channeled to the national body to purchase land in Canada. The local chapters would also be responsible for reporting news back to the people in their area. When

[49] Williams, *A History of the Negro Race,* II, 71; *Minutes of the Second Convention for the Improvement of the People of Color,* 16-17. There were forty delegates at the convention, representing seven states.

[50] *Minutes of the Second Convention for the Improvement of the Free People of Color,* 16; Williams, *History of the Negro Race,* II, 68-75; John Cromwell, "The Early Negro Convention Movement," *American Negro Academy Occasional Papers,* No. 9 (Washington: American Negro Academy, 1904).

[51] "The Address to the Free People of Color of these United States," quoted in Bella Gross, "The First National Negro Convention," *JNH,* XXXI (1946), 436. See also "The First Colored Convention," *Anglo-African Magazine,* No. 10 (1859), 308-10.

the business at hand was taken care of, the delegates agreed to re-assemble on the first Monday in June, 1831.[52]

Allen did not make the next meeting. The Philadelphia gathering, the capstone of his personal campaign for black unity, was his last; he died on March 26, 1831, three months before the second meeting convened. But he had made his mark on the convention movement and it remained visible at subsequent sessions where delegates continued to press the need for unity and moral reform. The fact that other churchmen in the anticolonization campaign—which was parent to the convention movement—shared these same concerns, improved the opportunities for creating a working relationship between them, the Garrisonians, and other abolitionists of similar persuasion. Together the black reformers and the white abolitionists kept up the attack on the A.C.S. during the 1830's, expanding their demands to include total, immediate emancipation.

If Allen reflected on the results of the colonization protest, he would have had to admit that they were, in many respects, inconclusive. The anticolonization attack had unified black opinion, it was true, but it had not brought any new members into the A.M.E. Church.[53] It had produced the convention movement, but in a way, the need that had created the conventions was a sad commentary on contemporary politics. And, unknown to the Bishop, the movement's effectiveness would be tempered in the late 1830's, as the popularity of the A.C.S. waned and dissension split the ranks of organized abolitionism.[54] Still, the black protest

[52] *Minutes of the Second Convention for the Improvement of the People of Color,* 16. See also Austin Steward, *Twenty-Two Years a Slave, and Forty Years a Freeman* (Rochester: William Alling, 1857), 165-67. Steward, who was a delegate to the meeting, reported that the convention lasted three days, during which time they discussed "the subjects of education and mechanism. Agricultural pursuits were also recommended. . . ."

[53] Williams, *History of the Negro Race,* II, 453. Between 1826 and 1836 the membership of the A. M. E. Church declined from 7,927 to 7,594. This loss was accounted for, in part, by a decrease in the Baltimore Conference of 333 members, reportedly sold into slavery. See also Payne, *History of the A. M. E. Church,* 109, 110.

[54] Litwack, *North of Slavery,* 235-39; Louis Filler, *The Crusade Against Slavery* (New York: Harper and Bros., 1960), particularly chapters VI & VII; Howard Bell, *A Survey of the Negro Convention Movement, 1830-1861* (New York: Arno, 1969), 52-55.

had forced the A.C.S. to revise its approach: colonization leaders had to confess that remarks about black inferiority would not encourage Africans to support their organization, nor would they let them go unchallenged.[55] But when that recognition finally dawned on them, it was too late: the Society had lost whatever appeal it once had, and no amount of revision or modification could enlist more than minimal black support.[56] Ambitious man that he was, even in old age, Allen might have congratulated himself on having been the one to convene the first black national convention, just as he had been the first to launch an independent African denomination. There was, after all, some value in precedent.

There were other areas, however, in which he had to share the credit with his clerical contemporaries. They were, as a group, generally interested in moral reform, and their public statements and sermons echoed that interest. Among them they developed an approach to social issues and religious questions that was uniquely their own. But there is a case to be made for singling out Allen even here, because as the instigator of the First National Negro Convention, he was historically the one most responsible for transferring religious interest in moral reform from the church and sharing it with the world of organized political activity.

[55] Litwack, *North of Slavery*, 28; Staudenraus, *The African Colonization Movement*, 189, 192-95.
[56] Staudenraus, *American Colonization Society*, Appendix. The A. C. S. continued to function until the close of the nineteenth century, with a small, but steady trickle of blacks leaving for Africa annually.

VII

PREACHING AND THEOLOGY

The history of the world shows us, that the deliverance of
the children of Israel from their bondage is not the only instance, in which it has pleased God to appear in behalf of
oppressed and distressed nations. . . .

Absalom Jones
Thanksgiving Sermon on the
Abolition of the Slave Trade

Whatever his personality type, the *effective* Black preacher
is a man who, if he is not born with charisma, acquires it
early and wears it with confidence.

C. Eric Lincoln
Foreword to *Black Preaching*
by Henry H. Mitchell

As IMPORTANT AS COLONIZATION AND ABOLITION WERE as community
projects, they represented only the more visible aspects of the
black preacher's professional work. Like the tip of an iceberg,
such activities revealed only a small, although very obvious, part
of the total: the more substantial portion of his ministry was less
public in nature, and consisted of serving the needs of his congregation. The preacher was primarily a local pastor, and the problems of his own parishioners generally had first claim on his time.

The way any particular preacher budgeted his time between
community and congregational activities was obviously a personal

decision, but in any church with more than a handful of members there were typically certain priestly functions that he alone had to perform. He buried the dead, baptized the young, counseled the troubled, and, perhaps most importantly from his point of view, preached to the faithful. Because for Allen, and many of his colleagues as well, it seemed that preaching provided the charge that fired the rest of their clerical interests. The sermon was usually the heart of the service—sometimes it was almost the entire service—and its appeal could be measured along with the preaching talents of the minister by the size of the congregation that returned Sunday after Sunday to hear him. Congregational approval, while hardly an infallible guide to a man's ability, was a valuable asset to those who enjoyed it because it made such necessary tasks as raising money that much easier. A really effective preacher, one whose charismatic qualities were supported by skill and sensitivity, was able to produce a kind of self-perpetuating cycle involving the interaction of his enthusiasm and the congregation's response to it. It was a process that seemed to operate with considerable success at Bethel, Philadelphia, where, according to the records, Allen usually preached to a crowded church.

His preaching style can't really be evaluated in any other way. Like many of the other Methodist clergymen of his day, he was especially fond of extemporaneous preaching, which at its best combined the speaker's inspiration in a fortuitous blend with the congregation's reaction. The Bishop preached several times a week, always without a manuscript, because he was convinced, he said, "that reading sermons will never prove so beneficial to the colored people as spiritual or extempore preaching."[1] Most of his contemporaries shared his opinion, with the result that they produced only a few written sermons to pass on to succeeding generations. The statements in Allen's memoirs suggest that he followed the Methodist evangelical style of preaching, measuring his own success, as others did theirs, on the basis of the number of souls that were "saved" and converts recorded. A good meeting, he believed, was one in which there was "much rejoic-

---

[1] Allen, *Life Experience*, 30.

ing." But each preaching occasion was a unique event, never recorded, and its elusive spirit never entirely recaptured again.

Some sermons were written down and subsequently printed, but
they offered a literary version of what was essentially an aural experience. As such, they fail to describe a man's preaching talents,
but they do point out what some of his theological interests were.
Allen's sermon on the occasion of a much publicized murder trial
in Philadelphia, for example, indicated that there was a theological basis to support his interest in moral reform. Taken together,
the sermons of Allen and his colleagues suggest that they developed their own theological interpretations and perspective, despite the fact that they were nominally identified with the doctrines of their particular denomination—in his case, Wesley's
Methodism. Their published homilies—admittedly limited evidence—reveal a developing open-ended system of black theology,
a system built around a dialectic involving the personal and the
collective, the individual and the community, or stated another
way, an oppressive culture and a liberating God.

Black preaching in Allen's day was almost never the expository
kind that tried to explain a theological proposition. It was usually
directed rather to an immediate situation, as in the case of Allen's
address following the murder trial, and its very timeliness was one
of the factors that determined its appeal. Many sermons did try to
teach a lesson, about the need for conversion, for example, or the
importance of moral reform, abolition, or anticolonization, but
their tone was more persuasive than didactic. Of those that managed to find their way into print, many were often designed for
a specific occasion, such as the celebration of the end of the slave
trade, or the death of some respected public figure, but unfortunately, most of them—whatever their subject matter—tended to
suffer from the same stylistic problems common to others of the
genre that were produced during the period. It required a certain
amount of intellectual discipline for anyone to sit down and read
a sermon, and for black readers the difficulty could be compounded by the fact that the author of the piece was usually trying to interpret a black religious experience in white literary
terms. The effort was probably just as frustrating for the writer
as it was for the reader.

The tenuous political situation of freedmen was partly to blame for the uneven quality of published sermons. Any black churchman who had the temerity to sign his name to an address made himself vulnerable to public criticism and censure, and in the existing climate of opinion, that could be extremely risky. To counteract such possibilities, many preachers first secured the endorsement of white clergymen and then composed their work with an eye toward white editorial approval. But that served as only a partial explanation for their rather stilted style: flowery prose was almost expected from preachers, and printed sermons, whether the work of black preachers or white, tended to have the same tedious quality. Printed sermons had the potential to take on life when their authors, perhaps inadvertently, employed a black idiom to discuss topics with particular racial implications. Of the two literary influences, white prose and the infrequently used black vernacular, the latter usually fared better in print. Descriptions of such things as slavery or the slave trade, experiences with which the preachers readily identified, were most vivid. William Miller, who was an A.M.E. minister before he joined the Zionites in New York City, made the following reference to slavery in one of his homilies:

> But meditate on the accounts you may have received from the West Indies, which some of you may have been eye-witnesses to, when, at the blowing of the horn, the slaves, young and old, men and women, naked and barefoot, running as it were for life, lest they should be beaten for being one moment behind their fellow-laborers. Picture to your imaginations the women enduring all the inclemency of the torrid zone, their bodies uncovered, and their young and tender off-spring tied to their backs, digging two or three feet with a hoe in a soil that almost resists the powers of the pick-ax; and if there is the least cessation in their most servile labours, — O said communication! they are laid down and receive corporeal punishment with the cart-whip, the sight of which is sufficient to produce a despondency in the unhappy slaves.[2]

Absalom Jones was somewhat more effective in describing the slave trade:

[2] William Miller, *A Sermon on the Abolition of the Slave Trade: Delivered in the African Church, New-York, on the First of January, 1810* (New York: John C. Totten, 1810), 10, 11.

He [God] has seen ships fitted out from different ports in Europe and America, and freighted with trinkets to be exchanged for the bodies and souls of men. He has seen the anguish which has taken place, when parents have been torn from their children, and children from their parents, and conveyed, with their hands and feet bound in fetters, on board of ships prepared to receive them. He has seen them thrust in crowds into the holds of those ships, where many of them have perished from the want of air. He has seen such of them as have escaped from that noxious place of confinement, leap into the ocean; with a faint hope of swimming back to their native shore, or a determination to seek an early retreat from their impending misery, in a watery grave.[3]

Allen's own literary attempts had the same uneven quality. Some were more successful than others, as two examples from his Addresses indicate: in a rather studied reference he said, "Our blessed Lord has not committed his goods to us as a deadstock, to be hoarded up, or to lie unprofitably in our own hands";[4] and then in a more imaginative simile he wrote, "we are not to lord it over God's heritage, as greedy dogs that can never have enough."[5] A phrase that he liked to use to encourage cooperation between preachers and laymen was "pull together for the glory of God. . . ."[6]

The content of black sermons, like their style, also suggested dual influences. In this case the two could be generally described as, on the one hand, revelation—or God acting in history—and on the other, the anxiety of the human condition—or man's desire for salvation and assurance. Sermons that fell into the first category were usually more concerned with matters of a political and social nature, while those in the second were likely to be addressed to problems with personal implications. Since black preachers themselves did not divide their sermons into categories any more than they did their ministerial work, there was a great deal of

---

[3] Absalom Jones, *A Thanksgiving Sermon, Preached on January 1, 1808, in St. Thomas's, or the African Episcopal Church, Philadelphia: On Account Of The Abolition Of The Slave Trade* (Philadelphia: Fry & Kammerer, 1808), 11, 12.

[4] Allen, "A Short Address to the Friends of Him Who Hath No Helper," *Life Experience,* 79.

[5] Allen, *Life Experience,* 35.

[6] Payne, *History of the A. M. E. Church,* 48, 49.

overlapping of these two main headings in almost any sermon, but generally there was a tendency to emphasize one more than the other in any given discussion.

In the case of those that dealt with revelation, there was a determined effort to draw a parallel between the Afro-American situation and God's deliverance of the Jewish people from either their Egyptian or Babylonian captivity. The illustration was designed to show that God was willing to intercede on behalf of the poor and oppressed, or as Jones described it; "the deliverance of the children of Israel from their bondage, is not the only instance, in which it has pleased God to appear in behalf of oppressed and distressed nations. . . ."[7] Miller emphasized the point in a sermon by repeating a quote that was popular among his colleagues; "Ethiopia shall soon stretch out her hand and come unto God."[8] For these preachers, at least, there existed the possibility that black captive suffering may have been part of a divine plan, the objective of which was not yet clear, although it was surmised that it could have been devised for chastening, instruction, or something of even greater significance. Jones speculated, "perhaps his [God's] design was, that a knowledge of the gospel might be acquired by some of their [slaves'] descendants, in order that they might be qualified to be the messengers of it, to the land of their fathers."[9] Miller reached a basically similar conclusion when he said that, while he was unwilling to thank slaveowners for their part in his captivity, he was still tempted to cry with David, "It is good for me that I have been afflicted, that I may learn thy statutes."[10] He apparently believed, as Jones did, that suffering could have been the means employed to inspire black Christians to "visit the land of their forefathers, propagating the word of salvation. . . ."[11] And like the Jews, the freedmen must accept their responsibility in God's plan by reminding themselves of their ancestral bondage, or as Jones maintained, "it becomes us, publickly and privately, to acknowledge, that an African slave, ready to

7 Jones, *Thanksgiving Sermon*, 10.
8 Miller, *Sermon on the Abolition of the Slave Trade*, 6.
9 Jones, *Thanksgiving Sermon*, 18.
10 Miller, *Sermon on the Abolition of the Slave Trade*, 13.
11 *Ibid.*, 14.

perish, was our father or our grandfather."[12] The point was made repeatedly: the God who revealed his compassion for the bound and oppressed in Israel, and again in the person of Jesus, would now intercede on behalf of the captive Africans. Sermons like those of Jones and Miller interpreted the past in terms of the present needs of the community; an example, perhaps of a black hermeneutic, if, as has recently been suggested, "the chief task of hermeneutics is to convey the revelation in its contemporary context. . . ."[13]

The other type of sermons, those, that is, that were addressed to people's private passions rather than community needs, have mistakenly identified the preaching of the black church with an exclusive concern for other-worldly objectives. Critics point out that instead of taking care of the business of political inequality, preachers too often diverted the practical interests of parishioners with "pie-in-the-sky" promises. African clergymen, in any case, had no monopoly on sermons that described the rewards of an afterlife: Methodist Bishop Asbury was only one of a multitude of white churchmen who thought it necessary, now and then, to remind his listeners of "the precious promises" awaiting the faithful in their heavenly home. And there was also a biblical basis of support for an interest in "last things." Obviously if that had been the sole focus of most sermons it would have produced a distorted religious perspective, one so busy looking skyward that it ignored the holes in the street, but that was not the case. Allen and his clerical contemporaries tried to deal with both public and private matters: preaching that was concerned with social and political issues had to share the pulpit with sermons that spoke to the personal needs of anxious or despairing members. To the sick, lonely, or despondent parishioner who came to the church for help, the preacher held out the comfort of an afterlife where "all sorrow and tears are wiped away."[14] To a woman who had lost a child, or a husband his wife, there was no solace in a sermon on colonization, and preachers like Allen recognized that fact. For them and

[12] Jones, *Thanksgiving Sermon,* 17.

[13] Henry H. Mitchell, *Black Preaching* (New York: Lippincott, 1970), 25. Mitchell discusses the meaning of a black hermeneutic.

[14] Allen, "Address to the People of Colour," *Life Experience,* 73.

others like them, the preacher seemed willing to forego, for the time being, a discussion of community problems, and preach instead about God's love and his saving grace. He was not willing to acknowledge any irreconcilable conflict between the two emphases.

Sermons dealt with the immediate and the particular, rather than the remote and the abstract, and there was no concerted attempt to systematize conceptual references. And yet, a certain system of sorts did emerge, one that might best be described as a kind of theological counterpart to W. E. B. DuBois' concept of "two-ness."[15] For DuBois inferred that the Afro-American was influenced by two forces in his socio-political life, and quite possibly the same situation prevailed in his religious life. He described it this way: "One ever feels his two-ness,—an American, a Negro; two souls, two thoughts, two unreconciled strivings; two warring ideals in one dark body. . . ."[16] Allen's version of black theology, dialectical in form, was similarly concerned with the conflict between two forces, an oppressive culture and a liberating God. In the pulpits of black preachers, the components of the dialectic received an interpretation rarely, if ever, duplicated in white churches, indicating that free churchmen rejected the substance, if not the forms, of white religion. No white preacher would have interpreted the Babylonian captivity, for example, in the same way that a black man would. When black clergymen referred to a cultural past, the historical culture they had in mind was, if not specifically African, certainly not European: the contemporary culture that they knew as a fact of life was characterized by white dominance and racial inequality. Their African ancestors had been brought to an alien culture, one in which the vestiges of Renaissance humanism and Reformation individualism had taken on New World forms among the white residents who appeared to be caught up in the rush for gain in a land of seemingly endless plenty. Masters who thought they should provide some instruction for their slaves were probably more successful in teaching, by example instead of precept, the nature of the acquisitive struggle rather than the tenets of orthodox Christianity.

15 W. E. B. DuBois, *Souls of Black Folk* (New York: Fawcett, 1961), 17.
16 *Ibid.*

Black churchmen necessarily came to share some of the prevailing interest in material gain, which was to be expected since they confronted the lack of goods as one of the basic problems their members faced. But they knew two definitions of culture: one was white, oppressive and acquisitive; the other was African, liberating and humane. The cultural reference of black theologians was therefore usually to the latter view of culture. When the preacher addressed himself to the needs of his community, he talked about an idealized society that had existed in the past, and could be reproduced in the future, if, with the help of divine intervention, committed black Christians worked to bring it to pass. For people like Allen, God was a present reality, an immanent force, who could help them out of their present difficulties, just as he had aided the Jews when they were in need. The Bishop's memoirs and addresses are replete with references to the daily presence of God in his rather routine activities: some were casual, even offhand, comments that indicated that he took such supernatural actions for granted. A few excerpts can illustrate the point: he observed, for example, that "my dear Lord was with me," that "the Lord blessed our endeavors," and that "the Lord would open some way for me to get my living," that "God . . . was our deliverer," and also "I know he was a God at hand and not afar off."[17] Such intercessory help did require as a precondition that the believer cooperate with God in effecting his own liberation. God would not do it alone, man could not: this appeared to be, in part, the theological rationale supporting Allen's belief in organized political activity.

If one component of the black theological dialectic viewed God in terms of his cultural relationship, the other, complementary, part referred to God and his concern for man. And in the process of dealing with man, black theology developed its distinctive views of God and Satan, conversion and human nature.

The black churchman's view of God seemed as characteristically dichotomous as the rest of his theological system. God, for him, was simultaneously the transcendent "Totally Other" and the pervasive spiritual immanence that was revealed in human

17 Allen, *Life Experience*, 18, *passim.*

acts of love and good works. The attributes most frequently associated with God were love and compassion, although as freedmen
who had personally suffered from the consequences of injustice,
they were sometimes inclined to point out the manifestations of
divine justice. The latter references, however, were usually
oblique, implying, perhaps, that while God was just, he was not
vindictive, and his system of justice did not always demand retri-
bution in terms of an "eye-for-an-eye and a tooth-for-a-tooth."

Their concept of man was vague by comparison, conceivably
because any comprehensive notions had to include black men as
well as white, male as well as female. The unconverted man was,
for Allen, a person who was "in love with this world" and its
treasures, but the believer was one who had been "saved" and
sanctified, and had cast off "the perishable riches of this world"
by building up "treasures in Heaven," through acts of "mercy and
charity." The Christian, the individual who renounced "Satan
. . . at . . . baptism," knew that at the final judgment his life
would be evaluated in terms of his service to "my brethren who
stand in need. . . ."[18] Viewed from this perspective, man was
neither innately good nor evil, but was rather the sum total of his
works. Despite their agreement on other issues, Allen would have
had little in common theologically with many of the white abolitionists who succeeded him in the movement in the late 1830's,
particularly those, who, like Ralph Waldo Emerson, entertained
Unitarian-humanistic assumptions about man's godly qualities
and their relevance to self-conscious introspection. The Bishop's
view of man was made up of different stuff. It produced some interesting, and perhaps unexpected, manifestations: it meant that
the black preacher might consider the slaveowner an "evil" person, but it was because of what he did, and not because he was
born with a predetermined evil nature. And judging from their
sermons, churchmen did not hold the female character in very
high regard, at least it did not seem so when compared with the
Bishop's response to Jarena Lee's request to preach. In an address
delivered by the Congregational preacher, Lemuel Haynes, as a
rebuke to Universalism, he referred to the descendants of Eve as

[18] Allen, "A Short Address to the Friends of Him Who Hath No Helper,"
Life Experience, 81.

people who had inherited her susceptibility to Satan. According to Haynes, the "great enemy to light" could "creep into houses and lead captive silly women laden with sin. . . ."[19] Generally, however, when the preacher referred to "man," whether in his fallen or redeemed state, he did so in a generic sense and intended to include women.

The condition of the slave also had to be accommodated within this system of black theology. That free churchmen regarded those in bondage as brothers and sisters is clear—most had been slaves themselves—but how they could minister to them in their present condition was a dilemma few seemed able to resolve. What kind of sermons could comprehend the needs of both the bound and the free? For someone like Allen, sermons with political connotations were not the only answer, because, while they might benefit the freedman, they offered frustration instead of help to the slave. People in all circumstances, he seemed to conclude, stood in need of a message that promised the kind of love and hope that was not focused solely on an afterlife, on streets of gold that lay beyond some pearly gates. He advised slaves to think of the "love of God" as the best source of comfort in their present condition, at the same time that he reminded the free people at Bethel to "help forward the cause of freedom."[20] The first injunction seemed prompted by a need to minister to the kind of personal despair that he knew all too well, while the second was a considered approach to the problems of social change. To tell the slave whose hopelessness threatened to overwhelm him that he was the captive of an unjust system, was to tell him something he already knew, just as he knew of certain ways that he could undermine, but not destroy, that system. Not everyone—even if properly indoctrinated—longed for a hero's death in what could only

[19] Lemuel Haynes, Universal Salvation: A Very Ancient Doctrine With a Short Account of the Life and Character of Its Author, 1802, MS, Congregational Library, Boston. The sermon subsequently went through several editions.

Haynes, born in 1753 to an African male slave and a white hired woman, served only white congregations in New England. His sermons, like this one which was designed to refute the claim for universal salvation made by Hosea Ballou, were usually involved doctrinal discourses.

[20] Allen, "Address to the People of Color," Life Experience, 73.

look like a futile assault on an oppressive system. Some care had to be taken for his present anguish, and if the church could not serve him, there appeared to be no other immediate source of help. To free and slave alike, the Black preachers of Allen's day offered a message of comfort and hope designed to give them strength to fight another day, for clearly, a long and difficult struggle seemed in store.

Their message to church members was not, nor could it be expected to be, universally effective; in every congregation there were people who became backsliders in the struggle with sin and society—sin being defined as moral turpitude and measured, in the final analysis, against the Ten Commandments. Personal or social pressures could, for some, blot out all thoughts of a better future, and the temptation was great to look for immediate relief in such temporarily pleasant but ultimately useless diversions as drinking or gambling. The preacher had two types of sermons to offer the potentially wayward member. If he was an unconverted person, he was urged to "seek the Lord" and live the redeemed life of a converted believer. And conversion implied more than a rejection of a certain type of behavior: ideally, it meant that the convert was preeminently a "new man," recently reborn. From that time on, if he asked, "Who am I?" he could reply that he was more than just a reformed drinker or gambler, but a "new creature in Christ," a person who accepted and respected himself even though the dominant white culture rejected his blackness. He was able to come to terms with himself in spite of what white society said about him. But to those backsliding members who claimed they were already converted, the preacher offered a different kind of message, one of caution and admonition: they were told that their disreputable behavior was a disservice to themselves, their family, and their community. Unless they mended their ways, they were warned, they stood in danger of being made captive by the wily Satan. The best soldier in the struggle for justice was therefore, first and foremost, the self-respecting convert, and then secondarily, the concerned member of the community. The individual who did not know and accept himself could be of little service to anyone else.

If sin was a problem for people, backsliders and believers alike,

Satan was assumed to be the source of it. Black churchmen regarded the presence of Satan to be as real as that of God, and
members were advised to guard against his tempting appeals.
Lemuel Haynes spent a great deal of time in one of his sermons
listing his qualities, and finally defined him as "the god of this
world who worked in the children of disobedience. He has his
people amazingly under his control." In an obviously sarcastic
conclusion to the sermon, Haynes invited critics to point out any
errors they found in his argument, which he offered to correct, because, he said, it had always been his policy *"to give the devil his
due."*[21] The devil, for Haynes as well as for others, was constantly
trying to seduce people into his service, perfidiously weaning
them away from God.

Black churchmen differed even among themselves on the interpretations they gave to their theological assumptions, partly because of their personal experiences and partly because of their
denominational backgrounds. It was never a closed system in any
case, and since it was improvised and open-ended, it resisted codification. And yet it was clear that they generally adhered to views
that were not consistent with those shared by their white denominational colleagues, or in Allen's situation, by the Methodist
Church. They made their mark on the quality of theology, just
as they had on the tenor of political activity. When Allen died,
the texts of most of his sermons, in a sense, died with him, leaving only those rare printed addresses as inadequate testimony to
his preaching ability and theological priorities. But when combined with similar statements from his colleagues, they describe
the outlines of a theology that appeared to be relevant to the
needs of their community of worshipers.

[21] Haynes, Universal Salvation, Haynes's sermon infers that the devil inspired
Ballou's contention for universal salvation.

VIII

ALLEN, ABOLITION, AND REFORM:
THE DECADE AFTER HIS DEATH

Tribute to Bishop Allen

When a good man dies, his country sustains a loss; but when not only a good but a great man has been summoned by the Angel of death to bid farewell to existence, humanity throughout the world becomes a mourner. In the death of RICHARD ALLEN, the first Bishop of the African Methodist Episcopal Church, religion has lost one of her brightest, most talented, and distinguished ornaments; philanthropy one of her firmest and most practical advocates and supporters; and the cause of African Emancipation one of the purest friends and patriots that ever exerted his energies in favor of civil and religious liberty.

> *The Liberator,* May 14, 1831
> (Quoted from the *African Sentinel*)

Benjamin Banneker and Richard Allen . . . were ornaments of their race rather than notable antislavery workers.

> Louis Filler
> *The Crusade Against Slavery*

WHEN RICHARD ALLEN AND HIS WIFE, SARAH, were buried in a tomb in the undercroft of Bethel Church, Philadelphia in 1901, the great gray stone building that now houses the congregation became, in a very literal sense, a monument to his ministry. It seems a fitting tribute, for if anything can be said to represent some tangible evidence of his life's work, it is Mother Bethel, the church he served for over 40 years. The original blacksmith shop that he first fitted out for congregational worship has long since disappeared, but an active membership has remained a constant from that day to this. To be sure, the organization of the African Methodist denomination was also a major achievement of his career, but Mother Bethel was where it all started, and it is somehow difficult to imagine how the denomination would have developed, if, indeed, it would have taken form at all, without the impetus provided by the Philadelphia church.

But memorials, however appropriate, are rarely, if ever, able to convey a sense of what a person's life was about. In Allen's case, with limited documentary evidence available to shed light on his daily routine, the difficulty of finding an adequate testimonial to his life and work is compounded. How, for example, is it possible to suggest what was involved for an ex-slave to challenge the white leadership of the Methodist Church and in so doing become himself a bishop? Or how is it possible to describe his ministry to individuals whom he feared might become targets for the Colonization Society, shipped away from their familiar surroundings to a place where it seemed no adequate provision had been made for their future well being? He was always an extremely busy man, with many interests, and for much, perhaps most, of what he did there is no satisfactory record. What the evidence does suggest, however, is his basic commitment to his ministry: it is otherwise impossible to explain the time, money, and emotional energy he expended on church business, always without compensation. What seems equally evident is that his own ministry suggested a type that was not at all uncommon among his clerical colleagues. He, as well as many of them, had a singular view of their mission, which was to serve the total needs of their constituency, members and potential members alike. They did not discriminate between religious work and secular activity; their outlook was comprehensive rather than exclusive. Allen himself recognized no inconsistency in a ministry that was designed to serve the needs of individuals, through such things as sermons on moral reform and advice on self-help, as well as the interests of the community, in colonization projects, convention meetings, and the like. His concern could be simultaneously otherworldly and very much this worldly: he was as capable of preaching a sermon that described the geography of Hell as he was of chairing a meeting that considered the Canadian climate in terms of its effect on black emigrants there.

Perhaps the most significant tribute to Allen's ministry was the extent to which those who followed after him, in the church and in the reform movement of the 1830's, adapted his ideas and approach to meet the demands of their own time. Because the men of that first generation of Northern free black leaders—the generation of Allen, Jones, Forten, Gloucester, Paul, and Williams—had initiated certain social patterns, it was comparatively that much easier for their successors to adopt or modify what had already been done. If the new spokesmen for free black society, the ones who were closest in time to the members of that first group, had rejected their ideas, it might be concluded that what had been said and tried had had a certain timely quality that became irrelevant as the times changed. The younger men did modify the old approach, but two basic concerns, for moral reform and political activity, remained an integral part of the new.

Important changes, significant for the future of the black church and black reform, occurred around the time of Allen's death to help account for some of the modification that took place. The leadership of the Northern free black community had, in a sense, come of age, and although the times were not auspicious for freedmen, new restrictions seemed to give rise to new leaders. Thanks to Allen, his successors now had a forum in which to exchange their ideas, the Negro Convention movement, and it provided the organizational structure for black abolitionism. The emergence of the Garrisonian brand of abolitionism also coincided with the year of Allen's death, through the appearance of *The Liberator,* the journal of opinion for moral suasionists. Other developments combined to add a note of urgency to the deliberations of the younger churchmen and reformers in the convention movement, and they included such things as the obviously accelerated pace of abolitionist activity, the renewed sense of militance among black spokesmen like David Walker, the abortive Nat Turner insurrection and its consequences, the news of British antislavery proposals, and particularly the disappointing racial policy of Jacksonian Democrats,[1] who treated "abolitionism [as] the great untouchable issue."[2] Some of the ominous signs that Allen and his contemporaries saw on the horizon became harsh political realities for their successors. The change in the climate of opinion necessarily helped to account for the change in approach.

But because the convention movement—the medium of expression for the black reform movement—had been born in the church, it was inevitable that it would retain certain distinguishing characteristics that marked its origin. The concerns of the reformers of the 1830's, many of whom were clergymen, were essentially similar to those of Allen, namely abolition, colonization, education, and temperance. Occasionally local auxiliaries or outgrowths of the convention would find a temporary attraction in other issues, such as women's rights, pacifism, or even wearing apparel or some other problem, but rarely did these matters become the focus of attention for very many groups or for very long.

Without treating the full spectrum of black reform, which has already been done successfully by Benjamin Quarles,[3] it is possible to gain a clearer perspective on Allen's ministry by looking at a few examples of community spokesmen who adapted his ideas and approach to the spirit of the 1830's. Labels are inadequate and inappropriate in this case: more to the point is to suggest the ways in which someone like Henry Highland Garnet, one of the more outspoken young activists, differed in his approach from James Forten, a representative, and perhaps one of the few surviving members, of the previous generation. Although both men shared many interests with Allen, neither held to a precise reproduction of his position: Garnet adopted methods that appeared increasingly divergent from Allen's as the decade wore on; and

[1] David Brion Davis, "The Emergence of Immediatism in British and American Antislavery Thought," *Mississippi Valley Historical Review*, XLIX (1962), 226-27.

[2] Arthur M. Schlesinger, *The Age of Jackson* (Boston: Little, Brown & Co., 1945), 190-91.

[3] Benjamin Quarles, *Black Abolitionists* (New York: Oxford University Press, 1969).

Forten, who cooperated with Allen on several projects, distinguished his approach to the extent that he emphasized his identification as an Episcopal layman. Still, their basic frame of reference was essentially similar, even though they represented two different points on the spectrum of black reform. What set them apart from each other was not a question of objectives but of techniques.

Colonization, the issue that had consumed so much of Allen's time, gave way to other matters, such as abolition and education, at convention sessions. Garrison and other speakers continued to point out the tragic flaws in the scheme, and if some freedmen still believed that emigration might have something to recommend it, no one was willing to offer what might be construed as a public endorsement of the A.C.S.[4] One proposal that was endorsed enthusiastically had to do with the founding of a college for blacks in New Haven, Connecticut. Forten had developed a seemingly congenial working relationship with Garrison—who had made a dramatic announcement of his conversion from a procolonizationist position[5]—and together with other abolitionists they drew up plans for the school, which were first introduced at the convention in 1831. But the project had to be abandoned before the college ever opened its doors because of the general public outcry raised against it by the citizens of New Haven.[6] The idea lingered on, however, even though the original proposal had to be scrapped.

A topic that appeared to be as important to convention dele-

---

[4] It seems inevitable·that some freedmen would have considered the advantages of emigration, particularly when they witnessed the restrictive legislation that states like Pennsylvania were considering. See Bell, *A Survey of the Negro Convention Movement, 1830-1861*, 273; it is the best scholarly account of the convention movement. Bell's study convinced him that "The zeal with which emigration was championed fluctuated with circumstances at home and abroad."

[5] There is fairly extensive testimony to support the conclusion that Garrison was persuaded to abandon his support of the A.C.S. by the arguments of black opponents of colonization. See, for example, *Journal of Charlotte Forten*, 14; Grimké, *William Lloyd Garrison, The Abolitionist;* and Lewis Tappan, *Life of Arthur Tappan* (New York: Hurd & Houghton, 1870). For Forten's relationship with Garrison, see Garrison Papers, Boston Public Library, Boston.

[6] *The Liberator,* July 9, 1831; also October 22, 1831; *Hazard's Register,* VIII (Sept. 24, 1831), 195-96; *Minutes of the First Annual Negro Convention.*

gates as it had been to Allen was temperance. At the 1832 meeting participants unleashed their attack on "that curse of the world . . . INTEMPERANCE" and reminded would-be imbibers of the evils attendant on alcoholic indulgence.[7] As the decade wore on, they stepped up their warnings against intemperance to include an appeal for total abstinence along with a suggestion to boycott those shops that sold liquor.[8] Garnet, who was a Presbyterian minister from Shiloh Church in New York City, became as ardent a defender of temperance as Forten and the men of the previous generation, although he called for a legislative solution to the problem instead of relying on individual conversions.[9]

As a result of the popularity of these single issues, however, schismatic tendencies began to develop which threatened to divide the movement into small groups focused on a particular "cause." Allen had not really been faced with a situation of comparable proportions, but his basic commitment to his ministerial responsibilities had, in any case, fixed his perspective. Those who accepted the temptation to work on a specific project, usually temperance or anticolonization, sometimes transformed local auxiliaries of the convention into societies with but a single objective.

Some clergymen did manage personally to bridge the gaps that threatened the unity of the movement by serving as leaders of several different local reform groups. Peter Williams and Christopher Rush, who were working in New York, could point to their colleagues in other Northern cities who were engaged in similar kinds of reform activities. There was George Hogarth of Brooklyn, for example, an A. M. E. minister who served as book steward for the denomination between 1835 and 1848, who also acted as an agent for *The Liberator,* organized local A. C. S. dissent, and helped to form the "Brooklyn Temperance Association for the People of Color" in 1831.[10] William Douglass, an Episcopal cler-

[7] *Minutes of the Second Annual Negro Convention; The Liberator,* September 22, 1832.

[8] Bell, *Negro Convention Movement; The Weekly Advocate,* January 28, 1837.

[9] Quarles, *Black Abolitionists,* 96. Garnet was known to address gatherings for an hour and a half on the "terrible effects of alcohol."

[10] George Washington Williams, *A History of the Negro Race,* II, 459; *The Liberator,* August 6, 1831.

gyman in Baltimore before he moved to Philadelphia to serve Forten's parish, was equally involved, as was Hosea Easton, the Boston Congregationalist, who had the added distinction of being one of the few men to serve as a delegate to national conventions on three different occasions.[11] Garnet and the man who had been his minister at Shiloh Church, Theodore Wright, were also frequently invited to address gatherings that had been convened to consider a particular cause, often sharing between them the spotlight in reform circles during this period before the popular Frederick Douglass commanded the center of the stage.[12]

An indication of the differences in strategy that began to distinguish Forten's approach from Garnet's became evident in the older man's participation in the American Moral Reform Society, an organization theoretically sponsored by the national convention but actually based in Philadelphia. Approaching seventy, Forten became the group's president in 1836, and led it through a series of discussions that ran nearly the whole gamut of reform interests, including abolition, education, pacifism, and women's rights.[13] For Forten, these meetings obviously recalled similar ones that he and Allen had conducted in the past for the Society for the Suppression of Vice and Immorality. He had had a long career as a social crusader when Garnet appeared on the scene, and his experience had convinced him that black self-help programs were more effective, more dependable, than political decisions. But even Garnet's own minister, Theodore Wright, had seen the value in this type of organization: joining with Peter Williams and Christopher Rush in 1833, he created with them a similar self-improvement group in New York, called the Phoenix Society, which proposed to "promote the improvement of the colored people in morals, literature and the mechanic arts."[14]

The interest that Wright and Garnet revealed in moral reform activity, was balanced by Forten's willingness to try political

[11] *The Liberator*, March 12, 1831; April 2, 1831; July 12, 1831; Woodson, *The History of the Negro Church*, 96; Douglass, *Annals of St. Thomas' Church*; Handy, *Scraps of A.M.E. History*. Also Bell, *Negro Convention Movement*.

[12] *The Liberator*, Dec. 3, 1831.

[13] Bell, *Negro Convention Movement*, 44, 45.

[14] Tappan, *Life of Arthur Tappan*, 159.

measures. At least twice during the decade he was prompted to publicize his views on political questions, relying on an approach that he had used before, namely, writing letters and drafting memorials. One case involved a Massachusetts law against interracial marriage, and the other was concerned with legislation in his own state designed to aid in the return of fugitive slaves. When his efforts yielded no noticeable results, he may have concluded that all of his impressions about the natural advantages of moral suasion were justified. The racial policies of the Jacksonian Democrats were proving to be a great disappointment to a man who could remember when the efforts of the post-Revolutionary War generation had helped to put Pennsylvania in the forefront of antislavery agitation. He summed up his own attitude in a resolution that he assisted in drafting on behalf of local black residents:

> We know that the most effectual method of refuting, and rendering harmless, false and exaggerated accounts of our degraded condition, is by our conduct; by living consistent orderly and moral lives.[15]

Younger men in the movement could respect his views, but they grew impatient with what they considered to be his overemphasis on the theoretical aspects of reform. Samuel Cornish, an editor of a newspaper started in 1837 called *The Colored American,* criticized Forten's Moral Reform Society in one of its issues. He, and a group of New York clergymen that included Wright, Rush, and Garnet, thought their present situation called for less discussion and more decisive action to hasten total emancipation and a better life for freedmen. They formed a group, called the Committee of Vigilance, which advised members to give aid and sanctuary to any fugitives who came to the area. Similar committees sprang up in other Northern cities, and together they served as links in the underground railroad.[16] Thwarting slave catchers, a subversive activity, was a hazardous undertaking, but certainly no more dangerous than the clandestine arrangements Sarah Allen had made

---

[15] *Hazard's Register,* IX (June, 1832), 361-362. See also Aptheker (ed.), *Documentary History of the Negro People,* 126-133.

[16] *The First Annual Report of the New York Committee of Vigilance, for the year 1837* (New York, 1837); quoted in Aptheker, *Documentary History of the Negro People,* 161-163; Tappan, *Life of Arthur Tappan,* 180-181.

to hide runaways. As an organized group project, however, it represented a departure from the Forten approach that consisted of drafting resolutions and supporting protests. Not really a rejection of Forten's ideas, their committee represented a different approach as well as a different stage in the development of black political consciousness, the outlines of which had been laid down by the men of the previous generation. Significantly, Wright, Cornish, Rush, and Garnet were numbered among the eight black clergymen who helped create the politically motivated American and Foreign Anti-Slavery Society in May 1840.[17]

Garnet's divergence from Forten's position—as revealed in the previous resolution—is perhaps no more apparent than in his celebrated speech before the Buffalo National Convention in 1843. In that address, which reportedly brought his audience alternately to tears and laughter, he advised slaves to rise up and overthrow their masters if they had to, and reminded them that they should personally prefer death to bondage. He said:

> You had far better all die, *die immediately,* than live slaves . . . there is not much hope of Redemption without the shedding of blood. If you must bleed, let it all come at once—rather, *die freemen, than live to be slaves.*[18]

Although the speech failed to win the approval of a majority of delegates to that particular convention, Garnet remained a potent force within political abolitionism, working in the so-called New Organization and persuading his colleagues to cooperate in an alliance with the Liberty Party.

The moral suasionists, with whom Forten had been identified, held to their opinions; unwilling to rule out politics entirely, they were still unconvinced that Garnet's approach or political remedies could solve their problems. Their interest in moral reform, they believed, was grounded in very pragmatic considerations about the needs of freedmen and slaves, and was little tained with the kind of abstract notion of self-purification that Wendell Phillips described when he said, "My friends, if we never free a

[17] Quarles, *Black Abolitionists,* 68. The other four were Stephen H. Gloucester, Andrew Harris, Jehiel Beman and his son Amos.
[18] Henry Highland Garnet, *An Address to the Slaves of the United States* (reprint, New York: Arno, 1969), 94.

slave, we have at least freed ourselves, in the effort to emancipate our brother man."[19] They seemed willing and able to comprehend the political activists within their ideological framework without sacrificing anything to consistency. And for those participants in the New Organization, the choice was not between an acceptance or repudiation of moral reform, moral suasion, and Garrison, but it was rather a decision to combine sympathy for that approach with other methods, so that support would not be "concentrated on one" man or position.[20]

What connection was there between the church and all this debate over alternative approaches to abolitionism? In the first place, it was an extension of a similar type of discussion that had long occupied the church, not over abolition necessarily, but certainly over colonization, to name just the most conspicuous example. And in the second place, it suggested that in the convention movement, as in the church, it was possible to find great numbers of people willing to support either approach, with seemingly few anxious to claim an exclusive preference for one or the other position. The commitment of all those involved in the black reform movement was to racial progress, and the church had already inadvertently conceptualized the outlook of the religious community in that regard. It was predicated on the interdependence of moral reform and political activism, and the reformers of the 1830's reflected this duality.

Allen was not faced with the kinds of choices that confronted his successors. He did not see options; what he recognized were opportunities and he grasped them. He was a preacher who measured his life by the test of experience, not doctrinal formulae or creeds, and he supported programs that he thought offered the best chance for success, an approach that necessarily limited his alternatives. After his election as bishop, the demands upon him forced him to budget his time to match his priorities. His first commitment, outside of his own family, was probably to his ministry, but he would have undoubtedly been hard pressed to decide

[19] Quoted in Quarles, *Black Abolitionists*, 53.
[20] The quote was taken from a statement by the New York abolitionists in the New Organization; D. L. Dumond, ed., *Letters of James G. Birney* (New York: Appleton-Century, 1938), I, 575-579.

whether the needs of his A.M.E. constituency or those of the larger community came first.

He would not have considered himself a "political" person; the only identification he made of himself was as "African" and "Methodist." And yet, in his day, the very act of establishing an African church was itself a kind of political statement. At the time of his death secular or political activity had already become an accepted part of the church's function. For the Wrights and the Garnets, their political preferences ran to abolitionism and not religious separatism, a development that was linked to the changes that had occurred in the social and political milieu. And it was these changes that helped to explain the shift in tactics. Tired of writing memorials and summoning mass meetings, they decided to employ more aggressive tactics. But their theological perspective remained essentially similar to Allen's, a comprehensive view of moral reform and political activism.[21] Their strategy changed with the times, their ideological reference remained tied to a black theological heritage. The same had been true for Denmark Vesey, the A.M.E. preacher in Charleston who had used the church to plan a rebellion. The fact that he belonged to the same denomination over which Allen presided as bishop demonstrated just how comprehensive their theological system could be. For some uninformed observers, however, it meant only that the church, like politics, was capable of producing strange bedfellows.

[21] In his article, "Religion and Resistance Among Antebellum Negroes," Vincent Harding seems to suggest that the black religious experience can be characterized by a quality of "doubleness"; that black religion has been either "otherworldly" and "compensatory," or revolutionary and socially conscious. Allen's ministry offers an example of a third type of black religious experience; one which combined both militant and otherworldly aspects within a single conceptual frame of reference.

BIBLIOGRAPHY

Manuscript Material

Manuscript material on Allen came primarily from two sources, Bethel Church in Philadelphia, and the Methodist Historical Society, also in Philadelphia. Bethel maintains an historical museum, containing Allen memorabilia as well as church records. The Journal of Proceedings, listing entries from August 1822 to January 1831, was in the possession of the church historian in 1968. The Methodist Historical Society, adjacent to Old St. George's Church, has most of the early records of the white church as well as those of the Philadelphia Conference. Since St. George's continued to list the people at Bethel on its membership rolls until 1816, its records provide an indication of what was happening at the time at Bethel.

Attempts to locate records at other churches produced little in the way of new documentary evidence but a great deal in terms of learning about the oral tradition of a particular church. Such was the case particularly at Abyssinian Baptist Church and St. Thomas' Episcopal Church. Most requests for information and help were warmly received by clergymen who seemed anxious to describe the particular contributions of their church, although it was disappointing to hear of the number of instances in which records had been either lost or burned.

Because most black churchmen preached extemporaneous sermons, only those designed for special occasions were written down and preserved. Most of them wound up as bound pamphlets, although there is a manuscript copy of Peter Williams's Discourse Delivered in St. Philips Church on July 4, 1830, in the Schomburg Collection of New York Public Library, along with some of Lemuel Haynes's sermons on Universal Salvation. Haynes's original sermon on the topic, delivered in response to an address by the Universalist Hosea Ballou, went through so many revisions that it is difficult to determine which was the first, although it appears to be the one in the library of the Congregational Historical Society in Boston. Two other sermons by Williams, one on the death of Paul Cuffe (October 21, 1817), and the other on the Abolition of the Slave Trade (January 1, 1808), are also in the Schomburg Collection.

The Methodist Collection in the main branch of the New York Public Library shed some light on the rise of African Methodism in that city. The Records of the John Street Methodist Church and the Miscellaneous Records of the New York Conference (1800-1860), reflect the problems black Methodists there faced as they worked out their own religious arrangement. Also useful were the Minutes of the Quarterly Meeting Conference of the Methodist Church, New York, 1804.

Material dealing with the controversy between black and white Methodists in Philadelphia is available in the Historical Society of Pennsylvania. Specifically, there are letters from the Rev. Robert Burch (December 16, 1815), the Rev. John Emory to the Philadelphia Conference (April 6, 1815), and Statements from two local lawyers who examined and then criticized Bethel's amended charter; Joseph Hopkinson (April 24, 1815), and S. Shoemaker (April 7, 1815).

A typescript of the memoirs of Absalom Jones, apparently garnered from a variety of sources, including oral testimony, is contained in a small collection on the first black Episcopal priest in the Church House of the Episcopal Diocese of Pennsylvania (Philadelphia).

New York Historical Society has some miscellaneous material that was helpful. These included C. C. Andrews, Minutes of the African Free School of New York, 1816 to 1832, and Samuel Davies, Letters from the Rev. Samuel Davies, etc., Shewing the State of Religion (particularly among the Negroes) in Virginia (1757). Davies, an Anglican priest, wrote these letters to the S. P. G. to thank its members for sending books that could be used to instruct slaves and poor whites.

The collections of some antislavery and abolition leaders were examined in the hopes of finding references to black churchmen involved in the reform crusade. A few were moderately helpful. The Benjamin Lundy Papers, on microfilm in Cornell University Library for the years 1814-1839, mention the Free Produce Society and the Free Cotton Society. The Gerrit Smith Papers, 1825-1848, in Syracuse University Library, refer to Smith's plan to make land available to free blacks and their response to that plan. The William Lloyd Garrison Papers in Boston Public Library provided useful background information, and also, through his correspondence with James Forten, some insight into Forten's position on various reform issues. Many of the black clergymen involved in the crusade are mentioned, with particularly popular and controversial figures, like Henry Highland Garnet, singled out for attention.

General Studies of Church Groups

The need to be selective is important when investigating accounts of any church group. Denominational apologists, while frequently revealing interesting "inside" information, can sometimes be carried away by their own enthusiasm. References to the growth of black congregations within Methodism and his attitude toward them are contained in Francis Asbury, *Journal and Letters* (Elmer T. Clarke, ed.), 3 vols. (Nashville: Abingdon, 1958). Other general works relating to the Methodist Episcopal Church during the period were S. A. Seaman, *Annals of New York Methodism* (New York, 1848), which contains a small, but valuable, collection of original documents, something that is also true for the book by J. B. Wakeley, *Lost Chapters Recovered from the Early History of American Methodism* (New York: Carlton and Porter, 1858). John Wesley's *Thoughts Upon Slavery* (London, 1774), makes it easier to understand why black people in America initially made an identification between Methodism and antislavery.

Studies that have an interdenominational interest include the following: Elmer T. Clark, *The Small Sects of America* (rev. ed., Nashville: Abingdon, 1937); W. E. B. DuBois, *The Negro Church* (Atlanta: Atlanta University Press, 1903), which emphasizes the influence of African culture on the black church in America; E. Franklin Frazier, *The Negro Church in America* (New York: Schocken, 1963), which rejects the idea that the church preserved an African heritage; Leonard Haynes, *The Negro Community Within American Protestantism, 1619-1844* (Boston: Christopher Publishing House, 1953), useful for its bibliography; Ruby F. Johnston, *The Development of Negro Religion* (New York: Philosophical Library, 1954), a sociological study, good for its definition of the role of the black clergyman; Mays and Nicholson, *The Negro's Church* (New York: Institute of Social and Religious Research, 1933), a critical evaluation of the church's preaching of other-worldly themes; William W. Sweet, *Religion in the Development of American Culture, 1765-1840* (New York: Scribner's, 1952); Carter G. Woodson, *The History of the Negro Church* (Washington: Associated Publishers, 1921), which remains the best general, historical account of the black church. Willis D. Weatherford's *American Churches and the Negro: An Historical Study from Early Slave Days to the Present* (Boston: Christopher Publishing House, 1957), is a more popularized treatment which focuses primarily on the South.

The best study of African Methodism was first published in 1888, the work of Bishop Daniel A. Payne, *History of the African Methodist Episcopal Church* (reprint, New York: Johnson Reprint Corp., 1968). It was he who discovered Allen's memoirs, stored away in an old trunk. He also wrote his own reminiscences, *Recollections of Seventy Years* (reprint, New York: Arno, 1968). But there are, in addition, other useful accounts of black Methodism, both the A.M.E. and A.M.E.Z. groups. The ones that were most helpful were: David H. Bradley, *History of the African Methodist Episcopal Zion Church* (Nashville: Parthenon, 1956), a sympathetic account by an historian of the denomination; James A. Handy, *Scraps of African Methodist Episcopal History* (Philadelphia: A.M.E. Book Concern, n.d.), an interesting book, but generally dependent on Payne's information; J. W. Hood, *100 Years of the African Methodist Episcopal Zion Church* (New York: 1895), a popular history by a bishop of the church; Grace Naomi Perry, "The Educational Work of the African Methodist Episcopal Church Prior to 1900" (unpublished master's thesis, Howard University, 1948); Christopher Rush, *A Short Account of the Rise and Progress of the African Methodist Episcopal Church in America* (New York: Marks Printer, 1843), a very useful history by the second bishop of the A.M.E.Z. Church who was one of its founders, and an active abolitionist; David Smith, *Biography of the Rev. David Smith of the African Methodist Episcopal Church* (Xenia, Ohio: Printed at the Xenia Gazette Office, 1881), which contains little tibdits on early A.M.E. history; J. Beverly F. Shaw, *The Negro in the History of Methodism* (Nashville: Parthenon, 1954), very generalized, but good for an introduction; Benjamin T. Tanner, *An Apology for African Methodism* (Baltimore: n.p., 1867); Richard R. Wright, *Encyclopedia of African Methodism* (Philadelphia: A.M.E. Publishing Co., 1947), a useful compendium of facts about the church by one of its scholarly bishops.

For a discussion of the black people who joined the Episcopal Church, see George F. Bragg, *A History of the Afro-American Group of the Episcopal Church* (Baltimore: Church Advocate Press, 1922). Bragg, who was a black priest in an Episcopal Church in Baltimore, also wrote an account of the activities of one of his predecessors, *The First Priest on Southern Soil* (Baltimore: Church Advocate Press, 1909). A few other works dealing with the Episcopal Church were also consulted, and they were: Charles Newton Brickley, "The Episcopal Church in Protestant America, 1800-1860" (unpublished Ph.D. dissertation, Clark University, 1949), which was useful for its discussion of the church's official attitude toward abolition; Richard James Hooker, "The Anglican Church and the American Revolution" (unpublished Ph.D. dissertation, University of Chicago, 1943); and C. F. Pascoe, *Two Hundred Years of the Society for the Propagation of the Gospel: An Historical Account of the Society for the Propagation of the Gospel in Foreign Parts*, vol. I (London, 1901), which described S.P.G. efforts to win black converts.

The *Journal of Negro History* has frequently published articles and documents that relate to various aspects of church history. Those of particular interest were: "Letters Showing the Rise and Progress of the Early Negro Churches of Georgia and the West Indies," I (1916); Joseph Butsch, "Catholics and the Negro," II (1917); Henry J. Cadbury, "Negro Membership in the Society of Friends," XXI (1936); Thomas E. Drake, "Joseph Drinker's Plea for the Admission of Colored People to the Society of Friends," XXXII (1947); Luther P. Jackson, "Religious Development of the Negro in Virginia from 1760 to 1860," XVI (1931).

Specialized Accounts of Local Churches

With the exception of the study compiled by the W.P.A. Writer's Project, most of the material used to gather information on the history of particular churches was in the form of pamphlet literature, not infrequently an anniversary sermon marking a milestone in the history of the church. The following titles, many long and descriptive, generally indicate the church or churches being considered: William T. Catto, *"A Semi-Centenary Discourse, delivered in the First African Presbyterian Church, Philadelphia, May, 1857* (Philadelphia: Joseph M. Wilson, 1857); Albert Cliffe, *The Glory of Our Methodist Heritage* (Nashville: Abingdon, 1958), a sympathetic history of St. George's Church, Philadelphia, by one of its former ministers; Fred Pierce Corson, "St. George's Church," in *Historic Philadelphia* (Philadelphia: American Philosophical Society Transactions, Vol. XLII, 1953); B. F. DeCosta, *Three Score and Ten: The Story of St. Philips' Church, New York City* (New York: 1889); Walter Brooks, "Priority of the Silver Bluff Church," *Journal of Negro History*, VII (1922); William Douglass, *Annals of the First African Church, in the U.S.A., now styled The African Episcopal Church of St. Thomas, Philadelphia* (Philadelphia: King and Baird, 1862), which is a valuable history by a scholarly rector of the church.

The *Annals* contains not only the minutes of the Free African Society, but also some of the early records of the church. Joy Street African Baptist Church in Boston, whose original building was sold and subsequently used as a synagogue, is discussed in Lee M. Friedman, "A Beacon Hill Synagogue," *Old Time New England*, XXXIII (July, 1942). Brief mention of the history of Joy Street Church is also made in Francis Jackson Garrison, *Address on The One Hundredth Anniversary of the Birthday of William Lloyd Garrison*, given at the Joy Street African Baptist Church, December 10, 1905 (Boston: n.p., 1906?). Baptists in New York City are the subject of John Dowling, "Sketches of New-York Baptists," *Baptist Monthly Record*, IV (1849). Jonathan Greenleaf discussed the emergence of separate black congregations in *A History of the Churches of all denominations in the City of New York from the first settlement to the year 1846* (New York: French, 1846). See also George W. Hodges, *Early Negro Church Life in New York* (New York: Privately published by the author, 1945); and John Street Methodist Episcopal Church, *Centenary Memorial . . .* (New York, 1868). One of the best historical accounts of the growth of black churches in New York City was compiled by the W.P.A. Writer's Project, "Negro Churches in New York City" (available in typescript, Schomburg Collection, New York Public Library, n.d.).

Works By and About Black Ministers

Finding printed material by and about the black preachers of Allen's day is almost as difficult as locating manuscript sources. Some have been the subject of articles, and a few have been described in books designed primarily for children, but only Allen has been treated to a scholarly biography, Charles Wesley, *Richard Allen, Apostle of Freedom* (Washington: Associated Publishers, 1935). Allen's memoirs, discovered by Bishop Payne, have been published separately as *The Life Experience and Gospel Labors of the Rt. Rev. Richard Allen* (2nd ed., New York: Abingdon, 1960). Also included in the Abingdon edition of Allen's autobiography is a pamphlet he co-authored with Absalom Jones describing the services rendered by black people during the yellow fever epidemic, *A Narrative of the Proceedings of the Black People during the late Awful Calamity in Philadelphia*. One of his addresses has been preserved, *Address to the Public and People of Colour* (Philadelphia: n.p., 1808). He also participated in planning the first Discipline for the church; Richard Allen and Jacob Tapsico, *Doctrines and Discipline of the African Methodist Episcopal Church* (Philadelphia: Cunningham,

1817). Correspondence by him and Jones concerning a British woman's request to preach is available in "Letters of Richard Allen and Absalom Jones," *Journal of Negro History*, I (1916). The life of Lemuel Haynes was described in a book by one of his white colleagues in New England, Timothy Mather Cooley, *Sketches of the Life and Character of the Rev. Lemuel Haynes* (New York: Harper, 1837). Other work dealing with Haynes includes, George Smith, *A Short Treatise Upon the Most Essential and Leading Points of Wesleyan or Primitive Methodism* (Poultney, Vt.: L. J. Reynolds, 1830), which contains a statement by Haynes supporting Smith's defense of himself against charges of immorality and heresy; W. H. Morse, "Lemuel Haynes," *Journal of Negro History*, IV (1919); and Richard Bardolph, "Social Origins of Distinguished Negroes, 1770-1865," *Journal of Negro History* XL (1955), which includes a discussion of Haynes. The following sermons by Haynes have also been preserved; *Discourses on Religious Subjects by the late Rev. Job Swift, and also a funeral sermon by Lemuel Haynes* (Middlebury, Vt.: Huntington and Fitch, 1805); *An Interesting Controversy Between Rev. Lemuel Haynes and Rev. Hosea Ballou* (Rutland: William Fay, 1805); *Mystery Developed; a Narrative of the Boorn Mystery* (Rutland: William Fay, 1805); and *The Nature and Importance of True Republicanism* (Rutland: William Fay, n.d.), this last a sermon that revealed Haynes's Federalist sympathies. Daniel Coker kept a journal which described his trip from New York to Africa, *Journal of the Rev. Daniel Coker* (Baltimore: John D. Toy, 1820). One of his sermons is contained in Aptheker's *Documentary History*. Absalom Jones had one of his sermons published, *A Thanksgiving Sermon Preached January 1, 1808, at St. Thomas's, or the African Episcopal, Church, Philadelphia on Account of the Abolition of the African Slave Trade* (Philadelphia: Fry and Kammerer, 1808). In addition, there is the typescript of his life, *Narrative of the Life of the Rev. Absalom Jones*. William Miller, an A.M.E. minister at one time, also preached on the slave trade, *A Sermon on the Abolition of the Slave Trade: Delivered in the African Church, New-York, on the First of January, 1810* (New York: John C. Totten, 1810). Two other A.M.E. preachers kept journals: one was the first woman preacher in the church, Jarena Lee, *Religious Experience and Journal of Mrs. Jarena Lee, Giving an Account of her Call to Preach the Gospel* (Philadelphia: published by the author, 1836); the other was a man who favored colonization, Daniel H. Peterson, *The Looking Glass: Being a True Report and Narrative of the Life, Travels, and Labors of the Rev. Daniel H. Peterson, etc.* (New York: Wright, 1854). Another black preacher who supported colonization, for missionary reasons, was Lott

Cary; see Miles Fisher, "Lott Cary, the Colonizing Missionary," *Journal of Negro History,* VII (1922). Some Southern black preachers who tried to develop autonomous congregations before Allen got his work started are discussed in the following: Howard H. Harlan, *John Jasper; a Case History in Leadership,* University of Virginia Phelps-Stokes Fellowship Papers, No. 14 (Charlottesville: University of Virginia, 1936); and John W. Davis, "George Liele and Andrew Bryan, Pioneer Negro Baptist Preachers," *Journal of Negro History,* III (1918).

The best discussion of preaching and sermons is Henry H. Mitchell, *Black Preaching* (New York: Lippincott, 1970). An earlier and equally useful analysis of sermons is James Weldon Johnson, *God's Trombones* (New York: Viking, 1927).

For a theological explanation of why black people chose to develop separate congregations see James Cone, *Liberation: A Black Theology of Liberation* (Philadelphia: Lippincott, 1970). Scholarly and readable, it is the best definition of what black theology is about. Vincent Harding also discusses religion as a potential force for resistance and liberation in "Religion and Resistance Among Antebellum Negroes," *The Making of Black America,* I, Meier and Rudwick (eds.) (New York: Atheneum, 1969).

For a view of what laymen, contemporaries of Allen, thought about the church, see Charlotte L. Forten, *The Journal of Charlotte Forten,* R. A. Billington (ed.) (New York: Collier, 1961), which contains an account of the entire Forten family; Prince Saunders, *A Memoir Presented to the American Convention for Promoting the Abolition of Slavery* (Philadelphia: Dennis Heartt, 1818), which discusses plans for an emigrant colony in Haiti; and also his *Address Delivered at Bethel Church* (Philadelphia, 1818); Austin Steward, *Twenty-Two Years a Slave, and Forty Years a Freeman* (Rochester, N.Y.: Wm. Alling, 1857), a participant's description of the First National Negro Convention in 1830. David Walker also had very definite ideas about the church; see *An Appeal,* Charles M. Wiltse (ed.) (New York: Hill and Wang, 1965). An understanding of his political, rather than religious, preferences can be gained from James Forten, *Letters from a Man of Colour on a Late Bill before the Senate of Pennsylvania* (Philadelphia, 1832).

The Racial Views of White Denominations

To understand one of the factors that helped to encourage black people to develop separate churches, it is helpful to look at some of the white denominational literature that attempted to deal with racial matters. The number of sermons and addresses on the subject by white churchmen may indicate their interest, but the contents reveal their inability to regard black people as equal members of the congregation. The following is just a sample of the material that is available: Thomas Bacon, *Sermons Addressed to Masters and Servants* (Winchester, Va.: John Heiskell, 1743); H. R. Bascom, *Methodism and Slavery: A Controversy Between the North and the South* (Charleston, 1822), which contends that the strong antislavery stand taken by the Methodist Conference in 1800 alienated white Southern Methodists; Bishop of London, *Letters of the Bishop of London: The First, To the Masters & Mistresses of Families in the English Plantations abroad; Exhorting them to Encourage & Promote the Instruction of their Negroes in the Christian Faith. The Second, To the Missionaries There. To Which is Prefix'd An Address to Serious Christians Among Ourselves* (London: Joseph Downing, 1729), the first letter of which said that baptism did not confer physical freedom on slaves; Nathaniel Bowen, *Pastoral Letter on the Religious Instruction of the Slaves* (Charleston: A. E. Miller, 1835), a statement by a bishop on how to instruct slaves in religion; Thomas S. Clay, *Detail of a Plan for the Moral Improvement of Negroes on Plantations* (Printed by the Presbytery of Bryan County, Georgia, 1833); Samuel Davies, *The Duty of Christians to Propagate their Religion Among Heathens* (London: J. Oliver, 1757), the work of an apparently earnest missionary for the S.P.G.; Charles Colcock Jones, *Catechism of Scripture, Doctrine and Practice for Families and Sabbath Schools* (2nd ed., Savannah: T. Purse and Co., 1837), contains a series of questions and answers designed specifically for slaves; and also C. C. Jones, *The Religious Instruction of the Negroes: A Sermon* (4th ed., Princeton: D'Hart and Connally, 1832), which went through many editions, and which represented a fairly popular Southern view that slaves should have enough religion to make them good servants, but not so much as to make them discontented; William Knox, *Three Tracts Respecting the Conversion and Instruction of the Free Indians and Negro Slaves in the Colonies Addressed to the Venerable Society for the Propagation of the Gospel in Foreign Parts in the Year 1768* (London: J. Debrett, 1789); William S. Plumer, *Thoughts on the Religious Instruction of the Negroes of this Country* (Savannah: Edward J. Purse, 1848); and Gerald DeJong, "The Dutch Reformed Church and Negro Slavery in Colonial America," *Church History* XL (December, 1971). For the purposes of this study, the most useful account of a denomination's changing policy toward blacks was Donald G. Mathews, *Slavery and Methodism: A Chapter in American Morality, 1780-1845* (Princeton: Princeton University Press, 1965).

Reports by Church Bodies

A.M.E. Conference records for the early years are spotty; the ones that are available are summarized in Payne, *History of the A.M.E. Church*. The situation is the same for the budget reports; for the early years, when the availability of funds was so unpredictable, they are not very helpful. See *Annual Reports of the Budget of the African Methodist Episcopal Church of the United States, 1816-1883* (Dayton, 1883). The *Minutes of the General Conferences* of the Methodist Episcopal Church for 1800-1830, available on microfilm, were useful for examining the shift in racial policy that took place during the period. Reports from other denominational groups, such as the Presbyterians and Episcopalians—where black members where proportionately fewer in number—were helpful for checking the status of a particular church or clergyman. The racial position of these various groups is discussed in Stokes, *Church and State in the United States*.

The Conditions of Freedmen

The best description of the life of Northern freedmen is contained in Litwack, *North of Slavery*. City registers and various forms of local histories offered some limited indications of the kinds of work black people were engaged in and where they lived and worshiped. The following would fit into this category: Moses King (ed.), *King's Handbook of Boston* (Cambridge: M. King, 1879); G. W. Watson (ed.), *Annals of Philadelphia* (Philadelphia: Carey & Hart, 1830); *Philadelphia Directory and Register, 1785-1837; Hazard's Register, 1830-1832*; David McNeely Stauffer (ed.), *Westcott's History of Philadelphia, 1609-1829* (Philadelphia: Sunday Dispatch), XXIV (1913); William Yates (ed.), *Rights of Colored Men: A Book of Facts* (Philadelphia: Merrihew and Gunn, 1838); *Philadelphia in 1824; or, a Brief Account of the Various Institutions and Public Objects in this Metropolis* (Philadelphia: H. C. Carey and I. Lea, 1824); *Sketches of the Higher Classes of Colored Society in Philadelphia* (Philadelphia: Merrihew and Thompson, 1841); James Hosmer Penniman, *Philadelphia in the Early Eighteen Hundreds* (Philadelphia: St. Stephen's Church, 1923). For specialized accounts of the situation in particular areas see: W. E. B. DuBois, *The Philadelphia Negro: A Social Study* (Philadelphia: University of Pennsylvania, 1899); Edgar J. McManus, *A History of Negro Slavery in New York* (Syracuse: Syracuse University Press, 1966); John Hope Franklin, *The Free Negro in North Carolina, 1790-1860* (Chapel Hill: University of North Carolina Press, 1943); Horace E. Fitchett, "The Traditions of the Free Negroes in Charleston, South Carolina," *Journal of Negro History*, XXV (1940); Aaron H. Payne, "The Negro in New York Prior to 1860," *Howard Review*, I (1923); Edward R. Turner, *The Negro in Pennsylvania, 1639-1861* (Washington: American Historical Association, 1911); Richard C. Wade, "The Negro in Cincinnati; 1800-1830," *Journal of Negro History*, XXXIV (1954); and James M. Wright, *The Free Negro in Maryland, 1634-1860*, Vol. XCVII of *Columbia University Studies in History, Economics, and Public Law* (New York: Columbia University Press, 1921). Lorenzo Greene, *The Negro in Colonial New England* (2nd ed., Ann Arbor: Atheneum, 1968), provided helpful background information.

Works that had some bearing on the story of Allen's life were Matthew Carey, *A Short Account of the Malignant Fever, lately prevalent in Philadelphia* (Philadelphia: Carey, 1794), in which Journalist Carey commended the freedmen for their work during the epidemic, but also charged them with asking too much for their expenses; Lydia Maria Child, *Isaac T. Hopper: A True Life* (Boston: John P. Jewett, 1853), which serves as a source for the account of Allen's difficulties with the slave catcher; and Burton Alva Konckle, *Benjamin Chew, 1722-1810* (Philadelphia: University of Pennsylvania Press, 1932), a description of the life of the man who first claimed the Allen family as his slaves.

In addition to *Freedom's Journal*, which appeared between 1827 and 1829 and offered an indication of what the current interests of freedmen were, the following shed some light on particular areas: Bella Gross, *"Freedom's Journal and the Rights of All,"* *Journal of Negro History*, XVII (1932); Charles C. Andrews, *The History of the New York African Free Schools* (New York: Mahlon Day, 1830); W. E. B. DuBois, *Economic Cooperation Among American Negroes* (Atlanta: Atlanta University Press, 1907); Stanley I. Kutler, "Pennsylvania Courts, the Abolition Act and Negro Rights," *Pennsylvania History*, XXX (1963); and William C. Nell, *The Colored Patriots of the American Revolution* (Boston: Robert F. Wallcut, 1855).

The Convention Movement

George Washington Williams described the proceedings of the first convention in his *History of the Negro Race*, but the most thorough account is contained in Howard Holman Bell, *A Survey of the Negro Convention Movement, 1830-1861* (reprint, New York: Arno, 1969). Briefer treatments, but still useful, are: Bella Gross, "The First National Negro Convention," *Journal of Negro History* XXXI (1946); "The First Colored Convention," *The Anglo-African Magazine*, I (1859); and John W. Cromwell, "The Early Negro Convention Movement," *American Negro Academy Occasional Papers,* No. 9 (1904).

Antislavery, Colonization, and Abolition

Benjamin Quarles', *Black Abolitionists,* is the most comprehensive study of the subject available. A brief, earlier account is Herbert Aptheker, *The Negro in the Abolitionist Movement* (New York: International Publishers, 1941). Archibald H. Grimké, in "Right on the Scaffold, or The Martyrs of 1822," *American Negro Academy Occasional Papers,* No. 7 (1901), discussed the Denmark Vesey affair, as did Richard C. Wade in "The Vesey Plot: A Reconsideration," *Journal of Southern History,* XXX (1964).

The best overview of colonization is provided by Phillip Staudenraus, *The African Colonization Movement* (New York: Columbia University Press, 1961), a work that extends, and also revises, much of the information offered by Early Lee Fox, *The American Colonization Society,* of the *Johns Hopkins University Studies in Historical and Political Science,* Series XXXVII, No. 3 (Baltimore: The Johns Hopkins Press, 1919). The founding of the A.C.S. is the subject of Isaac Van Arsdale Brown, *A Biography of the Rev. Robert Finley* (Philadelphia: John W. Moore, 1857). Although some writers on the subject of colonization have been able to maintain an objective view, many others have taken a stand strongly in favor of or opposed to the idea. William Lloyd Garrison consistently attacked colonization in *The Liberator,* and did so in greater detail in *Thoughts on African Colonization* (Boston: Garrison and Knapp, 1832). See also one of his speeches, *An Address, delivered before the Free People of Color in Philadelphia, New York and Other Cities during the Month of June, 1831* (Boston: Stephen Foster, 1831). G. B. Stebbins, *Facts and Opinions Touching the Real Origin, Character and Influence of the American Colonization Society* (Boston: John P. Jewett, 1853), is a collection of the views of those who opposed colonization. The anticolonizationist position is also considered in L. R. Mehlinger, "Attitudes of the Free Negro Toward African Colonization," *Journal of Negro History,* I (1916).

The position of John Russwurm, the editor of *Freedom's Journal* who decided to take up residence in Africa, is discussed in William M. Brewer, "John B. Russwurm," *Journal of Negro History,* XIII (1920). "Letter from John B. Russwurm to the Rev. R. R. Gurley, February 26,

1827," *Journal of Negro History,* X (1926), explains Russwurm's attitude. The prosperous condition of the Methodist churches organized by
black American emigrants in Africa is discussed in Ephraim Bacon, *Abstract of a Journal* (3rd ed., Philadelphia: Clark and Raser, 1824). A
defense of colonization by an Episcopal minister is contained in J. M.
Wainwright, *A Discourse on the Occasion of Forming the African Mission School Society* (Hartford: Published by the Directors of the Society, 1828). For other perspectives on colonization see H. N. Sherwood,
"The Formation of the American Colonization Society," *Journal of Negro History,* II (1917); and Rayford W. Logan, "Some New Interpretations of the Colonization Movement," *Phylon,* IV (1943).

The following material on white abolitionist leaders was useful for
providing a perspective on the white reform crusade: Barnes and Dumond (eds.), *Letters of Theodore Dwight Weld, Angelina Grimké Weld,
and Sarah Grimké, 1822-1844,* 2 vols. (New York: Appleton-Century,
1934); Dwight L. Dumond (ed.), *Letters of James G. Birney* (New York:
Appleton-Century, 1938); Archibald H. Grimké, *William Lloyd Garrison*
(New York: Funk and Wagnalls, 1891); Ralph V. Harlow, *Gerrit Smith*
(New York: Hold and Co., 1939); and for a comprehensive account, Louis
Filler, *The Crusade Against Slavery* (New York: Harper, 1960). Concerned with particular aspects of the reform movement are David Brion
Davis, "The Emergence of Immediatism in British and American Anti-
slavery Thought," *Mississippi Valley Historical Review,* XLIX (1962);
and Joseph R. Gusfield, "Temperance, Status Control, and Mobility,
1826-60," in *Ante-Bellum Reform,* David Brion Davis (ed.) (New York:
Harper and Row, 1967).

Antislavery activity was examined in Alice Dana Adams, *The Neglected Period of Anti-Slavery in America* (Boston: Ginn and Co., 1908);
Edward Needles, *An Historical Memoir of the Pennsylvania Society for
Promoting the Abolition of Slavery* (Philadelphia, 1848); Merton Dillon,
Benjamin Lundy and the Struggle for Negro Freedom (Urbana: University of Illinois Press, 1966); Russell Parrott, *An Address on the Abolition of the Slave Trade, delivered before the Different African Benevolent Societies, on the 1st of January, 1816* (Philadelphia, 1816); and
Clarice A. Richardson, "The Anti-Slavery Activities of Negroes in Pennsylvania" (unpublished master's thesis, Howard University, 1937).

The official papers and reports of abolition and colonization societies
were helpful for determining what issues the membership regarded as
particularly important at a given time. Among the sources that were
examined were: American Colonization Society, *Annual Reports;* and
its *Address of the Managers . . . to the People of the United States*

(Washington: James C. Dunn, 1832); American Convention for Promoting the Abolition of Slavery and Improving the Condition of the African Race, *Minutes of the Proceedings,* 1794-1829; its *Address to the Abolition and Manumission Societies in the United States* (Philadelphia, 1817); and also its *Address to the Free Blacks, and Other Free People of Colour, in the United States* (Philadelphia: Solomon W. Conrad, 1804); and from the Pennsylvania Society for Promoting the Abolition of Slavery, its *Constitution* (Philadelphia, 1787); its *Address . . . on the Origin, Purposes and Utility of their Institution* (Philadelphia, 1819); and its *Address to the People of Color in the State of Pennsylvania* (Philadelphia, 1838); the reports of local colonization groups, in Cincinnati, *Proceedings of the Annual Meeting,* 1833; in Maryland, *Third Annual Report of the Board of Managers,* 1835; and in New York, *Annual Reports,* 1830-1834. For the National Negro Conventions, the *Minutes and Proceedings of the Annual Conventions* were an important source of information. Also of some use was the *Memorial of the Free People of Colour residing in the County of Philadelphia: To the Senate and House of Representatives of the Commonwealth of Pennsylvania* (Philadelphia, 1835).

Other Sources

The following newspapers and journals contained information used in the study: *The African Observer,* 1827-1828; *The African Repository and Colonial Journal,* 1826-1860; *American Minerva,* 1796; *The Anglo-African Magazine,* 1859; *The Colored American,* 1837-1842; *Christian Journal,* 1818; *Freedom's Journal,* 1827-1829; *Genius of Universal Emancipation,* 1822-1830; *The Liberator,* 1831-1836; *The Minerva & Mercantile Evening Advertiser,* 1796; *New York Commercial Advertiser,* 1820; *New York Weekly Museum,* 1795-1796; *Niles Register,* 1816-1830; and the *Pennsylvania Journal,* 1790-1793.

Although developments within the black church reflected certain political concerns, governmental agencies, as such, had little to offer that bore directly on the role of the church. As a result, government documents were used only when specific issues were being examined. The following sources were helpful at certain points in the investigation: *Annals of Congress,* 6th Cong., 1st sess., 1800; U.S. House of Representatives, *Report on the Colonization of the Free People of Color,* 19th Cong., 2nd sess., 1826; U.S. House of Representatives Committee on Commerce, *Report of Mr. Kennedy of Maryland on the Memorial of the Friends of African Colonization* (Gales and Seaton, 1843); *Minutes* of the New York City Common Council for 1800 and 1803; Pennsylvania House of Representatives, *Report of the Select Committee on the Subject of Colonization* (Harrisburg: A. Boyd Hamilton, 1854); *A Digest of the Laws of Pennsylvania from 1700 to 1861,* John Purdom (comp.) (9th ed., Philadelphia: Kay and Brothers, 1862); *Constitutions of Pennsylvania,* Fertig and Hunter (eds.) (Harrisburg, 1916); Pennsylvania Supreme Court, *Reports of Cases Argued and Adjudged,* Benjamin Grant (comp.) January term, 1815.

INDEX